Literature of the 1900s

The Edinburgh History of Twentieth-Century Literature in Britain
General Editor: Randall Stevenson

Literature of the 1900s

The Great Edwardian Emporium

Jonathan Wild

EDINBURGH
University Press

For Michelle

Edinburgh University Press is one of the leading university presses in the UK. We publish academic books and journals in our selected subject areas across the humanities and social sciences, combining cutting-edge scholarship with high editorial and production values to produce academic works of lasting importance. For more information, visit our website: www.euppublishing.com

© Jonathan Wild, 2017, 2018

Edinburgh University Press Ltd
The Tun – Holyrood Road
12(2f) Jackson's Entry
Edinburgh EH8 8PJ

First published in hardback by Edinburgh University Press 2017

Typeset in 10.5/13 Adobe Sabon by
Servis Filmsetting Ltd, Stockport, Cheshire,
and printed and bound in Great Britain by
CPI Group (UK) Ltd, Croydon CR0 4YY

A CIP record for this book is available from the British Library

ISBN 978 0 7486 3506 1 (hardback)
ISBN 978 1 4744 3770 7 (paperback)
ISBN 978 0 7486 3508 5 (webready PDF)
ISBN 978 1 4744 1953 6 (epub)

The right of Jonathan Wild to be identified as the author of this work has been asserted in accordance with the Copyright, Designs and Patents Act 1988, and the Copyright and Related Rights Regulations 2003 (SI No. 2498).

Published with the support of the University of Edinburgh Scholarly Publishing Initiatives Fund.

Contents

Illustrations

Acknowledgements

I began the research for this book in 2007, and since that time a great number of individuals have helped me to get to grips with the literature of the Edwardian decade. These include four people who have read over and commented on the whole manuscript: Randall Stevenson, who proved an unfailingly generous, robust and companionable editor; Owen Dudley Edwards, whose remarkable knowledge of the period's popular literature enriched my understanding of the era; Alexandra Lawrie, a tireless, good-humoured, and acute reader of numerous drafts; and Michelle Keown, always the most eagle-eyed of proof readers, and an endless source of encouragement and support in professional and domestic spheres. I am equally grateful to the Department of English Literature/School of Literatures, Languages and Cultures for granting me periods of sabbatical leave to undertake research for this project. My friends and colleagues at Edinburgh, in particular James Loxley, Lee Spinks and Andy Taylor, have proved entertaining and stimulating company during the long gestation of this work. A necessarily selective list of others who have helped in various ways with this book includes Joe Bray, Keith Carabine, John Carey, Sarah Carpenter, Penny Fielding, Thea Fisher, Mary Grover, Faye Hammill, Mike Irwin, Laura Marcus, David McClay, Mark Nixon, Adam Reed, Jonathan Rose, Shari Sabeti, Roger Savage, John Shapcott, Anna Vaninskaya, and the committee and members of the Edwardian Culture Network. Much of the research for this book has relied upon materials at the University of Edinburgh Library and the National Library of Scotland, and I have greatly appreciated the diligence and professionalism of staff at both institutions; and thanks as well to the National Library of Scotland and to the Victoria and Albert Museum in London for permission to reproduce images from their collections. I also owe a great debt of gratitude to those undergraduate students who have taken my Edwardian Literature course, 'The Long Summer' – I've really appreciated having the chance to discuss Edwardian texts with such a talented and engaging bunch of people. At Edinburgh University Press, my particular thanks go to my Commissioning Editor, Jackie Jones, for her patience and forbearance, and Adela Rauchova for helping in the final stages of production.

Finally, I'm greatly indebted to my late mother, Dorothea Wild, whose unfailing interest in my work remains a continuing source of inspiration, and to my children, Nicholas and Antonia, for offering me the ideal distraction from matters Edwardian.

General Editor's Preface

One decade is covered by each of the ten volumes in The Edinburgh History of Twentieth-Century Literature in Britain series. Individual volumes may argue that theirs is *the* decade of the century. The series as a whole considers the twentieth century as *the* century of decades. All eras are changeful, but the pace of change has itself steadily accelerated throughout modern history, and never more swiftly than under the pressures of political crises and of new technologies and media in the twentieth century. Ideas, styles and outlooks came into dominance, and were then displaced, in more and more rapid succession, characterising ever-briefer periods, sharply separated from predecessors and successors.

Time-spans appropriate to literary or cultural history shortened correspondingly, and on account not only of change itself, but its effect on perception. How distant, for example, that tranquil, sunlit, Edwardian decade already seemed, even ten years later, after the First World War, at the start of the twenties. And how essential, too, to the self-definition of that restless decade, and later ones, that the years 1900–1910 *should* seem tranquil and sunlit – as a convenient contrast, not necessarily based altogether firmly on ways the Edwardians may have thought of themselves. A need to secure the past in this way – for clarity and definition in changeful times – encourages views of earlier decades almost as a hand of familiar, well-differentiated cards, dealt out, one by one, by prior times to the present one. These no longer offer pictures of kings and queens: King Edward VII, at the start of the century, or, briefly, George V, were the last monarchs to give their names to an age. Instead, the cards are marked all the more clearly by image and number, as 'the Twenties', 'the Thirties', 'the Forties' and so on. History itself often seems to join in the game, with so many epochal dates – 1918, 1929, 1939, 1968, 1979, 1989, 2001 – approximating to the end of decades.

By the end of the century, decade divisions had at any rate become a firmly established habit, even a necessity, for cultural understanding and analysis. They offer much virtue, and opportunity, to the present series. Concentration within firm temporal boundaries gives each volume further scope to range geographically – to explore the literary production and shifting mutual influences of nations, regions and minorities within a less and less surely 'United' Kingdom. Attention to film and broadcasting allows individual volumes to reflect another key aspect of literature's rapidly changing role throughout the century. In its early years, writing and publishing remained almost the only media for imagination, but by the end of the century, they were hugely challenged by competition from new technologies. Changes of this kind were accompanied by wide divergences in ways that the literary was conceived and studied. The shifting emphases of literary criticism, at various stages of the century, are also considered throughout the series.

Above all, though, the series' decade-divisions promote productive, sharply-focused literary-historical analysis. Ezra Pound's celebrated definition of literature, as 'news that stays news', helps emphasise the advantages. It is easy enough to work with the second part of Pound's equation: to explain the continuing appeal of literature from the past. It is harder to recover what made a literary work news in the first place, or, crucially for literary history, to establish just how it related *to* the news of its day – how it digested, evaded or sublimated pressures bearing on its author's imagination at the time. Concentration on individual decades facilitates attention to this 'news'. It helps recover the brisk, chill feel of the day, as authors stepped out to buy their morning newspapers – the immediate, actual climate of their time, as well as the tranquillity, sunshine or cloud ascribed to it in later commentary. Close concentration on individual periods can also renew attention to writing that did *not* stay news – to works that, significantly, pleased contemporary readers and reviewers, and might repay careful re-reading by later critics.

In its later years, critics of twentieth-century writing sometimes concentrated more on characterising than periodising the literature they surveyed, usually under the rubrics of modernism or postmodernism. No decade is an island, entire of itself, and volumes in the series consider, where appropriate, broader movements and influences of this kind, stretching beyond their allotted periods. Each volume also offers, of course, a fuller picture of the writing of its times than necessarily selective studies of modernism and postmodernism can provide. Modernism and postmodernism, moreover, are thoroughly specific in their historical origins and development, and the nature of each can be usefully illumined by the close, detailed analyses the series provides. Changeful, tumultuous and challenging, history in the twentieth-century perhaps pressed harder and more variously on literary imagination than ever before, requiring a literary history correspondingly meticulous, flexible and multifocal. This is what The Edinburgh History of Twentieth-Century Literature in Britain provides.

The idea for the series originated with Jackie Jones at Edinburgh University Press, and all involved are grateful for her vision and guidance, and for support from the Press, at every stage throughout.

Randall Stevenson
University of Edinburgh

Introduction

In the introduction to an edited collection of essays that appeared in the final decade of the twentieth century entitled *Seeing Double: Revisioning Edwardian and Modernist Literature* (1996), Carola M. Kaplan and Anne B. Simpson reassessed the writing of the early years of that century. This re-examination was necessary, they argued, because critics over the course of the twentieth century had consistently and wilfully undervalued Edwardian literature. Starting from the outbreak of the First World War, influential literary critics had declared it a 'truism to assert that the culture immediately preceding the chaos had offered an idyllic interval for a mindless British populace'. The legacy of this persuasive 'truism', Kaplan and Simpson continued, ensured that those Edwardian writers who in their day 'had been highly respected and widely read' had subsequently become 'grouped together' in an undifferentiated mass, 'their differences and disagreements forgotten' (Kaplan and Simpson 1996: viii). It is only in recent years that this disregard of the period's literary culture has shown signs of revision. Increasing academic interest in areas such as book history, popular and middlebrow literature, and a more general desire to extend and deepen our understanding of the twentieth century beyond an exclusive group of canonical texts, have all encouraged a revaluation of neglected Edwardian writing; the increasing proliferation of digital sources in recent years has offered scholars the perfect platform from which to undertake original research on often long out-of-print texts. The key aim of my work is to provide an understanding of what Edwardian literature in its various forms meant to the Edwardians themselves – following Kaplan and Simpson's lead, to try to understand those 'differences and disagreements' that made the period's writing so lively and variegated in its contemporary moment. To achieve this aim, I have attempted in the ensuing chapters to give a sense of the excitement, tension, frustration, wonder and pleasure generated by novels, plays, poems and essays in their original contexts. Equipped with a nuanced understanding of the significance of these texts to their producers and consumers, we are better prepared to assess what this literary culture might signify to us as its inheritors in the twenty-first century.

The subtitle of this book, *The Great Edwardian Emporium*, identifies a key element in its design. Like those vast new department stores which epitomised the thrill of modernity for Edwardian shoppers, the period's

Figure 1. Advertisement announcing the opening of Selfridge's in 1909. Image © Victoria and Albert Museum, London.

literary culture also looked to attract the eye of a fresh breed of consumers emerging in the new century. Many of those authors who came to exemplify Edwardian writing (including archetypal period figures, such as Arnold Bennett and H. G. Wells), would have recognised clear parallels between themselves and Harry Gordon Selfridge, the entrepreneur proprietor of the era's major new London department store. The publicity announcing the opening of 'Selfridge's' in 1909 proclaimed confidently that this 'New & Wonderful Shopping Centre' was 'NOW OPEN TO THE WORLD': the image accompanying the proclamation has a female figure representing London, dressed in elegant contemporary costume, holding a scale model of the cutting-edge building housing the shop, above the caption 'London receiving her Newest Institution' (Fig. 1). Although publicity of this type now appears laughably hyperbolic, in context, Selfridge's innovative approach to what his publicity described as the 'pleasures of shopping' (marketing it as a leisure activity, which would take place in a building incorporating up-to-date design and technical innovation) succeeded in offering shoppers a real sense of wonder; over one million people were estimated to have experienced this spectacle in the store's opening week (Woodhead 2008: 86, 90). Edwardian writers and publishers were equally alert to the possibility of breaking with the conventions that had governed and controlled their trade in the era of their Victorian forebears. Like Harry Gordon Selfridge, many of the new generation of literary professionals looked to celebrate modernity with fresh and dynamic forms of print. Viewed in this light, Edwardian consumers of contemporary literature might reasonably have considered themselves akin to those wide-eyed shoppers who attended Selfridge's grand opening; unlike their shopping counterparts, however, Edwardian readers accessed an imagined mutable space, replete with new floors, departments, staff and products which appeared in a rapid and colourful succession. Crucially as well, this virtual paper edifice was designed to attract consumers of all stripes, ranging from aesthetes with limitless resources who might purchase connoisseur editions at high prices to penniless browsers looking to borrow library editions without charge: the parallel between this latter cohort and Selfridge's democratic claim to offer 'London's Lowest Prices' provides a further instructive connection between otherwise separate entities. As the following chapters will demonstrate, Edwardian writers were generally comfortable in seeing themselves as retailers, often employing new and energetic literary agents (such as James Brand Pinker) to gain the best price for their wares. But the financial imperative of earning a living was typically balanced by a sense of the potential cultural and social importance of their trade. Wells epitomised this sense of mission in a 1911 speech, during which he decreed that the generation of writers who had come of age in the Edwardian epoch should 'appeal to the young and the hopeful and the curious, against the established, the dignified, and defensive' (Wells 1914a: 169). The great Edwardian literary emporium, much like its department store counterpart, was designed to profoundly transform the existing horizons of those who entered through its doors.

The outside world reflected in the texts of this decade was a decidedly unsettled one, with the beginning of the century coinciding with war in South Africa, and ending with anticipation of the Great War to come. As the narrator of Wells' 1914 novel, *The Wife of Sir Isaac Harman* proclaims, 'The first decade of the twentieth century was for the English a decade of badly sprained optimism'. Wells' narrator locates the source of much of this anxiety in what he describes as the 'acute disillusionments that arose out of the Boer War': 'Our Empire', he continues, 'was nearly beaten by a handful of farmers amidst the jeering contempt of the whole world – and we felt it acutely for several years. We began to question ourselves' (Wells 1914b: 292–3). The repercussions of this disastrous war are seen particularly in anxiety about Britain's position as an imperial power, and even more pressingly in fears about security on the home front; Britain's inability to wage an effective war in South Africa raised serious questions regarding the country's ability to protect its own borders. The building of a modern class of Dreadnought battleships (an initiative which dated from 1906) was intended to allay these fears, while offering physical reassurance about Britain's ability to repel invasion. A collective sense of unease regarding national security was exacerbated by the turbulent political landscape of the age. In the middle of the Edwardian decade, the landslide election victory for the Liberal party in February 1906 led to a radical and divisive programme of welfare reforms: these new initiatives included policies focused on the education and health of children; the Old Age Pensions Act (1908), which introduced pensions for the over-70s; new legislation covering employees' welfare, such as the 1911 National Insurance Act (instrumental in introducing compulsory health insurance for workers), and the 1909 Labour Exchanges Act (which introduced measures designed to help the unemployed back into work). Although many of these policies were subsequently lauded for the contribution they made to a more democratically organised society in Britain, at the time they were characterised by critics as the thin end of the wedge of socialist collectivisation. The key political battleground here was the manner in which these reforms would be financed, an issue which came to a head in the discussions surrounding David Lloyd George's 'People's Budget' in 1909. The Finance Bill proposed under this budget included measures such as the raising of the general income tax rate, together with a 'super-tax' of 6d in the pound for those individuals who earned over £5,000 per annum. The Bill unsurprisingly met with considerable opposition in the Conservative-dominated House of Lords, and this ensured that it was initially voted down. The broader significance of this political disagreement can be recognised in the clash it signifies between opposed social classes: on one side the 'people', who were destined to benefit from wide-ranging and tangible social reforms, and on the other side the patrician classes, keen to protect vested interests while vehemently resisting calls for reform of the upper house's power. Political fault lines such as this need to be considered in light of the changes brought about in British society by those Victorian Education Acts (dating from the 'Forster' Act in 1870) which had offered a platform for the intellectual growth and development of the working class. The emergence of an upwardly mobile lower-middle class (comprising in large part people of working-class stock) during the Edwardian period is proof of the rapid effect of this Victorian social legislation. As I argue throughout this book, many of the new generation of Edwardian writers, and the readers at whom their work was targeted, were graduates of the sorts of state-funded board schools which were established from the 1870s onwards. The coming to maturity and influence of this social class after 1900 is a narrative that has been largely underplayed in existing accounts of this literary period, and it is one that provides a keynote in my own interpretation. An important part of the same narrative can be seen in the agitation for women's suffrage that gained ground during the decade; many of the significant players in the 'Votes for Women' movement were drawn from the newly literate 'clerk' class. This new breed of politically active women, together with the equally vocal supporters of the period's other great lobbying faction, the Irish Home Rule movement, added greatly to the unsettled complexion of the Edwardian world as characterised by Wells and his contemporaries.

Alongside these social and political factors, numerous technological and intellectual innovations also contributed to the era's restless character. Edwardian writers from across a number of different literary fields were keen to incorporate the latest tangible incarnations of modernity in their work. These include modes of transport such as the motorcar, which although pre-dating the decade in its earliest manifestations, only came to prominence on British roads after 1900, and the aeroplane, whose arrival was signalled for many by Louis Blériot's successful cross-channel flight in 1909. New forms of media also became established at this time, chief among them the cinema and the popular mass-market illustrated newspaper, both of which were fixed institutions in British daily life by the decade's end. In science, Guglielmo Marconi established the first successful wireless broadcast across the Atlantic in 1901, and physicist Ernest Rutherford carried out the pioneering work on radio-activity that would later allow him to split the atom. Elsewhere, Albert Einstein's 1905 paper, 'On the Electrodynamics of Moving Bodies', introduced the theory of special relativity, a concept that would have a profound effect on the way in which we consider the relationship between space and time. In the social sciences, a number of influential intellectual theorists had their work widely published in English for the first time; among these were Friedrich Nietzsche and Sigmund Freud. In the fine arts, Cubism first appeared in the work of Pablo Picasso, Georges Braque and others from 1907, and Roger Fry's 'Manet and the Post-Impressionists' exhibition at the Grafton Galleries in London in 1910 introduced a British public to new forms of modern art for the first time; it was Fry's exhibition that inspired Virginia Woolf to famously aver that 'on or about December 1910 human character changed' ('Character in Fiction', in Woolf 1988: 421).

As this book will suggest, the sort of restless and innovative qualities evident across numerous aspects of Edwardian culture are consistently mirrored in the period's literature. But as the opening pages of my introduction also testify, existing historical surveys of twentieth-century writing tend to offer scant impression of literature's pivotal place in this dynamic landscape. The unfashionable nature of Edwardian literature has ensured that critical works focused directly on this period are relatively scarce. Even in the first half of the twentieth century, few critics showed an inclination to discuss the decade's literary history as a discrete entity; Frank Swinnerton's study of the succeeding literary epoch, *The Georgian Literary Scene* (1935), failed to inspire an equivalent Edwardian volume. Where Edwardian literature and writers were critiqued at this time, this usually happened in individual chapters within books with broader cultural and intellectual remits: cases in point here are the edited collection *Edwardian England A.D. 1901–1910* (1933), which includes a chapter on literature by the volume's editor, poet Lascelles Abercrombie; and Herbert Palmer's *Post-Victorian Poetry* (1938), which covers the verse of Edwardians alongside those of Georgians and Moderns. It was only in the second half of the twentieth century that the period's writing began a fitful progress towards revaluation. A key text in this respect is *Edwardians and Late Victorians* (1960), a collection of essays on literary topics edited by Richard Ellmann. Of particular interest among these essays is Ellmann's own chapter contribution to the book, 'Two Faces of Edward', which offers the first serious critical assessment of 'Edwardian' as a significant and stand-alone literary epoch. Samuel Hynes' *The Edwardian Turn of Mind* (1968/1991) builds upon Ellmann's essay while offering a broad synthetic evaluation of the era's cultural landscape. In placing writers and writing at the heart of the 'intellectual climate of Edwardian England' (viii) that he addresses here, Hynes establishes the significance of this literary period within wider contemporary contexts. Hynes subsequent collection of essays, *Edwardian Occasions* (1972), continued his wider project, this time in a text that offered 'the unity of one mind thinking about one period of literary history' (ix). Although the rarity of thinking such as this at the time is worth underlining, in the 1980s signs emerged that other critics were beginning to respond to the pioneering work of Ellmann and Hynes. John Batchelor acknowledges his debt to these predecessors in the opening page of *The Edwardian Novelists* (1982); he also cites Bernard Bergonzi's *The Turn of a Century* (1973) as another rare instance of a work focused on this era. Batchelor's study, while offering a useful introductory chapter on the period's fiction, then follows the 'great man' model of literary history in focusing the book's following chapters on Joseph Conrad, Ford Madox Ford, H. G. Wells, Arnold Bennett, John Galsworthy, and E. M. Forster. Jefferson Hunter's *Edwardian Fiction* (1982), by way of contrast, provides a thematically structured survey of its topic, demonstrating in the process an impressive knowledge and understanding of writers and texts drawn from well outside the mainstream. Further notable critical works first published in the 1980s and 1990s are Jonathan Rose's *The Edwardian Temperament 1895–1919* (1986), Peter Keating's *The Haunted Study* (1989), and David Trotter's *The English Novel in History 1895–1920* (1993). Rose's approach is much in line with the sort of broad intellectual history of the period covered in Hynes' *The Edwardian Turn of Mind*, but in common with its predecessor, Rose's text valuably establishes the social and political importance of contemporary creative writers by placing them at the forefront of a wide range of key movements of the period. Keating's *The Haunted Study* is subtitled 'A Social History of the English Novel 1875–1914', and therefore covers a broad time period in which Edwardian literature forms only a part of its focus. But Keating does give prominent space to the Edwardian decade, and in the process identifies a wealth of neglected texts, writers and issues which he painstakingly locates in their appropriate cultural milieu. Much the same can be said of Trotter's historical survey of the novel between 1895 and 1920. Trotter's work here is consistently suggestive and provocative, and as such it provides much inspiration for further academic study. This is equally true of two works whose usefulness as reference guides to the period's often neglected writers and texts are impossible to overstate: *Edwardian Fiction: An Oxford Companion* (1997), edited by Sandra Kemp, Charlotte Mitchell and David Trotter; and Philip Waller's monumental *Writers, Readers, & Reputations: Literary Life in Britain 1870–1918* (2006). For newcomers to the period's writing, Anthea Trodd's *A Reader's Guide to Edwardian Literature* (1991) offers a compact and sensible introduction to the major currents in the field, and is therefore a useful starting point for general Edwardian literary studies.

Aside from these broad surveys of the period's literature, a number of other monographs have appeared in recent years which are focused on particular forms or genres of Edwardian writing. Edwardian drama had already inspired a number of single-volume studies in the middle years of the twentieth century; these included *Carriages at Eleven* (1947) by W. MacQueen-Pope, and *Edwardian Theatre* (1951) by A. E. Wilson. Both of these works were largely designed to allow nostalgic theatregoers of the period to relive their youthful play-going days, and as such were primarily focused on the era's popular theatre, in particular its ubiquitous musical comedies. From the 1980s onwards, fresh academic interest was typically focused on the more innovative forms of theatre, in particular the so-called New Drama that emerged at this time. Jan McDonald's *The 'New Drama' 1900–1914* (1986), examines writers such as John Galsworthy and Harley Granville Barker, who attempted to modernise British theatre by making it newly relevant to contemporary society. Ian Clarke's *Edwardian Drama* (1989), also covers this territory, but places New Dramatists in context with those playwrights who were working at the more commercial end of the market; Clarke includes a chapter, for example, on Henry Arthur Jones and Arthur Wing Pinero, key advocates of the sort of 'well-made play' that the New Drama set out to challenge. Subsequent critical accounts of the period's drama have included *The Edwardian Theatre* (1996) edited by Michael R. Booth and Joel H. Kaplan, and *The Cambridge Companion to Victorian and Edwardian Theatre* (2004), edited by Kerry Powell.

Unlike theatre, Edwardian poetry has received little recent critical interest other than in studies of individual poets active in the period, such as Thomas Hardy, Rudyard Kipling and W. B. Yeats; the only genre-specific critical study of the era's verse to date is Kenneth Millard's *Edwardian Poetry* (1991). Meanwhile, gender issues in the period's literature have attracted a degree of critical attention since the publication of Jane Eldridge Miller's *Rebel Women: Feminism, Modernism and the Edwardian Novel* (1994) and Lyn Pykett's *Engendering Fictions: The English Novel in the Early Twentieth Century* (1995). Most recently, Anne Fernihough's *Freewomen and Supermen: Edwardian Radicals and Literary Modernism* (2013), has investigated sex and suffragism alongside a number of other radical issues of the day. Finally, in this necessarily selective overview of critical texts focused on Edwardian writing, Adrienne E. Gavin and Andrew F. Humphries' edited collection, *Childhood in Edwardian Fiction: Worlds Enough and Time* (2008), offers what is currently the only single-volume critical text dedicated to children's literature in the decade.

My own contribution to the history of Edwardian literature draws inspiration from and looks to build upon the work of many of the texts outlined above. The following chapters are organised around a selection of themes which permit a broad consideration of the period's literary culture in its historical contexts. In the first chapter I examine the response of writers to the Boer War (or the Anglo-Boer War, as it is now more commonly known) in particular, looking at the work that emerged during the time of the conflict. This chapter goes on to investigate 'invasion literature', a popular genre of writing that imagined an often vulnerable and unprepared Britain being attacked and conquered by rival imperial powers. The final section of this opening chapter then examines the idea of Empire as discussed in the fiction of Rudyard Kipling, Joseph Conrad and John Buchan. My second chapter begins by tracing the rise to prominence of two writers, Arnold Bennett and H. G. Wells, whose names have since become inextricably associated with the term 'Edwardian'. Their ability to profit from the favourable literary conditions in this period is examined in context with other writers of their class and generation who were, to use a characteristic phrase of the day, 'getting on'. The third chapter focuses on the appearance of much memorable children's literature during what has come to be known as its 'Golden Age'. Covering the work of three of the main innovators in this field, Beatrix Potter, E. Nesbit and P. G Wodehouse, this chapter shows how new writers reinvented existing popular forms of writing for children to make them attractive and newly relevant for readers in the new century. In the fourth chapter, I investigate Edwardian modernity via three areas which epitomised this quality for many readers of the day: sex, cars and money. My investigations into the first of these categories reveals the existence of a thriving and often quite explicit commentary on sex in the fiction of the day; the second section of the chapter, while concentrating on the motorcar as the embodiment of Edwardian technological modernity, also uncovers a wider fascination for the latest 'thing' in a range of contemporary publications; and the final part of the chapter concentrates on the issue of money (and the corruption that it often implies in the period's literature) in the New Drama of the day. Finally, Chapter 5 investigates the vexed question of the 'Condition of England' via an examination of 'England' as an entity in the period's poetry, its non-fiction topographical and nature writing, and lastly in that most Edwardian of literary forms, the country-house novel.

These focal points, while covering a wide range of topics, in no way offer an exhaustive overview of the Edwardian literary scene. The limited space at my disposal has dictated the selection of exemplary aspects of the period's literature, and this process of choice was a necessarily subjective one. Joseph Conrad articulated his own feelings about the subjective nature of writing in an 'Author's Note' he appended to *The Secret Agent* (1907) after the end of the Great War. Looking back on his novel from this perspective, Conrad remarked that the worlds he tried to evoke here offered an individual and therefore a partial viewpoint: 'I have attended to my business', he confessed, because 'I could not have done otherwise' (1907/2004: 232). The best any writer might achieve in these terms is to convey a reasoned understanding of the themes that they address, while drawing on what they consider to be the best materials and ideas at their disposal – attending honestly to their 'business', in Conrad's formulation. In constructing the Great Edwardian Emporium in the following pages, I have literalised Conrad's sense of attending to business, imagining in the process the sort of commercial enterprise that might symbolise the Edwardian literary scene. While there can be no grand opening of this virtual storehouse to match that of Selfridge's spectacular first day of trading in 1909, these introductory pages serve something of this purpose. But in this case, rather than signifying the opening of brand-new premises, my introduction represents instead the reopening and refurbishment of a long-neglected cultural edifice. Like any work of restoration, what is on show here cannot directly replicate the original entity, but it can offer a clear sense of the enterprise, displaying in the process the goods and personnel who occupied this cultural space. Beyond this Edwardian-centred reconstruction of the era's literary landscape, I have also remained cognisant of the question that C. F. G. Masterman asked in the opening lines of *The Condition of England* (1909): 'What will the future make of the present?' (1909/1910: 1). The act of refurbishing the Edwardian Emporium establishes the grounds on which this question can be addressed. By familiarising ourselves with the contexts in which Edwardians encountered and interpreted their own literature, we are best able to make our own informed judgements on the cultural edifice they left behind.

Chapter One

Department of War and External Affairs: The Anglo-Boer War and Imperialism

The literature appearing in Britain in the opening decade of the twentieth century was profoundly affected by events happening well beyond the geographical boundaries of the British Isles. The war fought in South Africa between British imperial forces and Dutch settlers (commonly known at the time as the Boer War (1899–1902) and now more generally referred to as the Anglo-Boer War) brought to a head many of the anxieties felt by ordinary British and British Empire citizens about the efficacy and sustainability of British imperialism. As this chapter will demonstrate, the war's role in focusing these anxieties is especially evident in the literature which emerged both during the conflict and in the ensuing years of the decade. This literary culture was profoundly influenced by wartime news media, in terms of its content, political positioning and style. We can recognise these effects explicitly in the fiction, discussed in the first section of this chapter, which drew directly upon the conflict for its subject matter. These Anglo-Boer War-centred novels and stories often replicated and extended the compelling narratives and distinctive textual forms evident in wartime reportage and feature writing. A line of direct influence between media coverage of the war and its aftermath can also be traced in in the popularity of 'invasion' fiction that appeared in this era. As the second section of this chapter will outline, narratives which imagined Britain under attack from rapacious imperial rivals (seeking blood after the exposure of British weakness during the war) exploited and extended fears whipped up by the Edwardian press. The works of Conrad and Kipling discussed in the third section of the chapter, while not directly focused on war-torn South Africa, appeared in the shadow of the conflict and its media reportage. Readers of this period encountered texts such as *Heart of Darkness*, *Lord Jim* and *Kim* (all of which originally appeared in serial form between 1899 and 1901) alongside incessant day-to-day media coverage of the often uncertain progress of the war. The forms of imperial critique found in these and other works in this chapter need to be understood in relationship with the dominant historical event occurring at this time. A better awareness of this relationship makes clear the extent to which a changing literary landscape responded rapidly to the demands of evolving readerships. In this way, the chapter suggests the importance of recognising Edwardian literature as a wartime and then an inter-war literature, as opposed to its more usual designation as a pre-war literary culture written in anticipation of the conflict to come in 1914. For the Edwardians, the Anglo-Boer War was a truly *great* war, and everything written or read during the period that touched on Britain's relationship with the outside world did so with South Africa much in mind.

Anglo-Boer War Literature

Until the Anglo-Boer War was overshadowed by later clashes fought on much grander scales, few commentators considered it to be anything less than a truly great imperial conflict. As Thomas Pakenham argues:

> It proved to be the longest (two and three-quarter years), the costliest (over £200 million), the bloodiest (at least twenty-two thousand British, twenty-five thousand Boer and twelve thousand African lives) and the most humiliating war for Britain between 1815 and 1914. (Pakenham 1982: xv)

When the first decade of the twentieth century began, the war had already been in progress for two-and-a-half months and, following a number of early military reversals for the British (culminating in the particularly disastrous 'Black Week' in mid-December 1899 (Pakenham 1982: 246)), the conflict appeared destined to continue far into the new century. While it is only possible here to sketch in some of the historical details relating to the political and military background of the fighting, it is at least necessary to offer a sense of why this war was publicly recognised at the time as much more than just another imperial conflict. Foremost among the reasons that set the Anglo-Boer War apart from other wars since Waterloo was the fact that the enemy was largely composed of the same north European Protestant stock as the British forces. Whereas earlier imperial wars had typically involved the forces of the Empire putting down rebellion by 'lesser' races, the Dutch-descended Boers were impossible to characterise in this dismissive way. In addition, the Boers, settlers in South Africa like the British, presented reasons for their occupation of the country that seemingly replicated those of the larger imperial power. The substantial numbers of pro-Boer supporters in Britain during this period pointed to these factors as key reasons why the Boers, largely small-scale farmers and agricultural workers, should be left to govern themselves in their own established southern African republics.

While the uncomfortable racial and moral proximity of British and Dutch-Boer settlers set this imperial war apart from many of its predecessors, the war was additionally distinctive because of the ways in which it was destined to utilise the technological and sociological developments of the late-Victorian era. This conflict might have been posthumously dubbed by J. F. C. Fuller the 'last of the gentleman's wars' (the title of his 1937 memoir of the war), but it was equally the first of the large-scale modern twentieth-century wars. The war's anticipation of these later conflicts is indicated by its employment of mechanised armaments, trench warfare, scorched earth policies and, most ominously, concentration camps. Moreover, the Anglo-Boer War anticipated ensuing world wars in the ways in which its events were recorded and repackaged for consumption on the home front. The reason why the war was so significant in this respect is that it took place at a time when the British news media was undergoing a period of revolution. The resulting transformation in the nature of the press ensured that the general public experienced the war through a lens quite different from that through which it had witnessed earlier conflicts. While Kenneth O. Morgan rightly interprets the Anglo-Boer War era as 'a seminal and crucial period in the evolution of the British press' (2002: 8), such a claim is also applicable to the readers of the wartime press. As I will argue in this section, after the war, in the early years of the new century, reading – and the nature of reading matter – would never be quite the same again.

The seeds of these changes in reading matter and reading habits can be traced back to the 1880s, when George Newnes first published the phenomenally popular weekly magazine, *Tit-Bits*. This paper, which offered its readers a miscellany of facts, puzzles and jokes, was targeted at the new reading public that had emerged following late-Victorian reforms in education. The success of *Tit-Bits* (its circulation in the 1880s and 1890s averaged half a million copies sold per week (Jackson 2001: 56)) spawned numerous other publishing ventures, also designed to attract an evidently vast market. Of these publications, the most important (and most lasting) was Alfred Harmsworth's *Daily Mail*, which first appeared in May 1896. The distinctive content and halfpenny price of the *Daily Mail* set it apart from existing newspapers (which typically cost one penny), and helped to secure its position as the first mass-circulation daily paper in the country. Harmsworth's paper included short feature pieces written in accessible English, human-interest stories, sporting news and a magazine page directed towards women readers.

Although this mix of materials might not appear especially revolutionary judged by subsequent standards of the British press, in the late 1890s the freshness of the *Daily Mail*'s format was perfectly judged to attract readers who sought entertainment as well as practical information. A measure of the paper's success can be gauged from the fact that during the Anglo-Boer War, the *Daily Mail* increased its circulation to over one million copies sold each day (Read 1999: 78); these sales figures were unprecedented at this time for any equivalent publication in the world. The astonishing wartime popularity of this paper alerted publishers to the potential scale of the current newspaper market and encouraged the launch of other mass-market dailies during this period; these included the *Daily Express* in April 1900 and another Harmsworth paper, the *Daily Mirror* (initially produced by women for a female readership) in November 1903.

The broadening of the franchise of newspaper readers at this time had a number of wide-ranging implications. We can, for example, recognise the potential political ramifications of international events being refashioned in print by a team of journalists and editors who were, in many cases, working for just a handful of press barons. The scale of this influence is clearly a matter for continuing speculation, but at least one critic has argued that the Mafeking celebrations (commemorating the relief by imperial forces of a besieged South African town in May 1900) 'were the product of the new newspapers' relationship with the new British publics they were creating . . . and the celebrations . . . actually reveal that such support was carefully manufactured through the press by a careful manipulation of public opinion(s)' (Krebs 2004: 7). Whether or not we agree that wartime journalism was as powerful as Paula M. Krebs' claim implies, the vast audiences reached by newspapers such as the *Daily Mail* certainly created the conditions in which this manipulation of public opinion might occur. We can also recognise the broader social and cultural implications of changes in print media at this time. Irrespective of how the press might or might not dictate public opinion, it is evident that vast numbers of individuals developed a daily habit of reading news media during the war; the remarkable volume of wartime poetry submitted to newspapers by members of the general public (discussed at length in M. van Wyk Smith's *Drummer Hodge: The Poetry of the Anglo-Boer War, 1899–1902*) hints at the scale of this cohort. It is also significant that this regular reading matter was typically *bought* by its readers, rather than being passively received from either school or church, or borrowed from a public library. Those readers who paid their halfpenny for copies of the *Daily Mail* and other popular papers during the war became (in many cases for the first time) active investors in the literary economy. Furthermore, as I shall go on to argue, the wartime subject matter was typically read in intensive ways, thereby developing new levels of engagement between readers and reading matter. While I would not claim that any marked broadening and transformation of the literary field at this time was exclusively the result of changes in wartime reading habits, the Anglo-Boer War undoubtedly alerted the publishing industry to significant changes in readerships, in reading tastes, and in book and magazine buying habits. Ford Madox Hueffer (later Ford Madox Ford) provides a clear illustration of the addictive, promiscuous, and evidently influential nature of wartime reading in an autobiographical work published in 1911 that looked back on his own experiences of the conflict:

> With the coming of the South African War we acquired the habit of skimming through from seven to ten papers a day – to get a little hope. I don't blame us. The man who could go through the period of Spion Kop without rushing anywhere to read the latest bulletin, or could keep in his pocket one single penny that might give him some glimmer of hopeful news, was something less than a man. I suppose I was as hot a pro-Boer as anyone well could be, but I know I came very near to crying with joy when Mafeking was relieved. (Hueffer 1911: 245–6)

Armed with this knowledge about potential readers – and, crucially, paying readers – Edwardian writers and publishers were energetic in their attempts to satisfy a virtually new and almost certainly profitable market. The dynamic climate brought about by writers, publishers and readers engaging in the cultural equivalent of a mating ritual at this time goes some way towards explaining the distinctive nature of the Edwardian literary field.

While it is difficult to quantify the extent to which the popularisation (and arguably democratisation) of British news media transformed sections of the population from irregular readers into print addicts, much evidence of changing trends in this field can be located in the period's fiction. What is particularly striking about those stories and novels which focus on the war is the extent to which they, like Hueffer above, register a contemporary obsession with newspaper reading. British Anglo-Boer War fiction typically includes episodes in which newspaper reading is defined – either implicitly or explicitly – as the key element in the public's experience of and engagement with the conflict. The impression conveyed here is of the general public experiencing a 'virtual' war, one that was played out in daily newspaper instalments. It is also significant that these fictional scenes of wartime news reading are included in texts intended for a wide variety of readers. These range from jingoistic accounts of the gallant Tommy, to novels evidently pitched towards the more literary end of the reading demographic. Across this range of imaginative texts, fictional readers use newspapers to satisfy a broad array of needs and desires. One of the earliest works to emerge in this field, A. St John Adcock's collection of stories, *In the Wake of the War* (1900), focuses on the reading that was taking place on the home front; the cover illustration of this work, featuring a young woman intently reading a newspaper, perfectly captures the mood of the volume as a whole (Fig. 2). Many of Adcock's diverse characters, drawn largely from among working-class and lower-middle-class Londoners, are depicted apprehensively scanning the pages of newspapers in search of information about relatives or friends involved in the fighting. In 'The Glory of Jack Dunn', an anxious grocer minutely follows the details of war gleaned from the evening papers to enable him to plot the movements of his son's regiment on a map pinned up on the wall of his shop. Elsewhere, two old friends (a plumber and an ironmonger) who have fallen out over disagreements regarding the conduct of the war are reunited when one of them reads a newspaper report of a battle and finds the names of their hero sons mentioned together ('A Treaty of Peace'). Other readers in Adcock's stories have their martial spirit piqued by reading war news: a veteran of Crimea and the Indian Mutiny, living in a London work-house, is whipped up by the press to such a state of excitement that he seeks to rejoin the regiment ('The Corporal Rejoins'). And in 'The Old Adam', an army reservist, now a member of the Salvation Army, is shaken out of his newly embraced religious pacifism when a newspaper report of the Battle of Colenso 'brought him to a sudden and inflexible resolve' to go to the front (Adcock 1900a: 95). Not all of Adcock's characters are convinced about the veracity of press reports: in 'The Shadow of War', a Lambeth mother refuses to place complete trust in the press for news of her soldier son ('Yer can't trust newspapers' (27)), and she walks instead to the War Office, where the list of killed and wounded is posted daily. But the general sense conveyed in Adcock's stories is of a home population neurotically picking over every available mote of war news provided by the press.

Taking into account the intensive reading witnessed in so many of Adcock's stories, it is particularly revealing that a number of his characters refer to their gathering of information from newspapers as 'watching' rather than 'reading' the news: a father criticises his daughter's relative lack of war knowledge by telling her: 'you'd know that if you watched the news half as closely as I do' (1900a: 57). Another anxious father 'watched the papers daily in fear and trembling' (151); and when a sweetheart is asked how she was able to greet her wounded beau on his return home, she replies: 'I watched the papers, dear' (135). One expla-

Figure. 2. Front cover of A. St John Adcock's *In the Wake of the War* (1900). Image reproduced by permission of the National Library of Scotland.

nation for this sense of the news being watched might be the extent to which illustration, and increasingly, photography were being incorporated into news media at this time: Morgan argues that the Anglo-Boer War was a news event 'you could see and not just read about' (2002: 9). But for Adcock's characters, the sense of *watching* the news appears to be evoked by vivid wartime textual reportage rather than via graphic images.

Many other works of fiction written in and around 1900 share Adcock's sense of the events of the war being *witnessed* in print by domestic readers. But, unlike Adcock's workhouse dwellers and small shopkeepers, the readers in many of these other texts are drawn from higher levels in the social scale. Whereas reading newspapers for Adcock's characters had often involved tracking the fates of relatives and friends, the middle- and upper-class individuals in other contemporary fiction are typically motivated by more self-serving concerns. The misguided anti-war politician in Fergus Hume's spy novel *A Traitor in London* (1900) is seen, for example, constructing his political speeches from among the 'clippings of editorial opinion and collected data' found in evening papers (87). Elsewhere, in this proudly pro-war novel, the same politician is incensed after reading an anti-Boer/pro-British article in the *Daily Mail*: 'This paper shows me how necessary it is for all men to protest against this unjust war, which has been forced upon the Boers' (20). The latter part of this novel (in which the politician is converted to a pro-war and pro-British stance following a revelatory visit to South Africa) indicates that Hume anticipated that his readership would share – or perhaps just unquestioningly accept – the *Daily Mail*'s hawkish political stance during the war. Guy Boothby's political thriller, *A Cabinet Secret* (1901), similarly includes scenes of a politician (here a Cabinet Minister) poring over a well-known London evening paper, the *Pall Mall Gazette*, for 'the latest war news': 'From what I found there', he avers, 'there could be no doubt that the situation was hourly increasing in danger' (61). Later, Boothby's Cabinet Minister records the sense of national crisis melodramatically conveyed to the public by the press: 'Day after day the news of reverses filled the columns of the Public Press, until it began to look as if the prestige of England would be destroyed for ever and a day' (123–4). A further important depiction of wartime newspaper reading in fiction of this type is found in E. W. Hornung's 1901 Raffles story, 'The Knees of the Gods'. In this tale, Raffles, the gentleman thief, and his partner-in-crime and chronicler 'Bunny', decide that it is their patriotic duty to give up their lives of crime during the wartime emergency. After hearing a newsvendor in Richmond announcing ''Eavy British lorsses! –orful slorter o' the Bo-wers!', they become preoccupied with following the events from South Africa in the press:

> We were never again without our sheaf of evening papers, and Raffles ordered three morning ones . . . We became strategists. We knew exactly what Buller was to do on landing, and, still better, what the other Generals should have done. Our map was the best that could be bought, with flags that deserved a better fate than standing still. (Hornung 1992: 256)

Like Adcock's Salvationist-turned-soldier, Raffles is inspired by reading newspapers to fight, and in his case die, in South Africa.

While the fiction of Hume, Boothby and Hornung clearly profits from the incorporation of melodramatic newspaper accounts of the nation in peril, other novelists provide more sober accounts of wartime reading. Ménie Muriel Dowie's *Love and His Mask* (1901) depicts a group of middle-class women, who, from the safety of their English village, have 'acquired a bewildering surface-knowledge of the South Africa question' (13–14). For these women, the political dimension of the conflict remains secondary to their thirst for information about the 'personnel of the Army', wartime 'hospital organisation', and 'the composition of the Irregular Forces', which was 'perhaps their speciality' (14). Dowie's novel also features a further wartime reading group often recorded in the period's fiction; this cohort, the army on active service in South Africa, is depicted by Dowie and others as avid readers of the London press:

> Every item of news from the London dailies was eagerly canvassed. They were starving for war news, all these soldier men . . . No one at home can believe – we who are furious if the afternoon paper cannot be had at the club within a moment of its reaching the street; we who grab our *Times* fiercely from the breakfast-table, or have had, possibly, a glimpse at the *Daily Mail* on our way to the bath – we cannot form any idea of the yearnings of Tommy for news of the other Tommies' doings! (66)

Dowie adds an intriguing postscript here by suggesting that the soldiers needed to read about the war to 'have some idea of the great work that is being done, of which they are a blind and willing instrument; how important or unimportant they can have but the barest idea' (66–7). The impression offered here is that the rendering of events into newsprint offered them coherent form and meaning that was lacking for individuals who were experiencing this action in its 'raw' state. In this interpretation, the newspaper correspondents are vital to the war effort in their ability to decode and in this way make sense of the otherwise meaningless data generated by the war. A further example of this is provided in George Cossins' *A Boer of To-Day: A Story of the Transvaal* (1900). The title character in this novel is a reluctant Boer soldier, who questions his own courage on the eve of battle. Thinking back over his life up to this point, he remembers a girl he had met in Britain before the war and who had snubbed him because he was a Boer. Stirred up by these unhappy memories, he resolved 'that she should read of him, should fear him, should yet bend her proud head in supplication before the discarded Boer' (210). For Cossins' Boer character, the outcome of his action will only hold meaning if it can be recapitulated in print for consumption in a distant English sitting room. Once again, the wartime journalist offers life and substance to an otherwise transitory action.

This fictional panorama of mothers, fathers, pacifists, politicians, spies, impressionable young women, amateur cracksmiths, and Boer soldiers all reading about the war (or self-consciously projecting their battlefield endeavours into print), suggests a society in the throes of cultural change. All of these forms of intensive reading practice depicted in the period's war fiction can be collected together to help us gain some understanding of an era in which print culture accessed via newspapers became, for scores of people, an indispensable part of their daily life. This sense of habitual reading was fostered particularly during the period in which the major sieges and battles of the conflict were taking place (from the end of 1899 until mid-1900). At this time, the unfolding events of war could be followed in much the same way as a developing serial story; the factual material being presented to readers had a similar blend of character and cliff-hanging event as that conventionally found in popular fiction. And in following the dramatic events of the war as they unfolded over a whole year, rather than merely a few weeks (as many jingoistic commentators had typically projected), individuals were able to build up and thereafter retain the habit of daily reading. In understanding the role that war coverage played in conditioning a new generation of regular readers, it is important to recognise the distinctive nature of the war as a reportable story during this era. No previous single news event of this sustained interest and duration had taken place since the broadening of the education franchise following late-Victorian Education Acts (dating from the passing of the 'Forster' Act in 1870) and the concurrent expansion of the media industry as outlined above. The war, therefore, allowed writers and publishers from across the literary world to capitalise on a reading market that had both expanded and, more importantly, seasoned over time.

That there would be considerable dividends for writers and publishers resultant upon this intensive wartime reading was entirely predictable. The novels and stories discussed above formed part of a deluge of books issued during the War that focused on the conflict. Reviewing the year's work for 1900, *The Literary Year-Book* noted that 'the flood of applications to publishers, more or less martial in their nature, shows little sign of diminution' (Morrah 1900: 15). This trend was also noted in a *Bookman* editorial in June 1900: 'fiction continues its popular career, and appears to be exempt from the fluctuations which affect other branches of literature' (Anonymous 1900d: 72). The close connections between media coverage of the war and the narratives encountered in much popular fiction suggest the reasons why appetites whetted by newspapers might equally be satisfied by the volumes of fiction then being published in increasing numbers. And those readers who did shift in their reading habits between newsprint and serial/magazine story or book were able to choose their texts from a fiction market increasingly structured in ways designed to satisfy individual tastes. This increased specialisation in the book trade mirrored the ways in which recent newspaper journalism had identified and exploited (and in many cases instigated) the specific tastes of its readers. Taking this into account, we can understand why fiction writers of this period were increasingly recognised by readers (and marketed by publishers) as specialists in particular genres of writing; see, for example, H. G. Wells' comments in the next chapter about his desire to break away from his designation as a scientific romance specialist.

As established writers in the genres of popular crime and sensation fiction, Hume, Boothby and Hornung clearly found little difficulty in incorporating war plots into their writing. Public anxiety about national security in time of war also allowed these and other writers to develop the Edwardian spy novel as a new sub-genre of existing popular fiction writing. The imperial romance, a form popularised in the 1880s and 1890s by H. Rider Haggard and G. A. Henty, was another category of fiction that lent itself to narratives of a war fought in far-off Africa: Hume Nisbet's imperial romance, *The Empire Makers* (1900), awkwardly grafts Anglo-Boer War scenes on to an evidently pre-existing lost world story. Morley Roberts' *Taken by Assault or The Fugitives* (1901), with its story of an English hero bearing up in the face of wartime anxieties, provides a more cohesively structured imperial romance than that offered by Nisbet. Similar tales of wartime derring-do are found in a number of boys' adventure stories, a genre which was also able to transfer seamlessly its characteristic plots of heroism and manliness to the Veldt. The incorporation of the names of key figures in the war into book titles provided an obvious selling point for juvenile novels of the time: see, for example, Herbert Hayens' *Scouting for Buller* (1902), and G. A. Henty's *With Buller in Natal* (1901) and *With Roberts to Pretoria* (1902).

Like these senior and junior branches of imperial adventure narratives, romantic fiction was equally well-placed to weave the war into its plots of love and loss: John Strange Winter's *A Blaze of Glory* and Anna Howarth's *Nora Lester* (both 1902) involve tangled love and inheritance plots set against the background of the Anglo-Boer War. A flavour of this material can be gained by the lament of a female character in Howarth's novel: 'I wonder if there is another country in the world where so many brave men lie buried!' (303). Readers who were curious about the actual experience of fighting in the war might have their interests satisfied by a number of works of fiction focussing on soldiers' accounts of life at the front: these include Andrew Balfour's *Cashiered and Other War Tales* (1902), a collection of stories which drew upon Balfour's wartime experiences as an army doctor. Thereafter, curiosity about the lives of the enemy might similarly be satisfied by reading those novels that focused on Boer life; novels in this category include Bertram Mitford's *Aletta: A Tale of the Boer Invasion* (1900), and Cossins' *A Boer of To-Day*. Elsewhere, J. A. Stuart's *The Eternal Quest* (1901) allowed devotees of the Scottish novel to combine their existing love of picturesque Highland settings with up-to-date accounts of courageous Scots soldiers in battle. And finally, although this overview by no means exhausts the various genres of writing absorbed by Anglo-Boer War fiction, the novel of ideas might be represented by both Charles Marriott's *The House on the Sands* (1903) and also, in miniature form, by Kipling's characteristically polemical war stories: these include 'The Way That He Took' and 'The Outsider' (both published in the *Daily Express* in June 1900), 'A Sahibs' War' (1901), 'The Comprehension of Private Copper' and 'The Captive' (both 1902) (all five stories can be found in Kipling 1999).

While it was therefore possible, during the conflict, to buy war fiction that suited a wide variety of tastes and interests, readers might also choose work which represented a broad range of political positions. Although major British book publishers were largely unwilling, during the war, to issue overtly pro-Boer or anti-war material, fiction writing at the opposite end of the political spectrum remained much in demand. A prime example of a work of this type is Nisbet's *The Empire Makers*, a rabidly imperialistic narrative predictably dedicated to the British businessman and politician Cecil Rhodes ('England's Greatest Empire Maker' (v)). This novel lays its political cards on the table in an emotional Preface which declares:

> If [this novel] can keep an Imperialist steadfast when persuaded by crafty traitors, if it can induce a wavering pro-Boer to be once more a faithful son or daughter to Justice and our Empire, then it has more than fulfilled the desires of ITS AUTHOR. (1900: viii)

Elsewhere in this Preface, Nisbet looks forward to the end of the war, which must bring about 'the triumph of our glorious Empire and the ultimate civilisation of those ignorant savages, the Boers' (vii). Nisbet's position here, while apparently representing the far extreme of xenophobic jingoism, was not actually excessive given the standards of the day. Evidence of this is offered in *From the Front: Stories from the Seat of War* (1900), an anonymously published collection of fictional letters supposedly written by a Captain in the Volunteer Horse. This text, like Nisbet's, offers a sense of being written for an audience already conditioned by the press to revile an uncivilised and unprincipled foe:

Your white-flag-red-cross-abusing Boer is generally an ignorant, poor devil, who is little better than an animal, and not nearly so good as a savage. Morally and physically he is unclean, and an act of kindness and magnanimity has no more effect upon his soul than a cake of toilet soap would have upon his body. (Anonymous 1900b: 85)

Much more surprising, perhaps, than these texts that played to the jingo gallery, are a number of works that appeared at a period of the war when British casualties were piling up at an alarming rate and which attempted to provide a balanced and compassionate perspective on the enemy. The most noteworthy of these is perhaps Bertram Mitford's largely overlooked novel *Aletta: A Tale of the Boer Invasion*. While Mitford's 'Introductory' preface insisted that his novel was 'devoid of any political purpose or leaning whatsoever' (np), its remarkably sympathetic portrait of the life of a Boer family in peace and war undermines this disclaimer. Indeed, the novel in many ways provides an antithetical political position to the above jingo texts, as Mitford's preface goes on to suggest:

There are Boers who do not go to bed in their clothes; who do wash, and whose persons and dwelling-houses are distinguished by the ordinary conditions of cleanliness and civilisation. There are Boers of good blood and unimpeachable descent; and whose women-kind show by no means badly in the matter of education and even of refinement. Stranger than all it may appear, there actually are Boers who do not devote their leisure moments to the pastime of flogging their native servants to death with sjambok. We feel moved to set forward these considerations, because an impression seems to have taken firm root in the British mind that each and every Boer is the blackest ruffian unhung. (np)

In presenting a direct counter-narrative to that offered by Nisbet and others, Mitford clearly felt that he was offering an important and timely service to an impressionable and often misinformed public. To further understand the need for urgency in Mitford's efforts, we must recognise the potential for social unrest on the home front that support for the war had generated. The celebrations inspired by the relief of Mafeking were only the most extreme forms of jingoism that occurred in 1900. A predictable outcome of this wave of often aggressive xenophobia was a desire among sections of the public to root out and attack suspected Boer sympathisers: Adcock's short story 'Monsieur' (which appeared in 1900 in his *In the Wake of the War* collection) for example, includes a mild-mannered French cornet player in a Mile End music hall who comes under attack by locals suspecting that he is either a 'Boer, or, at least a Boer partisan' (Adcock 1900a: 69). Even a text that is otherwise broadly imperialistic, such as Morley Roberts' *Taken by Assault*, has its hero recognise the potentially malign influence of the wartime press: 'Our lower papers pander to the mob, and there is no means of controlling them. So far as in me lies, I have done my best to counteract their influence' (Roberts 1901: 53).

Among the most remarkable attempts to counteract the potentially harmful influence of wartime propaganda can be found in Adcock's *The Luck of Private Foster* (1900). Adcock initially employs here a narrative designed to appeal to devotees of action and adventure plots. Having gained his audience's attention, he then uses much of his text to educate his readership about the complexity of a war fought between peoples of the same north-European racial type. One of the ways in which he builds this complexity into the narrative is by depicting the inter-linking of family and friends who are caught up on either side of the conflict. The title character, Foster, for example, discovers that his long-lost father is a Boer commander only after this individual has held him as his prisoner. Later, Foster's escape from captivity is facilitated by the sympathetic English wife of a Boer fighter. And towards the end of the novel, two brothers are depicted shooting at each other from opposing sides during the siege of Mafeking. This sense of the futility of a war often fought between 'equals' is summed up during a passage in which Foster reflects upon the kindness shown to him by a Boer Samaritan:

> He had never wronged me, nor I him, yet we ought to have been foes, and it was only a chance that he had not been one of the unknown men I had shot or bayoneted . . . and in this moment of insight I was vividly conscious of the soulless insanity of indiscriminate slaughter. (Adcock 1900b: 254)

Adcock, like Mitford, clearly felt in 1900 that there was a pressing need to address important issues about the actual nature of the fighting that were in danger of being occluded by a partisan and influential press. While Adcock's narrative is, in general terms, a politically conservative one (Foster says of the British government at one stage: 'we give them the power and must trust them' (258)), he, like Mitford, set about humanising the enemy in an effort to disarm what had become a dangerously malign stereotype.

The impression left by much Anglo-Boer War fiction is that its writers sensed – often in highly contrasting ways – the important role that imaginative literature might play in the coming century that was then in its infancy. In an environment in which daily papers might manipulate the minds of huge numbers of young and/or impressionable readers, many novelists were self-consciously working to address (and at times to fuel) potential extremism in society. The more general effects of this new sense of social responsibility were recognised by H. G. Wells in a talk that he gave to the Times Book Club in 1911, later revised for publication in his collection of essays entitled *An Englishman Looks at the World* (1914). Here he argued that, during the Edwardian period, the novel had come to be recognised as 'an important and necessary thing indeed in that complicated system of uneasy adjustments and readjustments which is modern civilisation'; indeed, he went on: 'in many directions I do not think we can get along without it' (1914a: 148). For Wells, the Anglo-Boer War had changed the way in which writers, and popular writers in particular, thought about their readers:

> So far from the weary reader being a decently tired giant, we realise that he is only an inexpressibly lax, slovenly and undertrained giant, and we are all out with one accord resolved to exercise his higher ganglia in every possible way. And so I will say no more of the idea that the novel is merely a harmless opiate for the vacant hours of prosperous men . . . by its nature I doubt if it ever can be. (150)

While Wells' remarks are couched in typically tongue-in-cheek language, they actually offer a serious perspective on the changing role that fiction might be expected to play in the new century. For Wells and others, the Anglo-Boer War signalled a watershed for writers and readers, whose experience of the conflict had in many cases signalled the massively increased power of print. In Wells' pregnant formulation, during the war 'something happened to quite a lot of us' (149).

Invasion Literature

The aftermath of what was almost universally recognised as a disastrous war for the British Empire provided plenty of scope for creative writers whose work reflected the new and dynamic imperatives defined above by Wells. Writers such as Kipling, for example, understood the increasing centrality of the printed word in the post-war period. In his poem 'The Lesson', originally published in *The Times* in July 1901, he offers an uncompromising assessment of the position of the British Empire following the war and suggests the consequences of a failure to learn from past mistakes:

> It was our fault, and our very great fault – and now we must turn it to use.
> We have forty million reasons for failure, but not a single excuse.
> So the more we work and the less we talk the better results we shall get.
> We have had an Imperial lesson. It may make us an Empire yet!' (Kipling 1990: 243)

Kipling's poem, published while the war was still in progress, recognised that the rebuilding of the imperial project might only take place if a collective memory of national failings was retained and acted upon. This same sense of the need to counter the tendency for national forgetfulness animated a broad range of imaginative writing inspired by the war. We can, for example, recognise this imperative to remember in a genre of writing conventionally classified as 'invasion literature'. In these texts, Britain (and by extension the British Empire at large) was threatened by invasion from one or more foreign powers. Writing of this type replicated the thrill of South African war reportage, but added piquancy by bringing the war onto the home front; the invasion of Britain invariably takes place in recognisable towns and cities, and results in the destruction of well-known local landmarks. Invasion literature is also characterised by the inclusion of a preface or afterword which underscores the perils of national apathy and points towards specific defensive (or offensive) projects for the government to address before it is too late. In this way, invasion stories effectively replayed and extended the sorts of thrilling newspaper coverage of the war that had proved so popular with readers. The reader's own recognition of the similarity of style and content between factual press reportage and imaginative fiction enhanced the work's excitement while simultaneously driving home the political message.

Like most genres of writing that now appear quintessentially Edwardian in profile, invasion literature was not an invention of the new century. The modern roots of the genre date from George Chesney's *The Battle of Dorking: Reminiscences of a Volunteer*, first published anonymously in *Blackwood's Magazine* in 1871. This tale, with its weakened British forces capitulating to a powerful German army in the apparently unremarkable Surrey town of Dorking, anticipated much of the invasion literature that emerged in the wake of the Anglo-Boer War. The timing of *The Battle of Dorking*'s publication, in the aftermath of crushing Prussian victories over France in the Franco-Prussian War, also foreshadowed the climate of international anxiety prevalent in Britain after 1900. But while Chesney's text was much discussed in its immediate period, it failed to generate the large volume of imitative invasion fictions produced during and after the war in South Africa. With considerable newspaper scrutiny focusing at this time on the hawkishness of Britain's empire-building rivals, the country's perceived openness to attack was an understandably rich subject for fictional treatment. The nature of the resulting productions can, to some extent, be gauged from titles of texts alone: these include *The New Battle of Dorking* (Anonymous 1900e), *How the Germans Took London* (Offin

1900), *London's Peril* (Allen 1900), *The Sack of London in the Great French War of 1901* (1901c), *The Coming Waterloo* (Cairnes 1901), *The Invaders* (Tracy 1901), *A New Trafalgar* (Curtis 1902), *Seaward for the Foe* (Hill 1903), and *Starved into Surrender* (Clarke 1904). The first wave of texts published at the beginning of the decade was, however, merely a prelude to the major period of invasion fiction publication which took place between 1906 and the outbreak of the First World War in 1914. I. F. Clarke argues that during this major phase of production, 'the growing antagonism between Britain and Germany was responsible for the largest and most sustained development of the most alarmist and aggressive stories of future warfare ever seen at any time in European history' (Clarke 1970: 138).

What these invasion stories suggest more generally is the rapidly changing relationship between news events and fiction publication. By the start of the twentieth century – and unlike the period in which Chesney's work emerged – writers and publishers were increasingly well placed to assess the demands of their growing audience and then swiftly commission new work to satisfy this market. The fluidity of themes and stylistic forms between factual newsprint and invasion literature provide telling clues to more general cross-currents of cultural influence. This slippage between factual news and its fictional counterpart can be witnessed in the manner in which writers of the latter material attempted to pass off their stories as fact. Erskine Childers' *The Riddle of the Sands* (1903), like a number of other invasion fictions, includes several authentic charts of the geographical area covered by the narrative. These often very detailed maps lend verisimilitude to their accompanying fictional narrative while also providing a direct visual counterpart to media coverage of war: battleground maps then formed (and continue to form) an integral part of war reportage. Childers carries this illusion of fact further in the first edition of the novel, when crediting himself on the book's jacket and title page as the material's editor rather than its author. Furthermore, in the book's original preface (dated March 1903), Childers looks to reinforce the authenticity of his work, while at the same time distancing himself from the book's authorship, by describing the text's originator as 'my friend 'Carruthers'' (17). This friend, Childers informs us, had told him that the details of a German invasion plan (unearthed in circumstances which threatened great personal danger) might best be presented to the public in the form of 'a bald exposition of the essential facts, stripped of their warm human envelope' (18). Childers' successful counter-argument to his friend's projected strategy, as outlined in this preface, was that 'the story should be made as explicit and circumstantial as possible, frankly and honestly for the purpose of entertaining and so of attracting a wide circle of readers' (18). This desire to move from hard news to a more attractive (and accessible) human interest form of news coverage appears to mimic the organising principle of Harmsworth's *Daily Mail*. According to Childers' pragmatic interpretation, it was worth sacrificing the high-minded Carruthers' original plan if the dressing of the narrative in a 'warm human envelope' had the capacity to grasp the attention of the general public at large.

A further connection between newspapers and invasion literature is the extent to which the latter was often written by current or former news journalists; these included Allen Clarke, A. J. Dawson, George Griffith, Headon Hill, William Le Queux, Max Pemberton, Louis Tracy and Walter Wood. The practical experience of journalism allowed a number of these writers to bring to their texts the putatively 'authentic' quality of news reportage. An understanding of the rhythm of news stories unfolding in daily sequence is especially evident in Le Queux's *The Invasion of 1910* (1906). Here, the novel's individual chapter titles echo the daily drip of newspaper headlines: 'Germans Landing at Hull and Goole' (154), 'Desperate Fighting in Essex' (171), 'British Success at Royston' (221), 'British Abandon Colchester' (235), 'Fierce Fighting at Chelmsford' (255), and 'The Feeling in London' (279). This familiar format becomes even more marked when we consider that Le Queux's story was first published in daily serial instalments in the *Daily Mail* between March and July 1906. The original idea for *The Invasion of 1910* was in fact developed by Alfred Harmsworth (now Baron Northcliffe), who then commissioned Le Queux (an established and prolific author of popular political thrillers) to write the serial under his direction for the *Daily Mail*. For Harmsworth, the serialised invasion narrative offered excellent opportunities to keep readers buying his paper during what promised to be a slack season for news stories following the excitement of the Liberal landslide election victory at the start of 1906. The method by which Harmsworth achieved his aims here demonstrates his consummate skill in anticipating and then satisfying the public taste. Apart from providing the public with an exciting tale written by a well-known popular writer, Harmsworth also ensured that readers from across the country were able to follow the progress of the fictional invasion as it arrived in their home town. Harmsworth wanted to ensure that the story remained in the public eye, and this invasion road tour certainly helped to maintain its profile over a period of months rather than just days. In addition to following the daily path of the invasion, Harmsworth created more localised talking points by, for example, employing sandwich-men dressed in Prussian uniforms and spiked helmets to advertise the story through the London streets (Clarke 1970: 145). This publicity for the serial and its long run in the *Daily Mail* helped to bring about one of the great publishing sensations of the Edwardian period. While popular reports of worldwide sales of the book reaching one million might have been exaggerated, something of the sensation that it caused can be gauged by the twenty-seven languages into which the tale was translated (144–5). While *The Invasion of 1910* was by no means the first example of a British newspaper serial becoming a popular success as a book, the ways in which its form was manipulated to increase the *Daily Mail's* circulation does suggest a new era in the relationship between seemingly distinct fields of print culture.

Given the growing influence of the newspaper market on the field of book publishing, it is unsurprising that the centrality of the press in modern society is consistently emphasised in invasion literature. But while, as argued above, the press in Anglo-Boer War fiction is seen to play a vital role in keeping the public informed, the writers of invasion fiction extend these claims for the importance of news media in the modern world. In part, this is achieved by characterising twentieth-century Fleet Street as the epitome of technological modernity. The speed at which the news can now be delivered is foregrounded in the first chapter of Le Queux's *The Invasion of 1910*; here, a special edition of the fictional *Weekly Dispatch* with the news of invasion is prepared overnight by a morally principled news editor, but his integrity will not allow the paper to be printed until confirmation is delivered by an eyewitness motorist speeding from Ipswich (1906: 11). Following the motorist's arrival at eight o'clock on this Sunday morning, the paper is then printed without delay:

> Then, just as Big Ben chimed the half-hour, the echoes of the half-deserted Strand were suddenly awakened by the loud, strident voices of the newsboys shouting – '*Weekly Dispatch*, spe-shall! Invasion of England this morning! Germans in Suffolk! Terrible panic! Spe-shall! *Weekly Dispatch*, Spe-shall!' (13)

The rapidity with which the news is able to hit the streets is deliberately linked by Le Queux to the speed of the motorist who delivers eyewitness testimony of the invasion:

> Of a sudden . . . came the whirr-r of an approaching car, as a thin faced, travel-stained man tore along from the direction of the Strand and pulled up before the office. The fine car, a six cylinder 'Napier,' was grey with the mud of country roads, while the motorist himself was smothered until his goggles had been almost entirely covered. (12)

The juxtaposition of the deliberately identified luxury Napier car and the up-to-the-minute news production is designed to provide readers with a frisson of the excitement of modernity. Also foregrounded here is the sense that the sort of Edwardian dynamism symbolised by the car and the newspaper press is lacking elsewhere in high levels of British society. When the motorist and news editor personally deliver their knowledge of the invasion to the War Office in Whitehall, they discover that this vital hub of national defence is closed on Sunday: a 'tall elderly man in slippers', evidently the caretaker, who answers the War Office door, tells the *Weekly Dispatch*'s news editor that he had 'better come to-morrow . . . about eleven. Somebody'll be sure to see you then' (13, 14). Taking into account this absence of reliable modern political leadership, the noble press in Le Queux's novel now forms a vital role in informing the public of future peril, while also stirring a sleeping government into some form of action; in *The Invasion of 1910*, the news editor subsequently motors up to the Permanent Under-Secretary for War's country retreat ('Sixty miles from London. We can be there under two hours!' affirms the Napier driver (15)) with the invasion news, and is greeted with incredulity by the flat-footed Minister: '"Impossible!" cried Sir James. "We should surely have heard something of it if such were actually the case! The coastguard would have telephoned the news instantly' (16). Later in the novel, Harmsworth's own papers, the *Daily Mail* and the *Evening News*, are placed honourably at the centre of events: the German proclamation of the war is taken from a barn door near the town of Billericay and delivered to the *Daily Mail*'s offices in the correspondent's motorcar so that it can be published without delay in a special edition (25).

A. J. Dawson's 1907 invasion tale, *The Message*, builds upon this idea of the press acting as substitute for ineffectual official channels of communication, by suggesting the vital role a newspaper might play in national reconstruction following an ignominious wartime capitulation to the Germans. In Dawson's novel, the avowedly imperial *Standard*, while unfairly mocked in the pre-invasion period as 'The Patriotic Pulpit' (170), goes on to play a central role in forming a united front against the invasion forces. While it is left to a pair of Canadian preachers to reignite the national sense of belief and duty among the British public, they rely on the *Standard* to deliver their message to a waiting public:

> For many months the *Standard*, now firmly established as the principal organ of the reform movement, devoted an entire page each day to the progress of our campaign . . . and the key-note thus given was taken by the Press of the whole country. (317)

The new social and political centrality of the press as conveyed in these texts also serves to raise to new heights the power and responsibility of newspaper editors and correspondents. These figures are seen as modern prophets, men empowered to bring about the salvation of the people if those people would only choose to follow them. In the anonymous novel, *The Sack of London in the Great French War of 1901* (1901), for example, a prediction of Britain's future invasion that had actually appeared in the *Morning Post* on Trafalgar Day 1900 is reprinted at length. The text's narrator, supposedly looking back on historical events from the future perspective of 1951, follows the prophecy of the *Morning Post*'s editor with note of weary resignation: England 'awoke to this fact, as usual, too late to remedy it' (46). This work is typical in incorporating real or imagined newspaper editorials or reportage from the newspapers into its narrative. In A. C. Curtis's 1902 novel, *A New Trafalgar: A Tale of the Torpedo Fleet*, for example, the narrator prefaces a newspaper account of the book's main naval battle with the following comment:

> if the Admiralty had not allowed a couple of press correspondents to be on board the British flagship to represent a large syndicate of all the London daily papers, no account at all intelligible to the ordinary reader would have survived, and it is from one of these correspondent's letters, published simultaneously in the morning papers, that the following account is taken. (238)

Curtis' sense here of the newspaper correspondent as friend to the 'ordinary' reader is echoed in several of these texts. Walter Wood's *The Enemy in Our Midst* (1906) is more specific in its recognition of the debt owed by the public to war journalists. In this novel, the initially sceptical Lord Halden is belatedly made aware of the scale of his own (and by implication, the general public's) indebtedness to reporters in wartime:

> I've hated war correspondents up to the present . . . but I never felt such gratitude for men as I feel for these. They have already gathered more information and told more news than the whole of our boasted military Intelligence Department put together. And that, I suppose, is because the men have to live by their brains, and have not been jobbed into office. (112)

Wood stresses here a form of social Darwinism that has made the dynamic modern newspaperman much fitter for the particular challenges of modernity than his decadent counterpart in the establishment. With vast constituencies of readers following their every word, newspaper editors in these texts were increasingly seen as, to follow Shelley, the unacknowledged legislators of the world.

The new century, in which newspaper editors (and, by extension, newspaper owners) were more and more recognised as powerful manipulators of public opinion, ensured that texts such as Kipling's 'The Lesson' were understood and acted upon in differing ways by readers. Although Wells claimed (in his 1911 speech to the Times Book Club) that the novel had the capacity to act as 'the social mediator, the vehicle of understanding, the instrument of self-examination' (Wells 1914a: 167–8), he also knew that the novelist's unique ability to put 'ideas into his readers' heads' (158) might bring about mixed results. At their worst, these results might lead individuals away from the enlightenment that Kipling sought as a lesson of the war, and towards further conflict. In an article published in the *Contemporary Review* in January 1910, Charles Lowe spelled out the ways in which hawkish invasion fiction would encourage this outcome:

> It may be argued that the spy and invasion fictions which have been pouring out of the Press are beneath contempt from the literary point of view, and so they are. But, unfortunately, the degree of harm that can be done by the printed word is not dependent on its literary value. In these days of popular 'education' such sensational writers who are readily believed by the masses who contribute to the formation of public opinion, which in turn tends to influence our rulers and our relations with other countries; and what these readers are wickedly taught to believe is that the Germans are arming and preparing to attack us by sea and land at the first available opportunity. Thus the pernicious publications referred to . . . constitute acts of criminal levity against the peace of two kindred nations – a poisoning of the wells of public truth – and that, too, at a time when each country is only too ready to believe the worst of the other. Such conduct is none the less a public crime for its being beyond the reach of the public prosecutor. (Lowe 1910: 56)

Seen through this lens, Wells' reader as 'undertrained giant' appears more akin to Frankenstein's monster. The noble desire to awaken the reader's potential is tempered here by the realisation that this instinct, once roused, may not be exercised in an *approved* fashion.

Imperialism in the Edwardian Writing of Conrad, Kipling, and Buchan

The Edwardian writings of Conrad and Kipling, unlike much of the war and invasion literature examined elsewhere in this chapter, remain prominent in critical consciousness. And although texts such as *Heart of Darkness*, *Lord Jim*, and *Kim* might appear far removed both intellectually and stylistically from the majority of the material discussed above, it is instructive to understand Conrad's and Kipling's fiction alongside its seemingly ephemeral counterparts. One way in which to gauge the proximity of these apparently separate forms of writing is by considering the nature and place of their original publication. All three of these texts were first published between 1899 and 1901 and, like a number of other works examined in this chapter, they initially appeared in magazine serial instalments. These key works of the period were, therefore, first read against a backdrop of rapidly changing historical events: in the case of *Lord Jim* and *Kim*, these included the main events of the Anglo-Boer War. It was therefore impossible for the initial readers of these wartime texts to overlook a sense of connection between the fictional lives of colonial subjects like Lord Jim and Kim, and the factual outcomes of British imperialism. While the topical connections to the war and its likely repercussions are more obliquely realised in Conrad's and Kipling's texts than in much of the fiction surveyed in this chapter, the issue of Edwardian imperialism remained a central preoccupation for the period's more literary writers, as well as its hacks. And while a perceived distinction between art and mere entertainment might suggest discrete categories of readership, Edwardian publishing practices (and the newly literate audiences that these practices increasingly targeted) ensured a blurring of what might be considered separate markets. The appearance of *Nostromo*, perhaps Conrad's most ambitious and challenging critique of imperialism, in the penny literary paper, *T.P.'s Weekly*, between January and October 1904, illustrates the difficulty of categorising discrete audiences in the period. The literary miscellany offered in *T.P.'s Weekly* and other popular Edwardian publications encouraged promiscuous rather than more strictly targeted reading.

The original publication of *Heart of Darkness* in *Blackwood's Edinburgh Magazine* between February and April 1899 offers an especially instructive case in this respect. *Blackwood's*, which would also publish *Lord Jim*, was a long-established and distinctly conservative magazine with a large circulation in the colonies. Given these credentials, it appears an unlikely location for the first appearance of Conrad's politically sceptical and stylistically innovative work. The seeming incongruity between subject matter and publication is increased when the first instalment of *Heart of Darkness* is examined alongside other material in this particular issue, which was a special double-number published to celebrate the magazine's 1,000th edition. Here we find, in addition to *Heart of Darkness*, a generous helping of fiction focused on *Blackwood's* favoured colonial or historical themes. This material includes stories by high-profile popular writers of the period, such as Hugh Clifford, Beatrice Harraden and Maurice Hewlett, whose reputations had been built upon work on these topics. Elsewhere, the Tory politics of the magazine are emphasised by the selection taken from the memoirs of long-serving conservative politician, Sir John R. Mowbray; and its international/colonial focus is foregrounded by articles entitled 'Romance of the Mines: Californian Gold Discoveries', 'Jamaica: An Impression' (by Conservative MP Ian Malcolm), and 'A Letter From Salamanca' by noted pillar of empire Lt-Gen. Sir Henry Brackenbury KCB, KCSI. The many pages of advertisements carried in this number of the magazine also evoke a world of traditional middle-class preoccupations and pursuits: among other products pitched here are church furnishings, hair oil, life assurance, patent medicines, guns, umbrellas, typewriters, whisky, boot blacking, musical boxes, kitchen ranges, Waverley pens, Lea and Perrins' Worcestershire Sauce, and Bryant and May's matches.

The opening page of the *Heart of Darkness* serialisation suggests that it will provide fiction in tune with these conservative ideas. The first lines depict a cruising yawl, the *Nellie*, waiting on anchor in the Thames for the tide to turn. On board, a group of apparently prosperous middle-class men (defined only by their professional roles as 'The Director of Companies', 'The Lawyer' and 'The Accountant') wait for the day's end in 'a serenity that had a still and exquisite brilliance' (Conrad 1899: 193). Any conservative-minded reader encountering Conrad's work for the first time here might be reassured by the narrator's description of London, the centre of the British Empire, as 'the biggest, and the greatest, town on earth'. But even on the first page of the serial the ominous keynotes of the work are evident. Darkness, foregrounded in Conrad's title, is immediately reinscribed in descriptions of the air above the metropolis: an atmosphere variously labelled as a 'dark' and 'a mournful gloom, brooding motionless' above. Elsewhere on this opening page, things are not quite as they first appear: the Director of Companies who 'resembled a pilot', seems to be merely playing the role of captain on the *Nellie*; his authority is mischievously undercut by the narrator who playfully remarks of him that 'on the whole river there was nothing that looked half so nautical'. In similar fashion, the reliability of Marlow (whose spoken narrative constitutes the bulk of Conrad's tale) is unsettled by the frame narrator's wry description of his appearance on deck; he had 'an ascetic aspect, and, with his arms dropped, the palms of his hands outwards, [he] resembled an idol' (193). The opening page of the *Blackwood's* serialisation alerts the attentive reader to what will be Conrad's distinctive refashioning of the imperial romance. Here, the characters will be actors playing out their parts in a drama, rather than more conventional heroes capable of fully inhabiting their roles.

It is, however, important to register the connections as well as the discontinuities between Conrad's tale and the established form of the popular imperial romance. Like Rider Haggard, Henty and other writers associated with this form, Conrad introduces a seemingly patriotic Englishman – Marlow – as his focalising character. Also in common with these earlier models, Conrad's tale involves sending this Englishman on a dangerous quest to a remote and unfamiliar location. Marlow himself seems at first well equipped to undertake the role of uncompromising and loyal imperialist: 'the Continent', he tells his interlocutors on the deck of the *Nellie*, with an air of instinctive prejudice, is 'cheap and not so nasty as it looks' (198); and with a similar sense of national assuredness and pride he suggests that the 'vast amount of red' on the world map denoting the British Empire is 'good to see at any time, because one knows that some real work is done in there' (199). Conrad, therefore, sets up Marlow in the early stages of his story as a typical member of his gender and class constituencies, one quite happy to accept the dominant hegemonic view of British imperialism as being above criticism. But far from affirming this position in line with more conventional adventure tales, Conrad's text instead foregrounds Marlow's growing scepticism at the actions of Europeans in Africa. Although the Belgian Congo setting of *Heart of Darkness* means that a direct critique of British imperial practice is avoided, only the most blinkered of readers of the serial could fail to register the wider applications of the tale. Indeed, as Marlow remarks of the fatally corrupted colonial servant whom Marlow encounters at the end of his river journey, 'all Europe contributed to the making of Kurtz' (497).

Conrad's text is consistently dense and elliptical – always suggestive rather than directly polemical. The texture of Marlow's voice and pattern of his language are typically conveyed by dashes and ellipses, forms of notation which leave meaning deliberately uncertain. But the corruption that Marlow witnesses is unambiguous, as is the hypocrisy and greed he encounters in his fellow European colonists. As Marlow remarks near the beginning of his talk, 'the conquest of the earth, which mostly means the taking it away from those who have a different complexion or slightly flatter noses than ourselves, is not a pretty thing when you look into it too much' (Conrad 1899: 196). The 'idea' which Marlow, by implication, suggests is underpinning British imperialism and therefore separating it from the more overtly corrupt practices of rival European powers, is a concept that 'you can set up, and bow down before, and offer a sacrifice to' (196). But the specific nature of this 'idea' remains undefined and tellingly elliptical in Conrad's rendering. And, as the rest of *Heart of Darkness* implicitly confirms, far from being underpinned by an uplifting and improving 'idea', imperialism in any form is likely to prove corrupting to both colonised and coloniser.

Kurtz's apparent decline into savagery, while working for an ivory trading company in a remote river station, undermines the consoling notion of imperialism as a civilising mission brought by indulgent white Europeans for the benefit of primitive black Africans. Indeed, Kurtz's injunction to 'Exterminate all the brutes!' (498), (scrawled on the last page of a report he was writing for future guidance' of the 'International Society for the Suppression of Savage Customs' (497)), presents a violent rejoinder to the benign and paternalistic imperative foregrounded in archetypal imperial ideology.

Before *Heart of Darkness* first appeared in book form in 1902 (published by Blackwood alongside two other of Conrad's *Blackwood's* stories, 'Youth' and 'The End of the Tether'), *Lord Jim* emerged in *Blackwood's* over a year from October 1899. This period coincided with the major battles and sieges of the Anglo-Boer War, before it shifted into its guerrilla war phase towards the end of 1900. While the serial version of the novel makes no direct comment on the news then emerging from South Africa (indeed, its Asian setting clearly works against such transparent applications), contemporary readers of *Blackwood's* would still have encountered *Lord Jim* against the backdrop of the African conflict. In this context, the gap between the romance of a colonial war in a distant land, as imagined by much of the contemporary news media, and the reality of a bloody conflict fought for uncertain and arguably corrupt aims, was brought into unusually sharp focus. Conrad's title character (whose tale is largely narrated by Marlow) encourages this focus because he, like many of the volunteers then enlisting for service in South Africa, is an unsophisticated young man whose impressions of the world are drawn from 'light holiday literature'. Popular reading of this type had inspired Jim to leave his country parsonage and pursue his 'vocation for the sea', in the same way that Henty's and Rider Haggard's heroes encouraged Jim's factual counterparts to fight in the Anglo-Boer War (Conrad 1899–1900/1981: 11). Jim's own imagination draws directly upon the 'sea-life of light literature', casting him in the role of 'a man destined to shine in the midst of dangers'. Here, safe in this imaginative realm, he variously saves 'people from sinking ships', confronts 'savages on tropical shores', quells 'mutinies on the high seas', and keeps up the 'hearts of despairing men' while stranded with them in a small ocean-tossed boat. In these projections, Jim always envisages himself as 'an example of devotion to duty, and as unflinching as a hero in a book' (11). Conrad's project in *Lord Jim* is designed to test Jim's book-conditioned sense of an ideal world against its much less reliable counterpart in lived experience. In this uncertain realm of real life, the choices Jim faces, and the morality underpinning these choices, are rarely clear-cut. And where they are apparently straightforward, the unpredictable nature of human response confuses the simple binary between heroism and cowardice that so often provides the bedrock of romance literature.

For Jim, the troubling relationship between romance and realism becomes evident when he abandons his apparently sinking ship, the *Patna*, leaving behind a boatload of passengers to their fate. While this act of ostensible cowardice is traumatic enough for a would-be hero like Jim, Conrad ensures that Jim's confusion regarding his agency in committing this act makes it doubly unsettling. Jim's reaction to his abandoning of the *Patna* lies between, on one hand, a straightforward denial of his action and, on the other hand, a simple admission of his guilt. In between these poles, Jim registers genuine bewilderment at his action, telling Marlow: "'I had jumped . . . '" He checked himself, averted his gaze . . . "It seems"' (Conrad 1899–1900/1981: 88). Just as Conrad's characters in *Heart of Darkness* are merely puppets playing out unfamiliar roles, Jim can only relate to himself as an actor unconsciously following a script he has had no hand in writing. Far from being exceptional, Conrad suggests that the confusion Jim experiences here is inherent in the interface between unreliable human nature and a chaotic outside world. Jim's typicality is identified throughout the novel, and in the last line of the 'Author's Note' that Conrad later appended to the novel, he is designated as 'one of us' (8). Like Jim, Conrad implies, we are all capable of culturally conditioned self-deception, vanity and an unshakable belief in the illusory ideas which dictate our actions. The tenacious nature of these misguided principles are underscored in a final act of book-inspired heroism, when an unarmed Jim is shot through the chest while offering his sympathy to a grieving and vengeful father. This act, which in adventure literature would prove the true mettle of the book's once-cowardly hero, is seen instead here by Marlow as an uncertain and ultimately futile gesture. While Marlow acknowledges the romantic nature of Jim's end ('not in the wildest days of his boyish visions could he have seen the alluring shape of such an extraordinary success!'), he also tells his audience that Jim the man was 'inscrutable at heart' (313). This lack of readability, we conclude, sets Jim, like us, apart from those more transparently legible heroes of adventure who had acted as his role models. That less complicated and more transparent figures of romance appeared alongside Jim, Marlow and Kurtz in the pages of *Blackwood's*, meant that readers would not have far to look in reminding themselves of the fictional characters that Conrad's fiction critiqued.

Kipling's *Kim* in many respects provides a more conventional and a more conservative rendering of the imperial romance than is offered by Conrad. *Kim*'s richly illustrated Indian settings, its *Bildungsroman* narrative featuring a charismatic young hero, and its description of the Great Game (the popular term used to denote imperial rivalries in central Asia during the nineteenth and early-twentieth centuries) in action, seem to identify it as a model of this genre of writing. In addition, the contemporary perception of Kipling as a cheerleader-in-chief for empire augments the sense that this novel will provide straightforward British imperial propaganda at a time when that Empire was in crisis: during the period between January and November 1901 (when the original British serialisation of *Kim* appeared in the mass-circulation *Cassell's Magazine*) the appetite of the British and Empire-wide public for the South African War had cooled as the conflict dragged on with mounting losses and little sense of a decisive ending. Kipling, who was then at the height of his popularity in the English-speaking world, had a remarkable opportunity to influence readers who were understandably wary about Britain's future as an imperial power. In wielding this influence, Kipling offers a clear vote of confidence for the potential of the British Empire as a force for good, but *Kim* equally suggests the considerable challenges incumbent on any imperial nation. This role was, as Kipling had already declared in his poem 'The White Man's Burden' (first published in *The Times* in February 1899), an onerous and often thankless one that could not be taken lightly. Kipling's design then in writing *Kim* was both to convey the nature of the burden and to demonstrate the vital and continuing necessity to shoulder this load in light of the reversals of the South African War. The novel sets out to convince its readers of the clear need for a fatherly hand in running India, and to confirm that only Britain had the requisite qualities to carry out this role. Notwithstanding *Kim*'s confidence on this point, however, the novel is equally clear that Britain has no inalienable right to rule India or indeed any part of its existing empire. If Britain wanted to succeed as an imperial nation, Kipling avers, it needed to work in partnership with native peoples in colonial lands. Rather than considering a country such as India a colonial possession which existed purely for exploitation, *Kim* makes clear that Britain needed to act as a sympathetic, resourceful and collegial guardian.

Kipling chose for *Kim* a distinctive and atypical central character to make his case. Kim, the son of a long-dead drunken Irish soldier and his nursemaid wife, is an outsider among members of the British establishment. His ramshackle upbringing, as a 'poor white of the very poorest' (Kipling 1901/1998: 1) among the prostitutes and opium addicts of the Lahore bazaar, makes plain his radical separation from counterparts in Henty's and Rider Haggard's work. Equally, even though Kim's facility for language and dark skin tone allow him to pass as a local boy, his European heritage sets him apart from the indigenous people of India. This partial stake in both east and west means that Kim provides a freshness of perspective unavailable from more conventional focalising characters, who were firmly rooted in either colonial or colonised camps. We recognise this in the way that, unlike more characteristic boy heroes of adventure fiction, Kim has no innate sense of the British right to rule; indeed, the final pages of the novel leave uncertain the nature of his future participation in the British cause. But Kipling, in contrast to Conrad, does present a clear sense of loyalty to the crown among non-European adults such as the Pashtun horse trader Mahbub Ali, and the Bengali, Hurree Babu, both of whom work tirelessly for the British cause. These individuals operate undercover in the fixed belief that British imperialism protects their place in India's racially diffuse and arguably vulnerable society. Other rapacious empire-building countries (here France and Russia) are identified in the text as lacking in the empathetic and altruistic qualities that characterise British rule. Tangible outcomes of these admirable qualities are demonstrated in ways calculated to convince readers who are sceptical about British imperialism. The British-built Indian railway system, for example, serves to connect a diffuse and geographically scattered population: a train carriage joined by Kim and the Tibetan Lama (whom Kim accompanies on his spiritual journey) is depicted as a locus for racial harmony and goodwill. Similarly, the Grand Trunk Road, a wonder of British engineering in its modern guise, functions as a vital artery on the subcontinent for commerce and family connection. Elsewhere, and in a more symbolic realm, the Lahore Museum curator (a character based on Kipling's father) offers a pair of spectacles to the Lama to allow him to improve his clarity of vision (Kipling 1901/1998: 11). This gesture of facilitation is made between individuals whose wisdom can benefit each other if they are mutually receptive. By contrast, those representatives of the Raj who lack the museum curator's empathy are (if they remain unenlightened) destined to lead the British Empire along the path of earlier failed imperial powers. Kipling's characterisation of Reverend Arthur Bennett, the Church of England chaplain who 'looked at [the Lama] with the triple-ringed uninterest of the creed that lumps nine-tenths of the world under the title "heathen"' (88), stands for an unthinking prejudice apparently all too prevalent among establishment figures: further evidence of Raj bigotry is provided by the English drummer boy encountered by Kim, who can only relate to him as an 'ignorant little beggar' who was 'brought up in a gutter' (103). Prejudice based on a sense of innate superiority, Kipling suggests, serves to undermine the work of the novel's enlightened figures, who are carefully balanced out on both sides of the racial divide.

These enlightened figures in *Kim* typically protect British rule in India by stealth. Colonel Creighton, for example, while working publicly as the head of the Ethnological Survey, also operates covertly as a spy master. As a surrogate father for Kim, Creighton recognises in the boy the special qualities that make him ideally placed to work as an agent in the Great Game. Creighton's fluent understanding of the vernacular and his wry sense of humour convince Kim and those around him that he is a man they can trust. Through Creighton's self-evident goodness and authority, Kim is drawn into espionage with little sense that he has made a conscious choice to risk his life in support of the British Raj. Kipling makes this loyalty appear natural – something that Kim, a boy of extraordinary native wit and charisma, will simply accept as the only reasonable course of action. Kipling's propaganda for empire is, therefore, seductively packaged in a manner designed to coerce an arguably disaffected wartime readership into accepting the self-evident rightness of continuing British rule. While there is clearly a need to be cautious about applying the India-specific issues addressed in *Kim* to South Africa, the timing of the serial's publication encourages a sense that Kipling presents his blueprint here for the future of the British Empire at large. This renaissance for the Empire (in Kipling's rendering) would be marked out by benevolent leadership, cultural and religious tolerance and understanding, and a sharing rather than an exploitation of natural resources. It is perhaps in this twentieth-century reinvention of imperialism as an enlightened and companionable concept that the quasi-mystical 'idea' alluded to by Conrad's Marlow in *Heart of Darkness* comes into focus.

John Buchan's 1910 novel *Prester John* also uses the imperial romance to present a fresh case for the British imperial mandate. In this instance, the focus is squarely on South Africa in the wake of the disastrous war. The background for the story and the shape taken by the narrative were inspired by Buchan's own time in South Africa during the earlier years of the decade, when he worked as private secretary to Lord Alfred Milner, the country's High Commissioner. At the end of the Edwardian decade, Buchan was able to reflect coolly on his South African experience and craft a story which might (like Kipling's *Kim*) make sense of post-war British presence in a distant colonial territory. In achieving this aim, Buchan wanted to attract the sort of young reader who was likely to form a part of the next generation of colonial settlers. To create a narrative appealing to this cohort, Buchan drew upon several forms of writing that had, as this chapter has confirmed, proved popular during the decade: these included war fiction, imperial romance and, more obliquely, invasion literature. Like many of the texts discussed above, *Prester John* originally appeared in serialised form under the title *The Black General*, published between April and September 1910 in the boy's weekly, *The Captain*. It was then issued in book form by the Edinburgh publisher, Thomas Nelson. For the tale's narrator and focalising character, Buchan chose Davie Crawfurd, a young Scotsman who escapes his destiny as an office worker in Edinburgh when he becomes an assistant storekeeper in the remote South African veld. Crawfurd's unease in making this bold move anticipates the likely reservations of those readers who were, like Buchan's protagonist, themselves potential colonists. It was important for Buchan in engaging with this sort of invested reader that he foreground Crawfurd's sense of his own ordinariness and lack of heroism in the novel. In the opening chapter, for example, Crawfurd is quick to declare himself 'a notable coward', someone who when faced with danger was 'hideously frightened' (Buchan 1910/1947: 20). Anxiety of this nature is returned to throughout the novel as Crawfurd, isolated in rural Transvaal, is forced to confront his lack of courage. At his most alarmed, he unconsciously recalls Conrad's own nightmare vision of the European alone in alien Africa: 'I had looked into the heart of darkness, and the sight had terrified me' (134). Buchan is determined here, and throughout the novel, to stress Crawfurd's status as one who was destined (like the bulk of the tale's readers) to play the role of a 'subaltern' rather than that of a 'great general' (97). But in making Crawfurd 'one of us', Buchan wants to identify the sort of prosaic and unexceptional individual who might be perfectly suited to a life in the colonies. Individuals of this type would, Buchan suggests, ultimately engage their latent masculinity in a profitable way on a worthwhile colonial testing ground.

Crawfurd's own masculinity is proved in a David-and-Goliath contest with the powerful and charismatic Reverend John Laputa, an American-educated black African, who leads an uprising designed to overthrow British rule. The type of intelligent and resourceful individual represented by Laputa appeared, by 1910, the central threat to the British in South Africa: the Boer settlers in the novel are no longer adversaries of the British, being depicted instead as 'honest, companionable fellows' (52). While Buchan does allow Laputa to articulate the case for black nationalism in a passionate speech overheard by an eavesdropping Crawfurd, the rebel leader's oratory is ultimately deemed hollow. But the effect of Laputa's seductive rhetoric is registered by Crawfurd in ways which suggest its dangerous persuasiveness: he declares himself briefly mesmerised with Laputa's oratory, confessing that he 'had a mad desire to be of Laputa's party' (129). With this clear threat registered, Crawfurd, in thwarting Laputa's rebellion, reinstates what Buchan considered the correct order of things. To underline this political position, Crawfurd, by way of conclusion, sets out Buchan's vision of 'the meaning of the white man's duty': 'he has to take all risks, recking nothing of his life or his fortunes, [leaving him] well content to find his reward in the fulfilment of his task' (238). But in addition to this spiritual reward, it is crucial that Crawfurd is also granted a specific financial prize (diamonds which he sells to De Beers for a quarter of a million pounds (241)) in recognition of his vital work in defeating Laputa. Equally, the paradise-like nature of the South African landscape depicted in the book – and characteristically likened to a pre-lapsarian version of Scotland – seems calculated to promise readers a more tangible reward than that suggested by Crawfurd, echoing Kipling, in his solemn declaration of 'the meaning of the white man's duty' (238).

Far, however, from a cynical attempt to co-opt reluctant readers to the case for empire, one senses Buchan's sincerity in offering these practical rewards alongside their spiritual counterparts. Any reader considering a future life in the colonies needed to be convinced that their lives would be comprehensively improved by this venture into the unknown. While for these readers, some degree of romance might be projected into settler life, the everyday anxieties articulated in Crawfurd's tale were more pressing concerns. Buchan's ordinary hero does play a full part in a romance plot but, unlike Conrad's Jim, he never loses himself and gives in to romance. Indeed, as the novel draws to its close, Crawfurd pointedly refuses to embrace the role of romance hero for which his place in the narrative has entitled him. When defending himself against the charge of a 'dull ending' (which an old Edinburgh friend suggests he had made following his 'tremendous time' in Africa), Crawfurd celebrates his plain nature: 'If I hadn't been a prosaic body, I wouldn't be sitting here to-night' (243). The spectre of Lord Jim hangs over these words, with their acknowledgement of the colonist's urgent need to temper the heady inspiration of imperial romance with a healthy dose of realism. A sense given here of the adaption of old literary forms to fit the requirements of a new post-war century provides a revealing context in which to consider Edwardian literature more generally. The Anglo-Boer War had, in many ways, provided the foundation upon which publishers, writers and readers might rapidly evolve, and the nature of this evolution will be discussed in the ensuing chapters.

Chapter Two

Department of Administration:
Office Clerks and Shop Assistants

When H. G. Wells looked back upon his life in *Experiment in Autobiography* (1934), he remembered the period of his literary apprenticeship with fondness:

> The last decade of the nineteenth century was an extraordinarily favourable time for new writers and my individual good luck was set in the luck of a whole generation of aspirants. Quite a lot of us from nowhere were 'getting on'. (506)

New openings in the 1890s provided Wells' generation from 'nowhere' with ample opportunity to embark upon their careers, and the early years of the new century allowed them to consolidate their positions in the publishing trade. Indeed, during the Edwardian period, Wells and his fellow literary newcomers began to take control of the field that they had inherited from their Victorian predecessors. The extent of the shift that had taken place in literary power structures is evident in the ways in which Wells' fellow former shopmen and ex-clerks were, by the close of the Edwardian decade, occupying key positions not only as writers of fiction, but also as essayists, reviewers, literary agents, editors, illustrators and publishers. A notable feature of this generation was their commitment, both as writers and as facilitators of writing, to raising the profile, in print culture, of the suburban and provincial worlds from which many of them had emerged. Although Wells and his friend Arnold Bennett led the charge to foreground literary representations of modern lower-middle-class life, many like-minded individuals followed in their wake. Beginning with an examination of the Edwardian careers of Bennett and Wells, the archetypal members of their class and generation of authors, this chapter then goes on to consider the emergence on the literary scene of several now-neglected writers, including W. Pett Ridge and Edwin Pugh, whose work was also primarily focused on 'ordinary' suburban life. The chapter concludes with an analysis of the role played by the new generation of literary agents and editors in shaping the literature of the day. The overall aim of this chapter is to register the significant shift that took place in the social and cultural fabric of the publishing industry in the first decade of the new century, and to trace its effects. To what extent, this chapter asks, did the office boys and counter-jumpers, who were so much a feature of the Edwardian literary scene, actually succeed in reshaping the literary world in their own image?

Bennett and Wells 'Pushing Up'

Arnold Bennett and H. G. Wells are names that have, since the 1920s, been synonymous with Edwardian literature. The roots of this synecdotal relationship can be traced back to Virginia Woolf's influential essay 'Modern Novels', which first appeared anonymously in the *Times Literary Supplement* in April 1919. Here, Woolf unflatteringly characterised Bennett and Wells (along with John Galsworthy) as 'materialists', who were producing fiction deficient in 'life or spirit'. It was for this reason, Woolf argued, that they 'have disappointed us and left us with the feeling that the sooner English fiction turns its back upon them, as politely as may be, and marches, if only into the desert, the better for its soul' (Woolf 1919: 189). While Woolf waited until her later essays 'Mr Bennett and Mrs Brown' (1923) and 'Character in Fiction' (1924) to classify Bennett and Wells as 'Edwardians' (opposing them to her exemplary Georgians, E. M. Forster, D. H. Lawrence, Lytton Strachey, James Joyce and T. S. Eliot (Woolf 1988: 421)), this period designation was already implicit in her 1919 essay. Although Woolf's definition of Edwardian 'materialists' began as an exercise in healthy provocation, it hardened over the twentieth century into a critical commonplace, one accepted often unquestioningly by later generations of critics and students alike. But the image of Bennett and Wells as complacent and prosperous literary 'uncles' (a label coined by Rebecca West in 1928 for a group of writers, also including George Bernard Shaw and John Galsworthy, that she dubbed the 'Big Four' (West 1928: 199)), was very much at odds with their literary profiles in the Edwardian period itself. V. S. Pritchett comes closest to recovering this now obscured image of Bennett and Wells in his remark that they were 'a pair of Lupins in their time' (1942: 91). This link to the rebellious and ambitious son of Mr Pooter, the conservative Victorian clerk in the comic novel *The Diary of a Nobody* (1892) by brothers George and Weedon Grossmith, offers a glimpse of Bennett and Wells as they might have appeared to readers on or about December 1900. The notion of Bennett and Wells as insubordinate Edwardian sons kicking against stuffy Victorian parents certainly captures their own sense of themselves at this time. Lupin Pooter's rejection of his father's cherished ambitions and ideals anticipates precisely the irreverent tone of Bennett and Wells as they mapped out their all-conquering literary careers. In their private correspondence, and in more public pronouncements about the literary field at the opening of the twentieth century, there is little sense of them as the establishment figures evoked in Woolf's ironic description of them as 'my elders and betters' (Woolf 1988: 432). Instead, in the early Edwardian period, Bennett and Wells railed against their own overbearing Victorian 'uncles', spurred, as Wells remembered in his autobiography, by their 'very lively resolve to "get on"' (Wells 1934: 629).

But their confidence in themselves as writers at the forefront of a new generation of novelists was tempered by a distinctly materialist need to earn a living. As Wells put it, 'we were both hard workers, both pushing up by way of writing from lower middle-class surroundings, where we had little prospect of anything but a restricted salaried life' (627). Both Bennett and Wells, born within months of each other in the mid-1860s, had emerged from distinctly unpromising backgrounds for literary aspirants. Wells, the son of a one-time cricket professional and shopkeeper, seemed destined in his early life to become a draper, having been apprenticed in this trade at fourteen – an unhappy phase of his young life, which would form the background to two of his Edwardian novels, *Kipps* (1905) and *The History of Mr. Polly* (1910). After escaping from this uncongenial fate, he became, in the mid-1880s, a schoolteacher, after training in Sussex and London.

Bennett shared Wells' shabby genteel social background, his father having been variously a potter, draper, pawnbroker and, latterly, a solicitor. Like so many of the coming literary generation at this time, Bennett became a clerk, working first for his father's legal firm in the Potteries and subsequently moving to an office in London in 1889. It was, with the benefit of hindsight, the great good fortune of Bennett and Wells to begin their literary careers in London in the 1890s. The burgeoning field of print culture at this time offered unusually rich opportunities for would-be writers looking to gain a foothold on the publishing ladder; Bennett himself noted in 1901 that the output of journalism was by that time 'probably twenty times that of twenty years ago' (Bennett 1901b: 127). In particular, the growth of the magazine and journal market during the 1890s allowed literary newcomers, often daytime clerks or teachers like Bennett and Wells, to publish sketches and stories for cash payments. Almost all of those writers whom Wells later identified as the generation from 'nowhere' (several of whom are discussed in the next section of this chapter) began their careers in this way, retaining their secure daytime jobs until they felt themselves safely established in literary work. In Wells' own case, popular publications such as the *Pall Mall Gazette*, its sister paper the *Pall Mall Budget*, the *New Budget*, and *Black & White* allowed him to consolidate his reputation as a story writer in the period before his first book volumes of fiction were published. Bennett also gained a foothold in the literary world via this route. After winning a twenty-guinea prize in a *Tit-Bits* writing competition in 1891, he went on to publish short pieces in papers including the *Star* and the *Sun*, before gaining his first real breakthrough in 1895, when his short story 'A Letter Home' appeared in *The Yellow Book*. In the year before this last success, and like many other budding writers in need of a regular income, Bennett had secured a salaried position in the literary marketplace, in his case as assistant editor and later editor of *Woman*, a popular weekly magazine.

By the end of 1900, therefore, both Bennett and Wells had good reason to be optimistic about their prospects. Wells' reputation as a writer of scientific romances was well established by this period, his having already published, among other works, *The Time Machine* (1895), *The Island of Doctor Moreau* (1896), *The Invisible Man* (1897), and *The War of the Worlds* (1898); the last of these texts can be considered as heralding the genre of invasion fiction in its modern form. Bennett's literary standing at this time, while far more modest than that of Wells, was apparently that of a man on the rise. Although his list of book publications by 1900 was limited to only a single novel, *A Man from the North* (1898), and a primer entitled *Journalism for Women: A Practical Guide* (1898), his evident ambition and industry suggested similar qualities to those that had prepared the ground for Wells' early success. These characteristics are amply evident in Bennett's journal entry for the final day of 1899:

> This year I have written 335,340 words, grand total. 228 articles and stories (including 4 instalments of a serial of 30,000 – 7,500 words each) have actually been published . . . My total earnings were £592 3s. 1d, of which I have yet to receive £72 10s. (Bennett 1932a: 100, 101)

Here Bennett, in characteristic fashion, brought the meticulously detailed eye of an accounts clerk to bear on his literary efforts. But while both Bennett and Wells had by 1900 established themselves as successful literary tradesmen, neither felt, at this stage of their careers, that they had achieved much more in print culture than a reasonably secure income and, in Wells' case, the literary celebrity that had accompanied his popular scientific romance fiction. There is a considerable sense of frustration expressed in their correspondence for this period that they had not yet done justice to what they saw as their own remarkable literary talents. Wells articulated this discontent in a reply to a compliment paid to him by Bennett in June 1900 regarding his works of scientific realism:

> [W]hy the Hell have you joined the conspiracy to restrict me to one particular type of story? I want to write novels and before God I *will* write novels. They are the proper stuff for my everyday work, a methodical careful distillation of one's thoughts and sentiments and experiences and impressions. But the other stuff which you would have me doing day by day is no more to be done day to day than repartees or lyric poetry. (Wilson 1960: 45)

This was more than simply a need to break out from a literary straitjacket: Wells sensed that a new phase of his career as a serious novelist should coincide with the start of the century. Bennett echoes these frustrations in a letter written in December 1899 to his friend Thomas Lloyd Humberstone: 'Just now I am consumed with a fever to chuck up women's journalism utterly, & go in for fiction & criticism only ... I swear I will get out of that damned office inside two years or shoot myself' (Hepburn 1968: 127). His desires on this front were fuelled by a belief, also expressed in this letter, that his forthcoming collection of literary criticism, with its 'curious mixture of worldliness & passionate feeling for pure literary art', would offer an 'exact' expression of himself to the reading public (1968: 127–8). By the time that this volume, entitled *Fame and Fiction: An Enquiry into Certain Popularities*, had appeared in 1901, Bennett had already resigned from his editorship of *Woman* and taken the initial steps on an independent literary career.

What seems particularly significant about the post-1900 phases of Bennett's and Wells' writing careers is the extent to which both felt a pressing need to redefine the nature of literary fiction in Britain in the new century. This comprehensive rethinking of the purpose of fiction was predicated on their shared belief that, towards the end of the nineteenth century, the evolution of British literature had failed to keep pace with a rapidly changing society. In particular, they argued that the development and concerns of their own social and cultural background, firmly located in the upper echelons of the working class and the lower reaches of the middle class, remained largely overlooked by British print culture to date. The ways in which Bennett and Wells addressed this apparent cultural gap demonstrates their marked differences as literary stylists, and equally their contrasting approaches to broadening the existing parameters of fiction. It is therefore useful at this stage to examine their Edwardian work separately, before concluding with a consideration of the shared aspects of their endeavours.

To take Bennett first, we can recognise the nature of his discontent at the current state of the novel in the title of a series of articles, 'The Fallow Fields of Fiction', which he published in the *Academy* during the summer of 1901. Bennett set the tone of his argument in the article's opening lines: 'Those who make it their business to examine the whole output of modern fiction must necessarily be depressed and wearied by the heavy sensation of its sameness, its futility, its lack of enterprise' (Bennett 1901a: 517). He went on to argue that contemporary fiction was currently dominated by 'love' plots involving 'permutations and combinations of two men and a maid, or two maids and a man'. These tedious permutations, he argued, were invariably employed as material for just 'five sorts of novels: the domestic, the historical, the criminal, the theological, and the bellicose', with 'not ten novels in a year [falling] outside these classes (we admit a few admirable exceptions)' (517). In moving beyond predictable plots with their casts of hackneyed characters, Bennett proposed that writers broaden the scope and ambition of their work to develop new forms of fiction more closely in dialogue with modern life.

While Bennett looked here to the French novel for stylistic inspiration, in particular to Honoré de Balzac's work, he went on to suggest the ways in which these continental literary influences might be developed for current day use. In adapting these models, Bennett argued, one might consider the potential of 'large co-operative' communities, such as those he had recently observed building the new Roman Catholic Westminster Cathedral, or equally, the network of individuals employed by 'the London and North Western main line' railway system. This latter organisation, connected together by its community of booking clerks, stationmasters, young engineers, 'wise greybeards', porters and directors, was, according to Bennett, a dynamic transport system that 'throbs from end to end with "the human interest"'. Taking this potential artistic fertility into account, he additionally suggested that a commercial organisation such as a railway company might provide the source material for a whole school of novels rather than being used to furnish a single text. Elsewhere in the 'Fallow Fields' articles, Bennett suggested other milieux as material for fresh twentieth-century fiction, including parish councils, corporate life, and the area on which he would concentrate in his own work: 'the municipal life of an industrial town'. This 'rich life-ore', Bennett claimed, 'might be "got" by any novelist who does not deem himself bound to do nothing that has not been done before' (Bennett 1901a: 57, 58). Whereas British interpreters of French literary naturalism (including George Moore, a writer much admired by Bennett) might well have taken up this challenge in the 1880s and 1890s, their work had tended instead to focus upon bohemian or slum life. According to Bennett, the resulting failure of both popular and more serious-minded British fiction to recognise and respond to the changing face of modern society had left it as a cultural form with only superficial relevance for its readers. Bennett summed up what he saw as the potentially wider significance of the novel in the following terms:

> In a world more complex than that of Balzac, a world where mutual compre-
> hension and imaginative sympathy are the conditions precedent to any real
> social progress . . . the supreme function [of our novelists] . . . is to promote
> by their imagination such imaginative sympathy . . . Novelists have work to
> do and they are not doing it. (Bennett 1901a: 518)

Only by writing fiction applicable to the world as it appeared to readers at the start of the new century, might authors move beyond the 'eternal and tedious monotony' which they currently evoked. In this way they might produce, as Balzac had already done in the previous century, work capable of acting on readers as 'a valuable stimulant and correc-tive medicine' (Bennett 1901a: 517, 518).

Bennett set out to reinvigorate current fiction by writing novels and stories centred upon the 'Five Towns' of the Staffordshire Potteries area of England, a location with which he was intimately connected. Here, in depicting the connected communities of this distinctive industrial area, he was able to flesh out the notions of liberal humanism (and, crucially, the limitations of these qualities) that his 'Fallow Fields of Fiction' articles had outlined. Over the course of the Edwardian decade, start-ing with *Anna of the Five Towns* in 1902, Bennett went on to write a number of texts set in the 'Five Towns', including *Leonora* (1903), *Tales of the Five Towns* (1905), *Whom God Hath Joined* (1906), *The Grim Smile of the Five Towns* (1907), and arguably his two most important works of fiction, *The Old Wives' Tale* (1908) and *Clayhanger* (1910).

The first of these novels, *Anna of the Five Towns* (*Anna*), was pains-takingly composed over a five-year period. Bennett's plot focuses mainly on the lives of a wealthy businessman, Ephraim Tellwright, his daughter Anna, and her suitor Henry Mynors, the owner of a pottery works. The relationships between these and other connected characters are played out against characteristic 'Five Towns' settings, such as a Wesleyan Methodist Sunday School and 'Revival', sewing meetings, visits to the municipal park, and a holiday to the Isle of Man. Bennett underpins all of the commonplace daily round he depicts with a sense of its rooted-ness in the surrounding pottery industry; Potteries people are described as products of the local clay, existing both 'in it and by it' (1902/1967: 115). The omnipresence of industry is underscored in an early passage by a narrator who anticipates our inability as readers to recognise the fitness of industrial landscape as a setting for art:

> Nothing could be more prosaic than the huddled, red-brown streets; nothing more seemingly remote from romance. Yet be it said that romance is even here – the romance which, for those who have an eye to perceive it, ever dwells amid the seats of industrial manufacture, softening the coarseness, transfiguring the squalor, of these mighty alchemic operations. (1902/1967: 25)

Bennett's use of the term 'romance' in this context is provocative, intended to invite readers to reconsider their existing understanding of this literary form. The quotidian world evoked in *Anna*, with its mundane daily routine, is established against the grain of more conventionally romantic literature, but with that form of writing always in mind. This is evident, for example, in Bennett's depiction of Anna's domineering father, the novel's putative villain. Whereas Tellwright's domination over his daughters and his designation as a miser (the novel's second chapter is entitled 'The Miser's Daughter') suggests his fairy tale-like role in *Anna*, this straightforward 'romantic' typology is complicated by the narrator. Rather than acting out of calculated melodramatic cruelty, Tellwright's behaviour is instead the product of more prosaic and arguably, therefore, more relatable causes:

> His treatment of his daughters was no part of a system, nor obedient to any defined principles, nor the expression of a brutal disposition, nor the result of gradually-acquired habit. It came to him like eating, and like parsimony. He belonged to the great and powerful class of house-tyrants, the backbone of the British nation. (1902/1967: 127)

Although this domestic tyranny appears instinctive and socially sanctioned rather than maliciously premeditated and deviant, its effects in the novel are profound; Bennett suggests that the results of this commonplace autocracy are much the same as those that would ensue from a more melodramatic form of despotism. The effect of this is signalled by Anna's powerlessness to exercise her own will and break away from her father, even after she inherits the distinctly romantic sum of £50,000 from her late mother's estate (41). Although the 'romantic' logic of the narrative (common to those 'two men and a maid' plots that Bennett had earlier derided) leads the reader to anticipate Anna's denouncement of her father and exercise of the power of her wealth in marrying the man she loves, the novel's conclusion offers a distinctly unromantic finale. This ending sees Anna accepting the prospect of becoming a 'good wife' in a loveless union with Mynors, an unromantic fate she accepts 'calmly and genially' (235). Anna's resignation here, the novel suggests, is the product not only of her father's crushing influence, but also of the traditional obedience and prudence inculcated in Potteries' women by the surrounding influences of Methodism and commerce. For Anna, these inexorable forces dictate what she understands as her 'duty', a quality in which the narrator declares, she 'had never failed' (235). 'Romance' is evidently a literary construction that shadows this text, but Bennett's resistance to its expected patterns allows him to construct a novel that responds more directly to the complex modern pressures under which individuals, especially women, negotiate their day-to-day lives. Bennett wants to enter into a dialogue here with his readers, asking them to question the narratives of the novels they habitually read, while offering them alternative paradigms for thought-provoking modern fiction.

While *Anna* offers a blueprint for Bennett's fresh approach towards the novel in the new century, its limitations are apparent when read against his later Edwardian Five Towns work. Wells recognised *Anna*'s central flaw when he suggested in a letter to Bennett that it was written too much under the spell of its influences; he singled out the work of George Gissing and George Moore here, although he might have added Balzac's *Eugénie Grandet* (1833), a novel with which *Anna* shares a number of key features and concerns. Bennett's consciousness of these models had, Wells argued, stiffened up the text and robbed it of much needed 'ease and gusto' (Wilson 1960: 85). In reply, Bennett defended his text, but acknowledged what Wells described as a 'certain consciousness of good intentions', admitting that this impulse had indeed coloured his writing (88). For his later fiction, Bennett worked hard to develop a style that was more detached from his acknowledged literary influences. A key aspect of this stylistically liberated and less studied later work was Bennett's desire to publish intellectually engaging fiction that would also be broadly accessible for what he dubbed the 'average reader' of popular literature – a category of readers that had greatly expanded in the wake of the 1870 Education Act, and subsequent legislation in this field. This democratic approach to creating substantial literary fiction was set out in the following terms in the opening chapter of *Fame and Fiction*: 'I believe that a novel could be written which would unite in a mild ecstasy of praise the two extremes [of current readership] – the most inclusive majority and the most exclusive minority' (Bennett 1901b: 16). The culmination of this phase of Bennett's work is found in *The Old Wives' Tale*, which Wells acknowledged had addressed his earlier reservations about Bennett's fiction: 'the knowledge, the detail, the spirit! from first to last it *never* fails' (Wilson 1960: 154). In this novel Bennett returned to the location (Bursley, a fictionised version of Burslem), social milieu, and points of focus (particularly the lives of lower-middle-class women) found in *Anna*, but he developed these elements over a broader canvas and through a markedly different literary style. This stylistic shift between novels is immediately evident in Bennett's choice of narrator: in *Anna*, as the passages quoted above suggest, the narrator is self-consciously formal ('Yet be it said that romance is even here' (1902/1967: 25)), whereas the narrator of *The Old Wives' Tale* is unceremonious, wry and ironic. These qualities, undoubtedly appealing to Bennett's 'average reader' in 1908, are evident in the passage introducing the novel's geographical setting:

> The Five Towns seem to cling together for safety. Yet the idea of clinging together for safety would make them laugh. They are unique and indispensable. From the north of the county right down to the south they alone stand for civilisation, applied science, organised manufacture, and the century – until you come to Wolverhampton. They are unique and indispensable because you cannot drink tea out of a teacup without the aid of the Five Towns; because you cannot eat a meal in decency without the aid of the Five Towns. (1908/1990: 39)

The confidence with which the narrator asserts the 'indispensable' centrality of crockery and its manufacture to the nation, appears a deliberate rejoinder to any snobbish reaction that a book seemingly immersed in vulgar commerce might evoke. This self-assurance on the narrator's part also throws into relief the introduction into the novel of its central characters, Constance and Sophia Baines, teenage sisters who live above their father's drapery shop in the town's main square. Baines' shop is meticulously evoked in ways that establish its dignity, significance and high standing in the local community. By setting up the shop and its occupants in this nuanced and fine-grained way, Bennett sought to dismantle those literary prejudices that had ensured, as Margaret Drabble has noted, that the shopkeeping classes of provincial England had 'hardly surfaced into literature at all' at this time (Drabble 1975: 95).

While the Baines' drapery shop may be resolutely local, the narrator ensures that the Baines family are also universally relatable; the death of the invalid patriarch, John Baines, for example, is synonymous with the ending of an historical epoch: 'Mid-Victorian England lay on that mahogany bed. Ideals had passed away with John Baines' (Bennett 1908/1990: 112). This desire to use the distinctly local to discuss the wider human condition, especially in its relationship to the passage of time, was inspired by Bennett's encounter in 1903 with an old and eccentric woman in a Paris restaurant. He speculated, in his Preface to *The Old Wives' Tale*, that this woman had once possessed the 'unique charm of youth', and that her current status as a 'stout, ageing woman [was] made up of an infinite number of infinitesimal changes, each unperceived by her' (Bennett 1908/1990: 32). Bennett's subsequent decision to write about such a figure, someone 'who would pass unnoticed in a crowd', inspired his depiction of the Baines sisters, themselves relatively insignificant figures passing through time. In *The Old Wives' Tale*, their spirited youth, as captured in the book's early chapters, solidifies during their 'stout' middle years, before their lives fade out in old age. The changing phases of their life occur quietly, like the ending of their once-cherished ideals, which pass away, the narrator suggests, 'not in the conventional pageantry of honoured death, but sorrily, ignobly, while one's head is turned' (Bennett 1908/1990: 112–13). The minute-by-minute quality of daily life is consistently set against a more epochal understanding of time's passing, with these two conceptions coming together at key moments, such as that in which Sophia confronts the dead body of her former lover Gerald Scales. At this instant, Sophia is able to overcome those local grievances against Gerald that had once preoccupied her (feeling now that 'the manner of his life was of no importance'), and focus instead on a broader truth evident in the certainty of his corpse:

> What affected her was that he had once been young, and that he had grown old, and was now dead. That was all. Youth and vigour had come to that. Youth and vigour always came to that. Everything came to that. (577)

Here and elsewhere in the novel, characters are slow to reconcile the microscopic detail of a lived life with the hidden truth of their existence, something Sophia characterises as 'the riddle of life' (578). Only, if at all, at moments of great personal crisis is some indistinct sense of 'what life is' – a declaration that forms the title of the novel's final section – available to them.

Although the novel's apparent social determinism suggests that this is a deeply pessimistic text, the narrator's approach couches human life in a sense of its predictable absurdity rather than its tragedy. The cyclical nature of life is emphasised in *The Old Wives' Tale*, with youth and modernity constantly usurping age and history, and this approach helps to place in broader perspective the transitory nature of day-to-day concerns. But equally, Bennett's text demonstrates the reasons why everyday things *do* matter; in this way it takes the everyday seriously. We can recognise this, for example, in the ways in which the writing of the word 'exquisite' on a shop ticket becomes a subject of intense debate and anxiety for the Baines family and their connections. This shop ticket, insignificant outside its historical moment, is seen in the novel as a battleground between opposing forces of youth and age; 'age' arguing that tickets such as these 'would outrage the decency of trade', and youth recognising this moment as a 'miracle' in the history of commerce (121, 122). Rather than using this episode to satirise the littleness of the event and the ridiculousness of the individuals involved, Bennett is instead interested here in the hidden significance of this seemingly trivial point of conflict. In this way, as John Gross observes, Bennett's novel dramatises the sense in which 'everything goes on as usual and nothing remains the same' (Gross 1969: 215).

This sense of real change in what first appears to be an emphatically static world is signified by the social mobility of Constance's son Cyril. Although a future in the family drapery shop seems mapped out for him at his birth, Cyril's interest in art and his subsequent move to London removes him from the Baines' social milieu and allows him instead to mix with the Peel-Swynnertons, a distinguished Potteries family belonging, in Sophia's mind, to a 'superior race' (Bennett 1908/1990: 473). Cyril's new social connections, unthinkable in the Victorian heyday of the Baines sisters, are by the Edwardian period in which the novel concludes, an 'unanticipated' but 'revolutionary' reality (481). For Bennett, the revolution that Cyril's social mobility points towards is a reflection of his own (and Wells') experience of 'pushing up', moving beyond the rigid social mores that characterised the Victorian era. A sense of silent but tangible social change is also central to *Clayhanger*, a novel which formed the first part of his Five Towns trilogy of novels focusing on the Clayhanger family; *Hilda Lessways* (1911) and *These Twain* (1916) form the subsequent volumes. With the central character of these volumes, Edwin Clayhanger, Bennett continued to build upon his key ideas regarding stasis and change, the influence of geography and heredity on human lives (focusing in the first volume of the trilogy on a father's influence on his son), and on the dissection of lower-middle class provincial lives. In *Clayhanger*, 'an epic of the commonplace' (as Walter de la Mare described it in his then-anonymous *Times Literary Supplement* review (Anonymous 1910: 328)), Bennett consolidated those ideas he had set out in 'The Fallow Fields of Fiction'. Along with his earlier Five Towns work, and especially *The Old Wives' Tale*, the publication of *Clayhanger* firmly established his Potteries scenes and people in the mainstream, not only of British fiction, but also in a more international dimension. The popularity of Bennett's novels in the United States, underlined by a successful tour he undertook there in 1911, confirmed his ability to transcend the local in his work, while putting his 'ordinary' everyday people firmly on the literary map.

Unlike Bennett, Wells already had an international profile as a writer by the beginning of the twentieth century, but, as he remarked in a letter written to James Nichol Dunn in February 1900, the work that had gained him this reputation was in his eyes merely 'crude & cheap' (Smith 1998: 354). While his popular literature had provided him with what he defined (in a letter written to Elizabeth Healey in May of that year) as 'the first excitement of [my] start into "literature"', this adolescent phase was now '*quite* over', and he looked forward to producing work 'with an increasing strength and quality' (355). His ambition in this line was to succeed a trio he dubbed (in a letter written to editor of *The Morning Post* in October 1900) as the 'living great masters' of English fiction: Henry James, George Meredith and Thomas Hardy (363). While these three ageing writers unquestioningly deserved respect from their younger peers, they would, in time, give place to emerging talents; indeed of Wells' 'three great masters', only two were active as writers of fiction in 1900, Hardy having effectively retired from novel writing following the appearance of *Jude the Obscure* in 1895. The next generation of writers, Wells wrote in his non-fiction work of social prophecy *Anticipations* (1901/1902), needed to come to terms with an increasingly diverse readership, which, while possessing 'no universal ideas, no universal conventions', would still be 'seeking to find themselves' (138, 139). The twentieth-century writer had a duty to help with this quest, and would be aided, Wells predicted, by the formation of a radical new world order that he dubbed the 'New Republic'. In this New Republic, 'contemporary literature' would form the very 'breath of civilized life', with those who 'sincerely think and write' making up the 'salt of the social body'; 'to mumble over the past, to live on the classics', Wells averred, 'is senility' (270). The high place that Wells set up for contemporary authors in his New Republic ensured that they would be well looked after by the state – a situation which contrasted with the current position of writers forced to exist 'within the limits of a particularly distressful and ill-managed market'. In a better-organised world, writers such as Wells himself would be able to reason directly with the public, without having to 'please and interest' them first (271). The emerging literature from this improved world order would be 'living literature', a form of writing unhindered by past conventions or tawdry commercial interests, one free therefore to address the pressing aspects of the day (272). Although Wells' New Republic remained a distant prospect at the start of the twentieth century, the vision he espouses here is useful in helping us to understand his sense of the primary role of the creative writer in contemporary society.

Wells' commercial popularity as an author at the start of the twentieth century, while a source of scant intellectual satisfaction, at least offered him a platform from which to publish work compatible with his New Republican ideals. Starting with *Love and Mr. Lewisham* in 1900, Wells went on to issue a series of broadly polemical novels (including *Kipps* (1905), *Tono-Bungay* (1909), *Ann Veronica* (1909), and *The History of Mr. Polly* (1910)), all of which focused on the complicated lives of contemporary individuals. Each of these novels pointed towards inequities in the current ordering of society, and each, like Bennett's own Edwardian novels, placed commonplace people from unfashionable places at centre stage. The first novel of this new phase, *Love and Mr. Lewisham*, was the product of much industry and ambition on Wells' part; he claimed at the start of 1900 to have been writing this text 'for a little eternity' (Smith 1998: 355). The time and effort Wells put into this work, and his sense of its significance in the development of his literary career, encourages direct comparison with Bennett's *Anna of the Five Towns*. Useful parallels can also be drawn between Bennett's extensive use of the Potteries people and settings, and Wells' own plundering of characters and scenes with which he was familiar: in *Love and Mr. Lewisham*, these include the Sussex school at which he was a pupil-teacher in the early 1880s, the Normal School of Science in South Kensington where he studied in the mid-1880s, and several nondescript areas of suburban south London, including Clapham and Battersea. But Wells had little interest in creating the minutely realised environments characteristic of Bennett's 'Five Towns'. For Wells, the settings he chose were simply useful stages on which to play out his account of Lewisham's early life and trials. While these settings are bound up with the events that take place in the novel, they are not completely integral to the substance of the work in the way that Bennett's geography and local environment certainly are. Wells is instead primarily focused on the effects on individual lives of society and its institutions at large. In this way, Wells' work is more reminiscent of the social-problem novels of earlier British writers, such as Dickens and Thackeray, than those continental writers, like Balzac, who had so profoundly influenced Bennett's work.

Wells' work also resembles that of his Victorian predecessors in the ways in which he uses comedy to enliven his social critique. Although *Love and Mr. Lewisham* is more restrained in its use of comedy than Wells' later social-problem novels, this mode still provides a keynote of the narrator's approach. Wells' distinctive comedic touch is evident, for example, in the novel's opening chapter, in which Mr Lewisham is introduced as an ambitious but impecunious eighteen-year-old assistant schoolteacher. His youthful ambition is symbolised by a document attached to the walls of his lodgings that he pretentiously calls a

'Schema'. This paper maps out the glittering career which will ensue from his current studies: a BA degree begun in 1892 at 'the London University', would be rewarded in 1895 with a 'gold medal' for out-standing scholarship, and then duly followed by '"pamphlets in the Liberal interest" and such like things duly dated' (1900/1994: 4). But this single-minded and meticulously plotted course of education and advancement is disturbed when, on a 'glorious' spring day, Lewisham hears the footsteps of Ethel. Although at this stage Ethel is a stranger to him, Lewisham is fatally distracted from his study by the sound of her movements outside his window:

> not only was the stir of Mother Nature's awakening in the earth and the air and the trees, but also in Mr Lewisham's youthful blood, bidding him rouse himself to live – live in a sense quite other than that the Schema indicated. (Wells 1900/1994: 6)

This moment dramatises the tension between Lewisham's monk-like pro-gramme of proposed self-improvement and his unruly sexual impulse. While Lewisham looks to further education as a means of escape from the uninspiring career awaiting him as a provincial schoolteacher, he falls prey, in this spring scene, to drives over which he has little control. Given Lewisham's modest social position, the novel makes clear, the insistent nature of his natural sexual impulse can only be legitimately addressed through marriage. And if his sexual tension is to be relieved in a marital union, then Lewisham would be forced to sacrifice his cherished intellectual ambitions, and knuckle down to a job that would bring security for his wife and family. The incompatible options that face Lewisham when mapping out his future prospects are described by the novel's narrator as 'on the one hand that shining staircase to fame and power, that had been his dream from the very dawn of his adoles-cence, and on the other hand – Ethel' (85). While Lewisham's dilemma is expressed here in characteristically tongue-in-cheek terms, the under-lying issue is deadly serious. Wells, who himself had made an unhappy marriage in 1891 to his cousin Isabel, was keenly aware of the gravity underpinning this comically bathetic remark.

At the conclusion of the novel, Lewisham's resigned acceptance of the end of his hopes for 'fame and power' (following marriage to Ethel and impending fatherhood), is underscored by a series of rueful thoughts on his recently rediscovered Schema:

> 'Yes, it was vanity,' he said. 'A boy's vanity. For me – anyhow. I'm too two-sided . . . Two-sided? . . . Commonplace!'
> 'Dreams like mine – abilities like mine. Yes – any man! And yet . . . – The things I meant to do!'

... 'Not for us – Not for us.
'We must perish in the wilderness – Some day. Somewhen. But not for us.
(Wells 1900/1994: 188)

John Batchelor argues that in abandoning his intellectual ambition in preparation for fatherhood, Lewisham has simply 'fallen into his appropriate role' in the Darwinian organisation of the world (1982: 43), but this interpretation seems reductive when considered alongside the novel's wider contexts. The lament for his lost life that Lewisham soliloquises at the novel's conclusion ('it is almost as if Life had played me a trick – promised so much – given so little!') is contested by a rival inner voice which attempts to quell this rebellion: 'No! One must not look at it in that way! That will not do! That will *not* do' (188). But the impatient and schoolmasterly tone adopted here by this inner voice suggests the difficulty of dismissing self-will in the face of all-conquering biological determinism. Although Wells the scientist might claim that a fundamental need to reproduce the species took precedence over the relatively insignificant desires of individuals, Wells the novelist remained sympathetic to Lewisham's personal plight. In a more fairly ordered society, Wells' narrator implies, young men like Lewisham would enjoy the freedom to achieve their public goals, while simultaneously satisfying their own private biological imperatives. Lives in this more sanely organised world would evolve unhindered by the misguided and restrictive social conventions currently in force.

Wells' later Edwardian fiction follows much the same narrative pattern as that established in *Love and Mr. Lewisham*. In these novels, individuals are initially entrapped, and then proceed to look for ways to escape the nets in which they are caught. The repeated narrative arc of imprisonment and attempted escape allowed Wells to examine a number of iniquitous aspects of society, demonstrating in the process what he saw as the rottenness at the core of much modern life. In *Kipps*, for example, Wells initially attacks the English private schools system, in which his title character is subjected to 'an atmosphere of stuffiness and mental muddle' (1905/1998: 9), before training his fire on an especially personal bugbear, the 'great stupid machine of retail trade'; the Folkestone Drapery Bazaar in which Kipps is indentured represents a 'vast, irresistible force which he had neither strength of will nor knowledge to escape' (35). Later in this novel, after Kipps unexpectedly inherits £26,000, the Wellsian narrator satirises the snobbish society into which the apprenticed draper is transported by this new wealth. Like Pip in Dickens' *Great Expectations* (1861), Kipps returns at the end of the novel to a more modest social position (in Kipps' case, after his fortune has been embezzled), and is evidently well-rid of the grand but ultimately hollow society into which he was inexorably drawn by his inheritance. Kipps, now happily married to his childhood sweetheart, opens a bookshop (an occupation for which he, as an avid reader, is ideally suited) and is thereafter able to live a life of simple contentment. This conclusion, like that of Wells' 1910 novel *The History of Mr. Polly*, imagines a society in which individuals are permitted to enjoy a purposeful life that is suitably adapted to their desires and talents. While Kipps (like Mr Polly) is evidently a 'Simple Soul' (a designation that forms the subtitle of the novel), this simplicity should neither condemn him at fourteen to an 'inexorable fate' (24) in the retail trade, nor instantly place him into the hands of exploiting 'superiors' if he should happen to receive a legacy. The freedom of choice that Kipps is able to exercise at the conclusion of the novel should be regarded, readers are invited to agree, as a fundamental right for all people, irrespective of their social background.

This rallying cry for all individuals to demand ownership of their future, and their emancipation from modern slavery in its various forms, is also at the heart of *Ann Veronica*. Here, Wells considers the pressing need for individuals to take control of their lives from the perspective of a twenty-one-year-old woman, who, in the novel's opening pages, decides to break away from her suffocating existence in the London suburbs. Although Wells covers much polemical ground here in tracing Ann Veronica's experience of areas such as the employment market, further education, the suffrage movement, Fabianism and vegetarianism, it is with the restrictions on female sexuality that the novel is ultimately concerned. For young women of Ann Veronica's suburban class, these limitations are particularly constraining, licensing their choice of certain *suitable* partners (such as the eligible but unappealing Mr Manning), and vetoing desirable ones (like Capes, Ann Veronica's tutor, who is separated from his wife). Wells rails here against the illogical social conventions which prevent a healthy and bright young woman from making a free choice of sexual partner in or outside marriage. Ann Veronica's decision to reject these prevailing conventions, and to follow instead her own natural biological instincts in choosing Capes, made the novel highly controversial in 1909; the *Spectator*'s editor, John St Loe Strachey, reviewed the novel under the heading 'A Poisonous Book', suggesting that it had inspired 'loathing and indignation' (Parrinder 1972: 169, 170). This controversy was exacerbated by the direct way in which Ann Veronica expressed her sexual instincts; unlike the demure heroines of numerous conventional novels of this period, Ann Veronica's declaration of her desire for Capes is strikingly unambiguous: '"I want you. I want you to be my lover. I want to give myself to you. I want to be whatever I can to you"' (Wells 1909/2005: 250). But this aggressive determination to overcome the rules of a restrictive society ends in what appears as a perfectly conventional bourgeois marriage to Capes (now divorced from his wife), who has given up his career as a scientist to become a successful playwright. Wells gives little sense here that Ann Veronica is in any way torn by the loss of her intellectual freedom and ambition in the face of future domesticity as a wife and mother. Instead she appears happily resigned in her coy declaration to Capes that she will now 'have to go carefully and bear children, and – take care of my hair – and when I am done with that I shall be an old woman' (291). Whereas Mr Lewisham had railed against any straightforward acceptance of his 'appropriate' role in life as father and suburban husband, Ann Veronica's willingness to embrace her equivalent female destiny suggests the limits of Wells' advocacy of personal freedoms. It also confirms the distinctly subjective and personal qualities that underpinned all of Wells' social fiction. Even in what is probably his finest novel, *Tono-Bungay*, Wells' narrator confirms Henry James' judgement on his work that it was 'simply at any and every moment "about" Mr. Wells's own most general adventure'. Although James (one of those three writers Wells had declared in 1900 as 'living great masters' of fiction) much admired the 'extraordinarily reflective' quality of Wells' work, he also lamented the lack of impersonality that this work evinced. Wells' inability to break away from his own personal preoccupations in constructing a novel, James considered, left his work fatally weakened – with the 'saturation' of Wells' personality overwhelming any claims that might be made for its artistic status (James 1914: 133, 134).

But any acknowledgement of the limitations of Wells' distinctly personal fiction must also take into account the significance of his novels in his Edwardian social and political contexts. As with Bennett, he felt he was writing on behalf of a whole class of people, who, like 'The Secret People' in G. K. Chesterton's 1907 poem of that name, had 'not spoken yet' (Chesterton 1927: 157). At the end of the Edwardian decade, Bennett and Wells, now both internationally established as writers at the forefront of their profession, published works which confirmed their continuing commitment to redrawing the existing literary landscape. In Wells' *The History of Mr. Polly* and Bennett's *The Card* (published in book form in 1911, but serialised in *The Times Weekly Edition* during the previous year), both writers returned to scenes and issues familiar from their earlier work. But these later novels demonstrate a fresh confidence and new optimism in depicting individuals from the suburban and provincial classes. We can recognise these qualities in the following passage from *The History of Mr. Polly*, which occurs when Wells' eponymous shopkeeper decides to break free from his oppressive life:

But when a man has once broken through the paper walls of everyday circumstance, those unsubstantial walls that hold so many of us securely prisoned from the cradle to the grave, he has made a discovery. If the world does not please you, *you can change it*. Determine to alter it at any price, and you can change it altogether ... And Mr. Polly ... saw through it, understood there was no inevitable any more, and escaped his former despair.

   He could, for example, 'clear out'. (1910/1999: 137)

This moment, either yearned for or achieved in all of Wells' earlier social fiction, takes on the decisive tone of a self-help manual in this novel, as the narrator steps out of the narrative frame. Mr Polly's ability to embrace personal happiness, in his role as handyman at a rural Kentish inn, also underlines Wells' commitment to the liberation of an apparently subjugated section of society. Bennett's own lower-middle-class hero Denry Machin, in *The Card*, also realises the potential freedom in his life, and acts upon this revelation to 'get on' in the world. Although this novel is written in the vein of Bennett's more light-hearted fiction (other examples of work written in this key include *The Grand Babylon Hotel* (1902), *A Great Man* (1904), and *Buried Alive* (1908)), there is a serious edge to his portrayal of a humble solicitor's clerk who refuses to accept his designated place in society. Indeed, *The Card* is a celebration of Denry's risk-taking attitude to life, tacitly approving his audacity in forging the results of a school scholarship examination, and mischievously adding his own name to a list of invitees to a municipal ball. Instead of receiving his deserved comeuppance, Denry's consistent failure to observe the strict laws governing his social class is rewarded with riches, civic honours and, crucially, the affectionate admiration of the local Potteries community. A contemporary and not entirely complimentary review of *The Card* summed up its 'very up-to-date gospel' in the following terms: 'if you want to make any success in life it is best done through cheek – always cheek' (NHW 1911: 327). But for both Bennett and Wells, 'cheek' had been a key weapon from the very start of their own literary careers, helping them to ensure that they did indeed 'get on'. Without 'cheek', they might never have left behind the solicitor's office and drapery counter, and, to paraphrase the narrator of *The History of Mr. Polly*, they would then have been unable to change, what for them, was an existing literary world that failed to please them.

Suburban Literature

The provincial and suburban scenes foregrounded in the Edwardian fiction of Bennett and Wells were complemented by similar material

appearing in the work of many other British writers at this time. After
1900, clerks, typists, drapers and shopmen regularly appeared in a wide
range of literature. While this section will go on to look at specific examples of provincial- and suburban-set literature in more detail, it is important to first sketch the wider field of this writing, beginning with the
serious suburban realism of George Gissing, a writer whose interest in
this section of society had pre-dated and influenced the fiction of Bennett
and Wells. Gissing, who died in 1903, continued in his final novels to
make an important contribution to the establishment of the contemporary lower-middle class as subject matter for significant literary texts; his
last, and posthumously published novel, *Will Warburton: A Romance of
Real Life* (1905), for example, concerns a gentleman forced by a reversal
of financial circumstances to become a grocer in south London. Other
contemporary fiction focusing on shop life included T. Baron Russell's
Borlase & Son (1903) (praised by James Joyce, in a *Daily Express*
review, for its 'actuality' and 'unsentimental vigour' (Barry 2000: 99)),
and Cicely Hamilton's play *Diana of Dobson's* (1908), which examined
the exploitation of female workers in the drapery trade. Like shops,
offices were increasingly seen as fertile locations for writers of literary
fiction; among the novelists whose work included substantial accounts
of white-collar work were Shan F. Bullock, whose *Robert Thorne: The
Story of a London Clerk* (1907) drew extensively upon his own background in the civil service; J. C. Snaith, another clerk-turned-writer,
whose *William Jordan Junior* (1907) depicted a literary-minded count-
ing-house clerk; and Frank Swinnerton, whose novels *The Merry Heart*
(1909) and *The Young Idea* (1910) offer positive portrayals of modern,
mixed-sex offices populated by bright young clerks. The female clerk,
usually designated in the period as a 'typewriter', also became a familiar
character in numerous Edwardian texts; representative examples include
Christine Seton and Estra Wilbraham's *Two Babes in the City* (1901),
E. Temple Thurston's controversial *Sally Bishop* (1908), Sophie Cole's
A Wardour Street Idyll (1910), and Inez Bensusan's one-act Suffrage
play *The Apple* (1909). More general depictions of Edwardian suburban
life are found extensively in the work of Edwin Pugh, whose naturalist-
inflected fiction included a novel focused upon alcoholism (*The Fruit of
the Vine* (1904)), as well as *The Broken Honeymoon* (1908), and *The
Mocking Bird* (1910); Horace W. C. Newte, who focused his attention
on the negative elements of suburban life in a number of Edwardian
novels including *The Square Mile* (1908), which examines the life of a
bank clerk; George Douglas Brown's deeply pessimistic *The House with
the Green Shutters* (published as Douglas 1901), which Bennett dubbed
'the first Realistic Scotch Novel' (Wilson 1960: 66); and May Sinclair,

whose novella *The Judgement of Eve* (1908) imagined married life in a 'creaking little villa built of sulphurous yellow brick' in Camden Town (36). Other texts that included a detailed evocation of suburban life were those that exploited the literary potential of boarding-house life; works in this category included Lucas Malet's *The Far Horizon* (1906), and Jerome K. Jerome's short story 'The Passing of the Third Floor Back' (1907), later adapted as an extremely successful play, which used this space to debate spiritual and moral issues.

While much of the comic literature of the era has faded from public consciousness, in its day it provided prolific entertainment for Edwardian clerks and shop workers during their journey to work or while they were relaxing on holiday. Writers of this material found lower-middle-class settings ideally suited to attracting a readership who evidently enjoyed seeing their own lives and localities in print. A popular form of suburban comedy that focused on quotidian detail was pioneered by Jerome K. Jerome in the 1880s and 1890s, and he continued to draw upon this comedy of recognition in his Edwardian writing; while *Three Men on the Bummel* (1900) and *Idle Ideas in 1905* (1905) provided sequels to his enormously popular Victorian publications, fresh work such as *The Observations of Henry* (1901) offered sketch comedy framed by the humorous experiences of a London waiter. Much of the comic material appearing in book form at this time (including Jerome's) began life in the newspapers and magazines of the day. This was the case with Barry Pain's 'Eliza' stories (such as *Eliza* (1900), and *Eliza's Husband* (1903)) which were originally published in the Jerome-edited paper *To-Day*, before being collected together as one-shilling paper-covered volumes. These accounts of the office and domestic life of an unnamed clerk, married to the feisty Eliza, offered a sharp satirical edge to subject matter previously treated more gently in the Grossmiths' *The Diary of a Nobody*. Another clerkly character, Troddles, the creation of R. Andom, featured in a series of popular Edwardian volumes, including *Troddles and Us and Others* (1901), and *On Tour with Troddles* (1909). Keble Howard's very successful comedy of the early married life of an insurance clerk and his wife, *The Smiths of Surbiton* (1906), inspired sequels which continued the story of the Smiths' suburban life. And finally, it is important to note the contribution to suburban-set comedy of F. Anstey, whose Edwardian work included *The Brass Bottle* (1900), *Only Toys* (1903) and a collection of stories and sketches entitled *Salted Almonds* (1906); Anstey's comic writing greatly influenced the fiction of E. Nesbit, whose suburban-based stories for children are discussed in the following chapter. Non-comedic writers of popular forms of genre fiction also favoured everyday suburban locations as settings for their work. Arthur Machen, for example, exploited the juxtaposition between the ordinary and the uncanny in 'A Fragment of Life', collected with other stories in *The House of Souls* (1906), and *The Hill of Dreams* (1907); and Algernon Blackwood worked to similar ends in many of his texts, including several of the ghost stories which appeared in *The Empty House* (1906). In addition, writers of Edwardian detective fiction, such as R. Austin Freeman and Baroness Orczy, were much inspired by Arthur Conan Doyle's Sherlock Holmes stories, which drew extensively upon suburban locations and characters. The inclusion of the name of an unremarkable south London suburb in the title of a 1903 Holmes story, 'The Adventure of the Norwood Builder' (collected with other stories in *The Return of Sherlock Holmes* (1905)), confirms Conan Doyle's continuing use of locations of this kind into and beyond the Edwardian period.

This overview is an exemplary rather than an exhaustive one, yet it does give a sense of the range of depictions of suburban location and lower-middle-class life that appeared in British fiction of the period. Moreover, it suggests the ways in which fiction focused on these places and people appeared alongside Bennett's and Wells' work in this area. W. Pett Ridge's name is little recognised now, but he was undoubtedly among the foremost writers of urban lower-middle-class life in the Edwardian era. In mastering this literary territory, Pett Ridge gained a distinctive reputation among the Edwardian press and public, which was neatly summarised in a review of his work that appeared in *The Times* in 1900:

> Mr Pett Ridge is a master of the social microscope . . . he lifts the roof off a row of the small semi-detached dwellings on which we look down from suburban trains. He is the Thackeray of the households of struggling clerks whose hard service is performed by the solitary maid of all work. (Anonymous 1900g: 9)

An alternative measure of his contemporary status can be gauged from the tribute paid to him by William Dean Howells, the respected North American writer and critic, who argued in 1910 that Pett Ridge had 'made himself a place in literature where he is unrivalled' (Howells 1910: 64). Other contemporary assessments of Pett Ridge's work defined the particular literary qualities which set it apart from that of other writers working in this field: a 1903 review of his work, for example, described him favourably as a literary cameraman, whose unique 'flashlight' left one 'in no doubt as to the identity of the photographer' (Anonymous 1903b: 104). Another feature that was also firmly associated with Pett Ridge's work was what G. K. Chesterton recognised as his 'humane irony'; this quality, invariably entwined with optimism, provides a keynote for his writing (Chesterton 1908: 10). Pett Ridge's work certainly offers an instructive contrast to that of Wells' politically motivated suburban fiction, and also to Bennett's stylistically measured interpretations of provincial scenes. Lacking these overt political and literary imperatives, Pett Ridge was free to craft a distinctive body of work saturated in suburban characters and settings. His 'ordinary' people, generally clerks, shop workers, waitresses and maids, tend to be broadly content with their status in life, and this contentment means that his characters are, to a large extent, liberated from the angst commonly afflicting the petit bourgeois elsewhere in the era's fiction. Pett Ridge's characters instinctively understand the fitness and utility of their everyday lives as they unfold in the modern city and emerging suburb. The remarkable body of work that Pett Ridge published in the Edwardian decade (including eighteen volumes of novels, short stories and essays), with its largely affirmative view of modern suburban life, offers a unique literary window onto the new social caste that was emerging in this space.

Pett Ridge's reputation which placed him among his era's most respected literary chroniclers of suburban life, grew out of his own deep connections with this social scene. Like Bennett and Wells, he had arrived in London in the 1880s (in his own case from rural Kent), before taking up employment as a railway clearing office clerk. Also in common with Bennett and Wells, he began his career as a writer by publishing short pieces in newspapers and magazines; his first published sketch, 'A Dinner in Soho', earned him one guinea when it appeared in the *St. James's Gazette* in the early 1890s (Ridge 1923: 9). While his first novel, *A Clever Wife* (1895), was respectably received, it was not until the success of *Mord Em'ly* in 1898 that his name became more widely established. *Mord Em'ly* focuses on the life of a female gang member in the East End of London, and for a time after its publication Pett Ridge was associated with the 'slum novel', a style of fiction much in vogue in the 1880s and 1890s. But while Pett Ridge continued to write about slum-dwellers in his fiction, his Edwardian reputation was largely built upon depictions of the respectable, but often hard-up, petit bourgeois. As a prelude to his work in the Edwardian decade, he published *Outside the Radius* in 1899, a collection of short stories that were linked by their common setting in 'The Crescent', a suburban street situated outside the four-mile radius from Charing Cross, beyond which London cabs were entitled to charge a higher than standard fare. The Crescent, populated by houses with archetypal suburban names such as 'The Firs, The Oaks, The Elms, The Beeches . . . Plas-Newydelln . . . La Maisonette . . . Beau Rivage . . . Ben Nevis, Beethoven Villa, St Moritz' (Ridge 1899: 6), was built twelve years before the period in which the book's stories are set, and this relatively 'historic' pedigree set it apart from other nearby streets which were 'one day blank spaces, next day a row of thirty-five pound villas' (3). The narrator, an avuncular figure who lives on The Crescent, anticipates the equivalent speaker in Bennett's *Anna of the Five Towns* with his assurance that this apparently unpromising literary locus will not disappoint his readers: 'I find that to declare life in The Crescent as dull and monotonous is a mere pretence; outwardly that may be so; in point of fact there are romances in every house' (20). The 'romances' unveiled here typically focus on resolvable misunderstandings that occur between family members or work colleagues. The details of these confusions, often involving the rituals underpinning courtship (and usually featuring clerks and shop assistants), offered Pett Ridge a rich seam of material for his fiction.

This is evident in many of Pett Ridge's Edwardian magazine stories, which were collected together in volumes bearing such evocative titles as *London Only* (1901), *Up Side Streets* (1903), *Next Door Neighbours* (1904), *On Company's Service* (1905), *Nearly Five Million* (1907) and *Light Refreshment* (1910). A brief examination of three stories taken from these volumes reveals much about Pett Ridge's mode of working in short fiction. In 'Trial and Verdict', for example (from *London Only*), a young woman on the 'green tram' heading for her family home in Finsbury Park coaches her prospective bridegroom on the best way to survive the first meeting with his future mother-in-law (1901: 29). The story concludes with the mother-in-law first uncovering the humble Devonian origins which the prospective husband had concealed, and then reassuring her anxious daughter that this revelation would not after all prove fatal to the match: 'I had just the same row with my people about your poor father. He wasn't anyone particular, but we were none the less happy because of that' (50). The breaking open of a bottle of ginger wine which was being kept for Christmas signifies the mother's happy assent to the couple's marriage. Another story, 'Repairing a Breach' (from *Up Side Streets*), depicts a couple whose engagement has been broken off because of an unresolved misunderstanding. After contesting a breach of promise hearing in court at Red Lion Square, the pair meet accidentally in an Aërated Bread Company (ABC) tea shop in Holborn; these cafés were a feature of London life for the clerkly class for many years. The man, William Wakeley, who lost the case and was ordered to pay damages to his former fiancée, Ellen Hird, has his affections for her reignited when he spots the 'admiring' glances given to Ellen by two young Chancery Lane clerks, who are described by the sharp-eyed narrator as wearing 'paper protectors on their cuffs and [having] the mark of the desk barred across their waistcoats' (1903: 158). Joining Ellen at her table, initially to thwart the 'insolence' of these clerks, Wakeley is gradually reconciled with his former fiancée and the marriage plans are reinstated along with the cancellation of the court damages. Finally, in a story entitled 'Capital Results' (from *Next Door Neighbours*), the marriage plans of a railway booking office clerk and a shop cashier are disturbed when the promise of promotion for the clerk encourages him to consider the marriageable prospects of another woman. This alternative target, a 'superb young woman' according to the clerk, appears a better fit for the sort of grand life that might be lived on a higher salary scale (Ridge 1904: 42); in this projected future, the clerk imagines liberation from the need to 'light his [own] oil stove and to measure tea from the caddy', or shine his own boots; he is depicted undertaking this last chore, while breathing 'on the uppers with gloomy resentfulness' (43, 44). The original pair in this story are reconciled when the clerk, over a cup of chocolate in an Italian restaurant in High Holborn, eavesdrops on his fellow railway office clerks, who reveal that his promised promotion was merely a practical joke on their part. Following the revelation of their 'spoof', the enlightened clerk returns to his senses and loses no time in inviting his reinstated fiancée to join him in 'house hunting to-morrow' (47, 48). All of these plot outlines suggest Pett Ridge's adherence to a largely unwavering formula for his short fiction. This involves highly specific London settings and interior spaces (typically offices, cafés, shops, boarding houses and maisonettes), the incorporation of fine-grained quotidian detail of the type that would best be recognised by a knowledgeable insider, the liberal use of idiomatic and apparently up-to-the-minute expressions, and a happy resolution usually involving moderate irony. By adopting this literary recipe, Pett Ridge ensured that his stories reflected at least some portion of the likely day-to-day existence and preoccupations of his readers. The infectious optimism and sense of fellowship with which this existence is reflected, underline his ambition to provide readers with a fresh and engaging literary window on their own lives. In this way, we can recognise that Pett Ridge's ubiquitous presence in the pages of Edwardian magazines, where his work often appeared alongside genre fiction or tales of aristocratic high life, was quietly political. But unlike the political sledgehammer often wielded by Wells in his fiction, Pett Ridge's politics are applied with a companionable touch. They take the form of a mild but persistent affirmation of the positive qualities of life – primarily the opportunity for happiness and contentment – that were characteristic features in his view of modern suburban existence.

Pett Ridge's stealthy politics of suburban affirmation are also widely evident in his longer Edwardian fiction. He published on average one novel per year in the Edwardian decade, and these works regularly demonstrate his particular interest in the life of 'ordinary' suburban women. The type of women in whom Pett Ridge specialised were, according to one contemporary reviewer, those who lacked a sensational 'past', being instead 'just the steady, every-day kind of persons who are to be found in large numbers in Kentish Town, Canning Town, and other populous London districts' (Anonymous 1907a: 849). His 1907 novel *Name of Garland* illustrates this type well, in its focus on Winnie Garland, a hard-working, shrewd and resourceful servant in a drapery emporium in Kentish Town, who has her promotion to the post of shop assistant prevented by her drunken father and step-siblings. This triggers a reversal of her social fortunes as she becomes a maid-of-all-work in a Camden Town lodging house. But the philosophical Winnie makes the best of this new situation, and ends the novel as a housekeeper who is happily embedded in the lives of a comfortably-off family in Hyde Park Gardens. *The Wickhamses* (1906) also focuses on a north London family, this time situated in Islington. The three motherless daughters of the Wickhams' printer patriarch 'push on' with their lives in ways which endorse the opportunity for class mobility in the new century; of the daughters, Mary marries well, Sarah becomes an illustrator and journalist, and Ruth becomes a teacher. *Sixty-Nine Birnam Road* (1908), meanwhile, investigates the life of an apparently mismatched couple: Ella, an intelligent and ambitious schoolteacher, is married to Fred, a hard-working but plodding railway clerk. In other hands (Gissing's for example), this story of suburban incompatibility would concentrate on the grimness of the entrapped couple's predicament, but Pett Ridge's divergent approach to this subject matter can be gauged from the following exchange, in which Ella outlines her aspirations for Fred:

> 'I want you to keep moving. I should like, Fred, to see you earning three hundred a year.'
> He drew in a breath between his teeth. 'That would take a bit of doing,' he said, thoughtfully. 'Men don't get along on the railway as they do in short stories.'
> 'Life is made up of short stories,' Ella insisted. (Ridge 1908: 60)

Neither Fred nor Ella is the recipient of the narrator's sympathetic patronage at the expense of the other. The faults of both parties are recognised as largely venial, and as such they simply 'mirror the life that we know', according to one contemporary review of the novel (Anonymous 1908d: 51). Faults such as Ella's misplaced social ambitions are, the narrative acknowledges, features that are all too common in modern suburban society, but they are equally issues which someone as intelligent and good-natured as Ella has the capacity to see through. This balancing out of the pressures of suburban living with its multiple pleasures is a mainstay of the novel, and Ella, who acts as the focalising character, is quick to defend suburbia when it comes under attack. When a snobbish acquaintance, for example, refers to '"the poor mistaken suburbs! the long straight roads with houses on either side all precisely alike. And the people in the houses, all of one pattern"' (Ridge 1908: 16), Ella is sparked into a passionate defence of this location:

> 'You're wrong,' she cried rapidly. 'You're altogether wrong. People take their souls and their own bodies and their lives with them, and whether they reside in Berkeley Square or at Forest Hill, they can be themselves, and they are not obliged to imitate their neighbours; they're not compelled to know them . . . ' She went on defiantly. 'There's as much intelligence in the suburbs as anywhere else in London; more. There's as much happiness in the suburbs as anywhere else in London; more. There's as much goodness and decency of behaviour in the suburbs as anywhere else in London; more.' (Ridge 1908: 16–17)

Ella's decision to 'stand up' for the suburbs (as another character interprets her words here) is endorsed throughout the novel, in spite of the fact that very little really happens at the level of plot (17). As one might expect of a novel which intends to hold up a mirror to suburban life, the major events that take place here comprise nothing more dramatic than Fred's promotion at work and the couple's seaside holiday.

The novel that perhaps best summarises Pett Ridge's approach to the female suburban character is *Nine to Six-Thirty* (1910), a work which foregrounds the contentious Edwardian issue of women's employment. As David Trotter has argued, the narrative of *Nine to Six-Thirty* offers an instructive contrast with Wells' *Ann Veronica*. In Pett Ridge's novel, the central character, Barbara Harrison, like Ann Veronica, embraces independent life in London as a way of breaking from her family home; Ann Veronica escapes from Morningside Park, a relatively affluent fictionalised South London suburb, while Barbara leaves the real-life London district of Stoke Newington. But whereas Ann Veronica longs to escape an intellectually stultifying location ('Ye gods! ... *What a place!*' (1909/2005: 7)), Barbara has no such aversions to Stoke Newington. Her reasons for leaving the suburbs are entirely grounded in the practical need to liberate herself from a family who effectively treat her as their slave. In escaping from this circumscribed existence, Barbara embraces the world of employment in ways that suggest the real opportunities it might offer for Edwardian women in her position. Whereas Wells sees female employment in *Ann Veronica* as just another form of servitude, Pett Ridge views it here as a potential agent of liberty. Barbara's own business career sees her join 'WARNETT's WORLD-WIDE WANDERINGS' travel agency in High Holborn as a letter-copying clerk, before progressing to become its manageress, and subsequently taking over the management of Mansford Bros, a colour printing business with offices in the same building. Pett Ridge is realistic about the perils of office work for women – Barbara is subjected to bullying and sexual harassment in equal measure – but she develops a real talent for business and becomes an adept 'player' in the commercial world. More than simply making a virtue out of necessity, as David Trotter shrewdly notes, Barbara's 'work experience shapes her identity' (1993/1998: 131). It does so to a point where Barbara's job takes the structural place that romantic love would occupy in a more conventional popular novel. While Wells cannot be accused of lazily reinstating this hackneyed reliance on the 'love' plot at the close of *Ann Veronica*, his recognition of the centrality of the sexual imperative in human interaction (focusing here on the need for human beings to reproduce the species), does dictate the novel's conclusion; its final page features a pregnant Ann Veronica, now married to Capes, willingly embracing domesticity at the expense of her independence. Barbara Harrison in *Nine to Six-Thirty*, by contrast, finds fulfilment in a business that seems to transcend the practical function it offers in providing her with a living: a clear illustration of this point comes when we are informed that Barbara 'fell in love . . . at first sight', with the 'fascinating . . . three-colour machines' in her office (Ridge 1910: 251). While marriage does await her at the novel's close (she, like Ann Veronica, having taken the lead in her choice of partner), this imminent union will not simply take the place of her business career. Indeed, Barbara defiantly states that, in spite of her impending marriage, she has also accepted a new business 'situation' which she thinks is 'likely to suit'. Her maid, Ellen, endorses Barbara's optimistic prospects, prophesying '"You'll soon be master, I lay a penny . . . Won't take you so very long before you get the reins in your own hands"' (343). Just as *Sixty-Nine Birnam Road* looked to 'stand up' for the suburbs, *Nine to Six-Thirty* defends the right of women, including married women, to make informed choices about employment.

Pett Ridge's defence of the life and work of suburban people was balanced out by other Edwardian writers of the period whose work, by contrast with his own, evoked a pessimistic vision of this section of society. Among those writers who followed Gissing in emphasising the dispiriting aspects of petit-bourgeois life, Edwin Pugh stands out as perhaps the most interesting. Pugh, in common with many of his literary peers, experienced a shabby genteel upbringing, followed by youthful white-collar employment, in his case as a clerk in a solicitor's office. His early success as a novelist with *A Street in Suburbia* (1895), published when he was just twenty-one, encouraged him to become a full-time writer, and by 1900 he was firmly established in this role. Like Pett Ridge's work, Pugh's early-Edwardian subject matter straddled slum and suburban life, but his 1908 novel *The Broken Honeymoon* is firmly located in the lower reaches of respectable society. Pugh's novel uses the techniques of literary naturalism, and as such, it offers an important contrast with Pett Ridge's work. While the central characters of Pett Ridge are rendered with considerable sympathy, Pugh's forensic literary lens, by contrast, emphasises the weakness and decay of his protagonists. In *The Broken Honeymoon*, a solicitors' clerk, Ferdinand Smallpiece (who provides the novel's first person narration), marries Rosetta Conover, his landlady's daughter. Pugh's approach to this subject matter is outlined in a contemporary review of the novel in the *Academy*, which cautioned that 'the reader in quest of amusement would do well to let this novel alone . . . Not one sordid or squalid detail is missing': the reviewer added, presumably with Pett Ridge's work in mind, that:

> Suburban life is stripped of that veil of illusion with which many modern romantic writers have sought to invest it and we see the thing as it is – or rather as it appears to Mr. Pugh – grim, loathsome, and repulsive. (Anonymous 1908a: 473)

The suburban life in question is focused on the Conover home, 'Rocklands', a 'jerry'-built house in Tufnell Park, which is dissected with awful precision in the novel's opening pages (Pugh 1908: 7). Rosetta's mother is a 'slatternly trollop' whose dress features 'a sodden lumpy tail [that] for ever dangled and flopped in her wake as she slommocked about' (1–2); the father is a 'feckless creature of a colourless type, hen-witted, dictatorial, peevish' (3); and of their twelve offspring, 'seven of them were luckily dead' (4). The squalor of their outwardly respectable semi-detached villa is described in detail with the shabbiness of rooms and furnishings maliciously exposed; a typical minute observation takes in a 'cracked art-pot' on a bamboo pedestal, from which 'dirty water' had dripped on to 'the carpet and lain there and soaked in, staining its chequered brown surface with a sprawling patch of bilious yellow' (12). Added to a depressing inventory of suburban degeneracy are more personal and indignant reflections on daily life as a lodger in this squalid Edwardian villa house:

> It is saddening to find that your razors have been used for some inscrutable purpose and rendered blunt, and then slyly restored to their case in a damp

condition; that your brushes are greasy and wet and your sponge sodden; that your tooth-brush tastes of brick dust and your shaving-soap has shrivelled into nothingness. (31)

The tone of Pugh's narrator echoes that of late-Victorian comic clerk characters, but his voice lacks either the knowing irony that characterises Jerome's *Three Men in a Boat* (1889), or the underlying foundations of contentment that underpin the diary entries of the Grossmiths' Mr Pooter. For Pugh's clerk, the keynote is one of a barely suppressed rage which singularly fails to leaven the grimness of boarding-house life. Any vestiges of comedy that appear in Pugh's novel are hard-won; the ghastly mysterious object that Smallpiece senses under his foot while walking in a dark passage in the house that 'felt like a small, hard, round pudding in a bag', offers the reader only the blackest of comic reflections (10). Pugh's facility (and evident first-hand knowledge) in offering such vivid impressions of clerkly life results in a text which provides few redeeming features of this existence. Even Smallpiece's genuine love for Rosetta is blighted by their sexual incompatibility, a misalliance evidently brought about by the cancerous atmosphere in which their courtship takes place. Although the couple's broken honeymoon is apparently repaired at the novel's close, this ending fails to convince in light of all that has gone before.

For Pugh, and for Pett Ridge, the opposing visions of lower-middle-class life were, to some extent, the product of their own innate temperaments; biographical accounts of Pett Ridge suggest that he was an individual of sunny disposition given to joke-telling, whereas Pugh's alcoholism and inability to make ends meet from his writing presumably fuelled the pessimistic streak in his work. Pugh's biography also suggests the perils of the literary profession for the new generation of writers at this time; Frank Swinnerton felt that Pugh 'had not quite the moral stamina to support' the demanding life of the professional novelist (Swinnerton 1937: 241). This judgement is corroborated by evidence of Pugh's repeated requests for financial assistance from the Royal Literary Fund, and his grim alcoholic demise. But Pett Ridge's successful career as a writer suggests that other members of Wells' generation 'from nowhere' were indeed still 'getting on' well into the twentieth century; Pett Ridge published on average one book per year until his death in 1930, invariably focusing attention on his characteristic suburban subject matter. Indeed, the inter-war period in which Pett Ridge died might be considered a golden age of suburban writing, with popular middlebrow authors such as Victor Canning, E. M. Delafield, Stella Gibbons, J. B. Priestley, R. C. Sherriff and Dorothy Whipple ensuring that the lives of their lower-middle-class and provincial characters increasingly occupied the mainstream of the era's literature, rather than its periphery.

The Edwardian Literary Industry

Bennett's and Wells' generation of writers from 'nowhere' were certainly 'getting on' around the turn of the twentieth century, and much the same can be said of other influential literary professionals who emerged at this time. These individuals, who had started off in the literary world without much in the way of position or influence, subsequently helped to establish the wider publishing networks within which Bennett's vision of a more representative literary field was constructed. They included critics, magazine editors, publishers, illustrators and literary agents. An exemplary sample of literary professionals who became established figures in the Edwardian era might include former bank clerk Dixon Scott, who became a distinguished critic on the *Manchester Guardian*; John Lane, who had worked as a railway clearing office clerk (like Pett Ridge), before founding the publishing house that bore his name; Wilfred Whitten, employed in his father's tea company before transforming the *Academy* into one of the most dynamic arts publications of its day, and subsequently setting up the popular one-penny literary paper *T.P.'s Weekly*; and James Brand Pinker, a former shipping clerk who became one of the most influential literary agents in the world. We can glimpse something of the workings of these literary networks in the review by Dixon Scott in the *Manchester Guardian* of Bennett's *The Card*. Dixon Scott, writing from the north-west of England, approached this novel from Bennett's own provincial perspective, rather than adopting a more detached metropolitan standpoint:

> To appreciate Mr. Bennett's art, a purely provincial product, to see all that it stands for and all that it is bringing us, you too must be provincial – seeing London, as a consequence, a third storey, not a basement and first cause. (Scott 1911: 7)

Bennett's Bursley, viewed from this revised perspective, becomes the centre of life, rather than its unfashionable periphery. Bennett recognised the importance of this shared common ground between writer and critic when noting in his journal that Dixon Scott's review was 'one of the best I ever had, and no effusiveness either' (Bennett 1932b: 4); Bennett had earlier lamented, on reading a lukewarm review of *Clayhanger* in the *Manchester Guardian*, 'now if they had given my book to Dixon Scott' (Bennett 1932a: 384).

The sense of a new fellowship between a generation of writers and literary professionals who had, to some extent, gatecrashed their way into the existing literary world, is especially evident in the relationship that James Brand Pinker built with the clients of his literary agency. Pinker's connections were developed at a time in which a new sense of professionalism was evident in the publishing industry. This professionalism had developed as a by-product of the increasing complexity of the literary marketplace around the turn of the twentieth century. With expanding opportunities in home and international markets, and rapid advances in printing technology, the old and characteristically amateur dealings between writer and publisher became rapidly anachronistic. In this modern publishing environment, there was a pressing need for individuals who would act as middlemen between interested parties in an increasingly complex literary field. The literary agents who took on this role were employed by authors to navigate the intricacy of the publishing trade on their behalf and, if successful, to maximise the profit that writers were able to gain from their work. An effective agent, typically acting for ten per cent of the writer's earnings, would build a partnership with clients whose success and productivity were inextricably linked to his own. For writers of Bennett's and Wells' class and generation, therefore, the symbiotic relationship between writer and agent often took on a significance which transcended that of a simple business partnership. Pinker's social and occupational background made him ideally suited to build the intimate connections with clients needed for an effective literary agent. While his origins remain somewhat indistinct, it seems probable that he was born into a London lower-middle-class family in 1863 (Gillies 2007: 88). Pinker certainly shared a commercial background with Bennett and Wells, having been employed as a clerk in the London docklands during the late 1880s. He then began his literary career as a journalist in Constantinople, before, following a financially advantageous marriage, returning to London to work as assistant editor on *Black and White*, an illustrated weekly paper founded in 1891. During this period and throughout the first half of the 1890s Pinker gained considerable expertise and understanding of the British publishing scene at a key phase in its development. The knowledge and connections gained here ensured that when Pinker decided to open up his literary agency in 1896, he was so confident of its success that he resigned from a well-paid and prestigious editorship on *Pearson's Magazine* to embark on this new venture.

When Pinker opened his agency, the major existing player in this field was A. P. Watt, who had established his firm in 1875. Instead of directly challenging Watt's share of the market, Pinker built his list from the fresh talent he had encountered during his magazine editorships. We can recognise the contrasting approaches of Watt and Pinker from the entries advertising their firms that appeared in *The Literary Year-Book* for 1901. Watt prefaced an impressive and extensive list of clients with the confident assertion, 'An idea of the field now covered by the operations of Messrs Watt & Son will be given by the following list of some of the clients of the firm' – this list included literary heavyweights such as Conan Doyle, Hardy and Kipling. Pinker's entry in *The Literary Year-Book* was, by comparison, markedly modest and low-key. Following a brief but pointed list of his practical credentials for the job, the entry continued:

> Mr. Pinker has always made a special point of helping young authors in the early stages of their career, when they need most the aid of an adviser with a thorough knowledge of the literary world and the publishing trade. (Morrah 1901: 119)

Pinker's pitch, while seemingly artless, was, in fact, carefully constructed to attract those would-be professional writers who were looking for help from a friendly and sympathetic literary insider. In this respect, Pinker's background as the editor of a reputable and large circulation weekly paper, and also a 'reader of manuscripts for a well-known publishing house', ensured that his credentials were doubly attractive to the novice author (118). As an established literary gatekeeper, Pinker might offer practical advice about placing magazine stories for the best price, while also assisting new writers in publishing their prized book-length work. Furthermore, potential clients who looked to authorship as a means of escape from commercial occupations would be understandably encouraged when they discovered that, as a former clerk himself, Pinker understood the particular needs and ambitions of this generation of suburbans and provincials. This sense of a common heritage of class and experience provided the glue that fixed in place many of the new publishing partnerships and allegiances that were developing across the industry in this period.

An early list of Pinker's clients underlines for us the importance of shared experience in forming these new cultural networks. Whereas Watt's clients at the turn of the century included the Prime Minister and the Poet Laureate, Pinker's list was dominated by new writers who had benefited from the recent expansion of print culture. These included former clerks such as Pett Ridge, Edwin Pugh and W. W. Jacobs, alongside many others who had begun in the 1890s to eke out their earnings from fiction with more regular work as magazine editors and journalists; among them were J. MacLaren Cobban, H. B. Marriott Watson,

L. Cope Cornford, A. J. Dawson, Ernest Rhys and Nora Vynne. One of Pinker's most notable early clients was Wells, whose age, class, education and employment background made him an excellent match with other writers on Pinker's list. Wells probably encountered Pinker for the first time when he published an early story entitled 'Through a Window' in *Black and White* in the summer of 1893 (see Wells 1895a). No correspondence seems to have survived from this stage of their relationship, but Pinker's editorial role on the magazine at this time suggests both Wells' early debt to him and, equally, Pinker's timely recognition of Wells' talent. The approach that Pinker made to Wells when inviting him to become his client in 1896 offers a further revealing example of the formation of cultural networks at this time. In this letter, Pinker cannily mentions his 'friend' Marriott Watson, who, he reminds Wells, has 'written to you of my enterprise, [and] thought you might place your affairs in my hands' (Mackenzie and Mackenzie 1973: 113). Pinker clearly knew that Marriott Watson was a trusted confederate of Wells, who (as literary editor of the *Pall Mall Gazette*) had been a great advocate for Wells' early work. Relations between Wells and Pinker broke down over time, but their connections were reasonably harmonious and mutually profitable for the first eight years or so of their dealings. It is clear from Wells' correspondence at this time that Pinker enabled him to maximise the profit received from his writing, while leaving him with the time and opportunity to produce this work. In a letter Wells wrote to Harry Quilter in December 1898, he shrewdly remarked: 'there are things called serial rights & America which he [Pinker] understands & I do not & for the English book rights he gets me about ten times what I used to get for myself' (Smith 1998: 335). Aside from Pinker's evident understanding of the complexities of the book trade, his services often went far beyond organising his clients' literary affairs. In December 1899, for example, Wells wrote to Elizabeth Healey that he had delegated many of the legal responsibilities associated with the building of his new house upon his literary agent: 'I have had days of incapable rage with these sinuous tricky creatures [solicitors] and at last I have cast these cares upon the good Pinker who does all my publisher hunting and my mind is comparatively at peace again' (Smith 1998: 347). Several of Pinker's Edwardian clients would come to rely on him for services that went well beyond the ability to maximise profits for written work; Wexler notes, for example, the remarkable extent of Conrad's dependence on Pinker (Wexler 1997: 41).

Bearing in mind Wells' confrontational temperament, perhaps the most surprising aspect of his relationship with Pinker was that it lasted as long as it did. It seems that it was only Wells' impatience at what he perceived to be Pinker's failure to market his work satisfactorily in America that brought about the eventual breakdown in their relationship. But a measure of Wells' earlier contentment with Pinker's services can be recognised in the fact that, a couple of years before ending his contract, Wells was prepared to recommended the agency's services to Bennett. Pinker, grateful to have another promising young talent on his books, wrote to Wells thanking him for 'sending Bennett along', adding the pregnant phrase, 'I think I can do something for him' (Harris 1960: 71). Over the following twenty years, until his death, in fact, Pinker proved the truth of his word, and the correspondence of over 2,600 letters is ample testimony to the remarkable and enduring success of this partnership (Hepburn 1966: 1). One might go as far as to say that this relationship between writer and agent became the most successful of its type in British publishing history. The fruitfulness of Bennett's relationship with Pinker tells us a considerable amount about the changing literary field in Edwardian Britain, and also hints at the experience of many other clerk-turned-writers on Pinker's books who benefited from his ability to navigate the increasing complexities of the publishing world. We might take the publication of *The Sinews of War*, the serial Bennett co-authored with Eden Phillpotts in 1906, as an example of the sorts of rewards now emerging for ambitious young writers with hard-bargaining agents. The seeds of the publication of the story date back to December 1905, when Bennett wrote to Pinker about a 60,000-word mystery story that Phillpotts had pitched to him as a potential collaborative project. In this letter Bennett claimed that 'the thing is to be rather exceptionally strong . . . He [Phillpotts] offers me halves and personally guarantees me a minimum of £450. He will draft the entire book, & I shall write it' (Hepburn 1966: 64). At the time Phillpotts was a more established literary figure than his proposed collaborator, and Bennett was flattered by this invitation; as Bennett went on in his letter to Pinker: '[Phillpotts] has always praised my work enthusiastically but this is the greatest compliment he has ever paid me' (64). Bennett clearly took on the lion's share of the writing for this serial, but even when taking this extra work into account, the project was still highly lucrative. In January 1906, Pinker sold the rights for a twenty-instalment serial for £450 to *T.P.'s Weekly*. In line with Bennett's request, the word count here was fixed at 80,000, and he managed to complete the writing between January and April of that year. Although, as Bennett wryly remarked to Pinker in a letter dated 6 March, Phillpotts' four days' work on the project would provide him [Phillpotts] overall with an whopping '£250 a day for his trouble', Bennett himself was in no mood to complain about being short-changed. Indeed, Bennett remarks, 'as the whole affair will take me just 2 months and four days, I shall be very well paid' (70). The serial rights were just the start of the bargaining for this work that Pinker was able to do. He also sold off the British book rights to T. Werner Laurie, and Phillpotts' own agent Curtis Brown sold the American rights to the firm of McClure, Phillips, ensuring that Bennett's total earnings for the story by the end of 1906 were £775 (72). The high prices achieved here were only available to established literary figures whose names were calculated to increase magazine circulation figures, yet it is also clear that multiple sales of single pieces of writing were an established feature of the publishing trade by the 1900s. Writers and agents such as Bennett and Pinker were thus able to double and even treble their profits from single pieces of writing.

It is difficult to gauge the level of influence that an individual agent might have on the nature of a writer's literary production, but the Bennett–Pinker correspondence does indicate the sorts of manipulation that might take place in this respect. Bennett, while very knowledgeable himself about the nature of the publishing market (and keenly aware of his remarkable ability to produce large quantities of saleable work at speed), clearly trusted Pinker's judgement in terms of what material to produce and when. An overview of their discussions during April 1904 regarding forthcoming publication schedules clearly illustrates this point. Pinker at this juncture wanted to limit the appearance of new Bennett texts, but Bennett himself disagreed: 'I am very strongly of opinion that it is a great mistake to pile up books in waiting for another book which is intended to make a boom . . . One cannot produce too much sound work' (Hepburn 1966: 48, 49). Although Bennett argued his position here very forcefully (even remarking in a letter written to Pinker three days after the one quoted above, that 'you don't yet realise what an engine for the production of fiction you have in me' (50)), he was also prepared to give way to his professional adviser: 'It is absurd to pay an expert for advice & then only to take the advice when it agrees with your own views. You will therefore have your way as regards the output for this year'. Bennett's apparently light-hearted postscript to this letter – 'The truth is you twist me round your little finger' – contains more than a grain of truth (50–1). We can trace throughout their correspondence Pinker's quiet manipulation of Bennett's literary output; in the process we witness Pinker *managing* his client's career, rather than simply selling off Bennett's work as it arrived at his office. Pinker's wish to limit the output of a productive client might appear perverse or even foolish, perhaps, in an agent who stood to gain a percentage fee on all of the books published by that client, but his strategy here takes account of the broader picture. He looked to maintain and build upon Bennett's existing status in a market that might be damaged by putting out too much material in a short period of time. Bennett's broader support for Pinker and his ilk remained solid throughout his lifetime, and as early as 1903, he promoted the concept of literary agency in his primer entitled *How to Become an Author*:

> The value of a good literary agent to a rising or risen author has been demonstrated beyond all argument. The question of the literary agent is no longer a 'vexed question'; it is settled ... The editor and publisher who 'cannot understand why authors should be so foolish as to pay 10 per cent. of their earnings to an agent,' are marked men in genuine literary circles. (Bennett 1903/n.d.: 195)

While the evolutionary changes in publishing that brought Pinker to the fore in this period were not universally celebrated (Wells remained highly sceptical about the value of agents, following his period as Pinker's client), Bennett's advocacy of literary agents was broadly accepted as an orthodoxy by his fellow Edwardian writers. For a rising author, the acquisition of a reputable agent, from this time onwards, seemed as necessary as the possession of a typewriter.

Wilfred Whitten's career as an Edwardian editor and critic provides further telling evidence of the rise to literary prominence at this time of 'outsiders'. Like others discussed in this chapter, Whitten established his literary credentials in the 1890s, and consolidated his position in this field at the start of the new century. Born in Newcastle in 1864, the son of a prosperous tea merchant, Whitten reluctantly joined his father's firm after completing his schooling. This reluctance on Whitten's part to inherit the role of respectable Victorian merchant stemmed from what he saw as the incompatibility of the business world with his passion for literature. As a bookish child who had spent much of his youth reading the works of Charles Lamb, William Hazlitt, James Boswell, Benjamin Disraeli and Thomas Carlyle, the life of a north-eastern tea merchant held only limited appeal. Whitten, therefore, took the opportunity, on the retirement of his father in 1886, to leave the family firm and move to London, where he felt better able to connect with the literary world. Like many other literary aspirants of his generation, Whitten was initially employed in white-collar work in the metropolis, but he was also able to develop his talents as a writer after his daytime office work. In Whitten's case, the initial rewards from nocturnal authorship were gained by writing 'turnovers' for the London newspapers such as the *Globe*: these were articles on seemingly ephemeral topics which necessitated page-turning (hence 'turnovers') and were a familiar feature in newspapers of the day. During the 1890s, further publishing opportunities emerged for Whitten and his peers as fresh publishing ventures appeared on a weekly basis; Whitten and Wells, for example, both contributed to the *New Budget*, an illustrated weekly founded in 1895 by *Punch* cartoonist Harry Furniss. But it was while working on the *Academy* that Whitten was able to develop the style of literary publication with which he would become popularly associated during the Edwardian period. The *Academy* was a well-established, respectable, but arguably rather dated periodical when it was taken over in 1896 by John Morgan Richards, a wealthy American drug promoter. The new editor installed by Richards, Charles Lewis Hind, was charged with redesigning the publication to appeal to the tastes of a new generation of readers. Hind's revamping of the *Academy* included the incorporation of literary prizes and competitions for its readers, lists of bestselling books, columns of literary gossip, portrait supplements and short, often pithy, anonymous reviews. The resulting publication became something of a landmark in broadening the appeal of the British literary magazines, and in doing so anticipated much of the direction of this market during the coming decade. Whitten's experience at the *Academy* gave him the confidence to establish a new literary paper, *T.P.'s Weekly*, in 1902. Here, as acting editor under the well-known journalist and politician T. P. O'Connor, Whitten designed a penny literary paper which would have a widespread popular appeal. The evident physical (and price) disparity between the three-penny *Academy* and the one-penny *T.P.'s Weekly* suggests the differing markets aimed at by these publications. Although the *Academy* had in many ways pioneered the popularisation of the literary paper, it still retained its focus on the sort of 'serious' culture that might well appear forbidding for a young Board School graduate. *T.P.'s Weekly*, by contrast, was calculated to address the putative concerns of its culturally unsophisticated readers by appearing more like a newspaper than a learned review. This impression is immediately conveyed by the modest quality of its newsprint paper, by its illustrated advertisements for tobacco, bleach and biscuits, and most evidently by its short and enticingly subtitled paragraphs; this lightened the appearance of the paper by breaking up longer blocks of text, and was clearly intended to replicate the format of a daily newspaper. In this way, the familiarity of the textual format of *T.P.'s Weekly* permitted a seamless shift for its readers from their reading of newspapers to Whitten's broadly accessible articles on serious writers such as Shakespeare, Milton, Byron and Browning.

In terms of the content of *T.P.'s Weekly* more generally, articles on higher literary culture tended to be included alongside a number of lighter and more topical items: the issue dated 1 July 1904, for example, includes travel tips for those holidaying in the Lake District; a literary notes and queries section; an article for the budding writer entitled 'Why Short Stories Are Rejected'; a number of brief and largely descriptive reviews of new works; an instalment of Conrad's *Nostromo* currently under serialisation; an article by Ernest Rhys on Swinburne's lyric poems; and a leading article signed 'John O'London' entitled 'Intellectual Honesty', which focused on the French critic and historian Hippolyte Taine. The Taine article is revealing in dealing with a literary figure, who, although probably unfamiliar to the core readership of *T.P's Weekly*, is discussed in a way calculated to make his work relevant and appealing to this cohort. The tone adopted in Whitten's introduction to this article perfectly captures his method of approach: 'It has just been my fortune to spend a whole day alone. Under such circumstances the book in one's hand, if it be a good one, seems perfectly alive and intimate, and is certain to give a lasting impression': the book in question was R. L. Devonshire's translation of Taine's *Life and Letters* (1902). Following this companionable opening, Whitten established Taine in early life as a 'young man of fine intellect and lofty aspirations'. For those of *T.P.'s* readers with literary ambitions, Taine is posited as an exemplary figure; the article endorses this inspirational theme with lengthy quotations from Taine's own work designed to demonstrate his 'exultant belief of the power of thought and investigation'. Finally, having established Taine's solid credentials for his autodidact readers, Whitten concludes: 'I am content to point out that for the man who desires an exemplar of the intellectual life, at once strenuous and honest, this book waits' (Whitten 1904: 17). The rhetorical flourish with which Whitten signed off here is characteristic of his work elsewhere during this period. While the breezy nature of the article's opening sentence baits the hook, the ensuing seriousness of purpose is calculated to inspire self-improvement and ambition. For those readers who were inspired by Whitten to take up further literary study, one shilling reprints of significant works of literature in series such as World's Classics (from 1901) and Everyman's Library (from 1906) ensured that those on a limited budget now had unprecedented access to books.

One recognises in much of Whitten's work on *T.P.'s Weekly* a strong sense of mission on behalf of his Board School graduate readers. He clearly believed, like Bennett and Wells, in the potential for literary culture to improve the lives of his readers. While it is impossible to gauge with any accuracy the scale of influence on readers of Whitten's work here (and from 1919 on *John O'London's Weekly*, the popular literary paper that bore his pseudonym), it seems reasonable to claim that he was among the foremost tastemakers of his era. For the majority of Whitten's core readers whose formal education had incorporated only a tantalising glimpse of literary study, the weekly textual lectures he provided offered a precious opportunity to broaden their existing cultural knowledge. Alongside other like-minded figures in the field of publishing, Whitten helped to facilitate the sort of literary revolution that Bennett and Wells had mapped out at the turn of the twentieth century. These networks of new literary professionals ensured that what had appeared in the 1890s to be a gold rush of opportunity for would-be writers, journalists, illustrators, publishers and agents was consolidated and secured in the ensuing epoch. The varied and successful careers of the figures examined in this chapter demonstrate that the apparent power shift in this field was far from a temporary realignment of a more permanent existing order. These individuals proved, as the twentieth century developed beyond its Edwardian beginnings, that aspirants from 'nowhere' were not merely 'getting on', they were in fact taking control.

Chapter Three

Children's Department: Edwardian Children's Literature

By any standards, the Edwardian decade was a remarkably fertile one for the publication of children's literature which was to have an enduring appeal. Although any notion of an established canon of British children's literature is necessarily subjective, the following would have a strong claim on any such grouping: Beatrix Potter's *The Tale of Peter Rabbit* (1902), and her subsequent series of illustrated animal tales; E. Nesbit's family and fantasy stories including *The Wouldbegoods* (1901), *Five Children and It* (1902), *The Phoenix and the Carpet* (1904), and *The Railway Children* (1906); Kipling's *Kim* (1901), *Just So Stories* (1902), *Puck of Pook's Hill* (1906) and its sequel *Rewards and Fairies* (1910); J. M. Barrie's Peter Pan, who appeared in various textual incarnations, beginning with *The Little White Bird* in 1902; Hilaire Belloc's satirical verse collected in *Cautionary Tales for Children* (1907); Frances Hodgson Burnett's *A Little Princess* (1905) and *The Secret Garden*, which first appeared in serialisation in 1910; Kenneth Grahame's *The Wind in the Willows* (1908), which (alongside Hodgson Burnett's works) quickly established itself as a standard text for children; John Buchan's updating of the imperial romance, *Prester John* (1910); and finally, two bestselling works of non-fiction, H. E. Marshall's popular history of England *Our Island Story* (1905), and Robert Baden-Powell's Scout movement manifesto, *Scouting for Boys* (1908). These writers and texts appeared at a time when many of the giants of Victorian children's literature had recently died, leaving the field open for new and distinctive work; notably G. A. Henty (died 1902), arguably the most popular boys' author of his era; Kate Greenaway (1901), an enormously influential illustrator of books for younger children; and George MacDonald (1905), a pioneering writer of Victorian fantasy literature. As well as benefiting from this departure of the old guard, Edwardian writers also had at their disposal a new range of technical and stylistic innovations, upon which they could draw to inflect the look and often the feel of their work. The emergence of the three-colour reproduction process, for example, allowed the publication at affordable prices of large numbers of richly illustrated books. Alongside new printing techniques, designers were also developing fresh and inventive formats for books intended to appeal to children of all ages; innovation in this area included Dean's Rag Books, a series of cloth-printed nursery texts, which proved popular with infant consumers from their debut in 1903.

Because children's literature in the Edwardian period was such a vibrant field in terms of its contents and design, this chapter will necessarily take a selective approach to the topic. By focusing on the work of three children's authors of the period – Beatrix Potter, E. Nesbit and P. G. Wodehouse – the chapter investigates in detail the key developments with which these writers were particularly associated. In the first section, for example, an analysis of Beatrix Potter's animal tales illustrates the ways in which new production techniques comprehensively transformed the appearance of children's books at this time. This section then moves beyond Potter to examine the often-spectacular effects of these new reproduction processes that illustrators such as Arthur Rackham and Edmund Dulac were able to achieve in what has become known as a 'Golden Age' of children's illustrated books and magazines. The following section investigates the fiction of E. Nesbit, looking at the ways in which she modernised several forms of writing – in particular the fantastical tale and the family story – that had long proved popular with child readers. Nesbit revolutionised the familiar narratives associated with these forms by populating them with the sorts of modern urban children, narrators and settings with which her twentieth-century readership might identify. In the chapter's final section, one of the most enduring genres of children's literature, the school story, is discussed through the work of P. G. Wodehouse. His later success as Britain's pre-eminent comic novelist in the twentieth-century has largely obscured Wodehouse's contribution to Edwardian children's literature, but he, like Nesbit, was an important moderniser in this field. Alongside Angela Brazil, whose popular girls' school stories helped to define the modern schoolgirl in literature, Wodehouse established the grounds for school fiction in the ensuing decades.

Before concentrating on the work of these writers and themes, it is first important to outline some of the wider trends that made Edwardian children's literature so distinctive. Among these was a readiness by writers and publishers to incorporate the technological wonders of the age in books designed for children of all ages; it is clear from the titles alone of Florence K. Upton's popular Golliwogg books, that even the youngest of readers were able to witness the latest marvels in transport:

The Golliwogg's 'Auto-Go-Cart' (1901) was followed in 1902 by *The Golliwogg's Air-Ship*. For older children, books that might be collected as part of a series offered windows into modern applications for the latest technology. Notable among these are Archibald Williams' series of popular science texts: *The Romance of Modern Invention* (1902) was followed by 'Romances' of *Modern Engineering* (1904), *Modern Locomotion* (1904), *Modern Exploration* (1905), *Modern Mechanism* (1906) and *Modern Mining* (1907). Alongside these scientific non-fiction texts were numerous works of fiction designed to appeal to boys with an interest in cutting-edge technology. Most popular among these were several written by George Herbert Ely and Charles James L'Estrange, both editors at Oxford University Press, who published their work under the collective pseudonym 'Herbert Strang': the *Bookman* declared in August 1906 that Herbert Strang was 'rapidly attaining to the position so long held by Mr. Henty' as the most popular writer of books for boys (Anonymous 1906a: 160). As the following titles suggest, Herbert Strang often blended exciting overseas adventures with up-to-the-minute modes of transport: *King of the Air; or, to Morocco on an Airship* (1907), *Swift and Sure: The Story of a Hydroplane* (1909), *Round the World in Seven Days* (1910), and *The Cruise of the Gyro-Car* (1910).

The popularity of Edwardian children's books that focused on technological modernity were balanced out in this period by a growing demand for books focused on the natural world; this trend, as the final chapter of this book will suggest, was marked by work centred on the English countryside and its flora and fauna. Typical among these were three volumes of Arthur Ransome's *Nature Books for Children* (1906), published long before his popular *Swallows and Amazons* (1930–47) series of novels. Many of the books which belonged to this new generation of nature-writing incorporated the latest printing technology, which permitted, among other things, detailed photographic images to be published alongside corresponding text; representative examples of this format of book production are volumes by Rev. C. A. Johns and others entitled *I Go A-Walking Through the Lanes and Meadows* (1905), and *I Go A-Walking Through the Woods and O'er the Moor* (1907). In addition to the era's new wave of richly illustrated nature books, the emergence of the Boy Scouts (and other youth groups focused on outdoor activities) created a ready market for literature able to explicate field craft. Apart from Baden-Powell's Scout books, and the movement's official magazine, *The Scout* (which appeared weekly from April 1908), E. Thompson Seton's Woodcraft Indian books and nature novels were equally influential in encouraging children to venture out of doors. The new wave of interest in nature at this time also accounts for the popularity of a number of texts focused on the lives of animals: these included several by Seton himself, including the North American-set *Monarch, the Big Bear of Tallac* (1904), and *The Biography of a Silver-Fox* (1909); Jack London's perennial favourites, *The Call of the Wild* (1903) and *White Fang* (1906), both of which feature the lives of dogs in the Yukon; and the South African-set hunting-dog tale, *Jock of the Bushveld* (1907) by J. Percy Fitzpatrick. The popularity of this genre of writing is indicated in a contemporary review of *Jock of the Bushveld* which claimed that 'Nature books have been somewhat overdone of late, for now every animal tells its biography in print' (Anonymous 1907c: iv). The extraordinary popularity of fairy books in the Edwardian decade also has clear links to the decade's renewed interest in nature and the natural world. In the 1908 Christmas season alone, a wide range of fairy books appeared with titles such as *The Fairies' Fountain and Other Stories, Legends from Fairyland, Fairy Tales from South Africa, The Russian Fairy Book, The Welsh Fairy Book*, and *Fairies – of Sorts*. This boom in Edwardian fairy literature was, to a considerable extent, inspired by Andrew Lang, whose 'Coloured' Fairy books led the market in fairy literature from their inception with *The Blue Fairy Book* in 1889. Lang provided his young readers during the decade with a well-stocked palette of colours (comprising *Grey* (1900), *Violet* (1901), *Crimson* (1903), *Brown* (1904), *Orange* (1906), *Olive* (1907), and *Lilac* (1910)), thus ensuring that fairy literature remained much in much vogue throughout the Edwardian period.

A further area of children's literature that deserves special mention are those texts originally appearing in North America which enjoyed extraordinary popularity among British children. Aside from Jack London's animal tales, probably the most enduring of these, in terms of lasting popularity, were L. Frank Baum's series of *Oz* books, beginning with *The Wonderful Wizard of Oz* (1900). Two other North American books which made a great impact on British readers at this time were Kate Douglas Wiggin's *Rebecca of Sunnybrook Farm* (1903), and L. M. Montgomery's Canadian-set *Anne of Green Gables* (1908), and its sequel *Anne of Avonlea* (1909). The popularity of these novels for girls suggests the wider demand at this time for writing designed to appeal to young female readers. This profitable market was capitalised upon by many Britain-based writers, including Mrs George de Horne Vaizey, whose spirited heroine Pixie O'Shaughnessy first appeared in the *Girl's Own Paper* in 1900; Angela Brazil, whose numerous school stories featuring hockey-playing girls began with *The Fortunes of Philippa* in 1906; and the highly prolific L. T. Meade and E. Everett-Green, both of whom specialised in fiction for a variety of girl readers. Many of these writers benefited from a healthy demand for children's literature by the Edwardian magazine market. As was the case with the ex-drapers and former clerks discussed in the previous chapter, new writers hoping to specialise in children's literature would often begin their professional careers by submitting material to established publications such as *The Boy's Own Paper* and *The Girl's Own Paper* (begun respectively in 1879 and 1880, but still selling well in the new century). But budding writers might also offer their work to a number of fresh Edwardian periodical publications, such as *The Captain* (from 1899), and *C. B. Fry's Magazine* (from 1904). Of more lasting significance, perhaps, in terms of the history of children's periodical literature, was the appearance of the *Gem* in 1907 and its sister paper the *Magnet* in 1908. These cheap weeklies (the *Magnet* was initially priced at one halfpenny and the *Gem* at one penny) were largely written by Charles Hamilton (under various pen names including Martin Clifford and Frank Richards). The *Magnet* introduced the popular schoolboy character Billy Bunter, who appeared in weekly instalments in the paper until 1940. George Orwell's 1940 essay, 'Boys' Weeklies', addressed the important political ramifications of these seemingly ephemeral publications, assuming that their deeply conservative ideology worked to manipulate the minds of succeeding generations of lower-middle-class and working-class children (Orwell 1976). While much of the literature produced for children in the first decade of the twentieth century must, like the *Gem* and the *Magnet*, have initially appeared transient, this chapter attempts to understand why it, in fact, so often outlasted its historical moment.

Beatrix Potter's Animal Tales

It is perhaps in the look and feel of books published after 1900 that the shift from Victorian to Edwardian is most readily apprehended. As an article in the *Edinburgh Review* in 1908 stated:

> Some future historian of our art and literature, reviewing these early years of the twentieth century, will rejoice in at least one portent salient enough to give character to the period. The development of mechanical colour-printing has justified already the utmost predictions of those who, a few years ago, foretold its coming greatness. The process has only come into general use for book-illustrating during the last six or eight years; yet it has been estimated that anything between five hundred and a thousand books adorned by its means with coloured sketches are now being issued annually by the London publishing firms. (Anonymous 1908e: 209)

This abrupt transformation in the appearance of the era's books is particularly evident in literature designed for very young children. While the Victorian nursery book was typified by the coloured wood engravings by illustrators such as Kate Greenaway, Walter Crane and Randolph Caldecott, books for pre-school children in the first decade of the twentieth century were able to incorporate new technical innovations in the colour reproduction of their illustrations. Beatrix Potter proved to be a revolutionary figure in this field, both as an individual determined to bring these new printing techniques to her work, but also in the way she managed to balance the visual dimension of her books with the accompanying text. It was in this skilful marriage of distinctive pictures and deceptively acute prose that Potter was able to secure the remarkable popularity of *The Tale of Peter Rabbit* (1902) and the series of animal books that it spawned. To fully understand the reasons why *The Tale of Peter Rabbit* (*Peter Rabbit*) so quickly established itself as a standard work of children's literature, it is first necessary to outline the contexts in which it emerged.

When publishing *Peter Rabbit*, Potter insisted on the use of a then relatively new and largely untried form of colour reproduction in commercial book publication: the three-colour process. This process is outlined by Harry G. Aldis as follows:

> Three blocks, representing the primary colours, are employed. The negatives for these are taken through filters of coloured glass or glass cells containing coloured liquid, in addition to the ruled screen. Each of these light filters allows only certain colours to pass through to the negative and stops the passage of all others. The colours of the original are thus automatically dissected and grouped in three categories representing approximately the yellows, the reds and the blues, each of which is contained on a separate negative . . . The various colours and tints of the resultant pictures are formed by the combination of these three colours printed over each other and varying in proportion according to the density of the printing surface of the respective blocks. (Winckler 1980: 125)

Until Potter's book exploited the possibilities of this new process, woodblock engraving was the standard technique used in the reproduction of coloured illustrations in children's books; this involved the printing of individual colours in succeeding layers from an engraved wooden block. The work of the foremost late-Victorian children's book illustrators suggests the distinctive appearance of images produced using this method. While the effects produced here might be highly successful when handled by a skilled printer, there was a degree of inflexibility with this technique which severely limited its application. Wood-block engravings could not provide delicate tints and colour shades, and individual colours printed from the block tended to be locked within the lines of their designated frame. These limitations in reproduction were clearly problematic for illustrators who wished to work with art materials which relied upon a more subtle approach to tone and form. For Potter, an artist whose preferred medium was watercolour, the advantages of incorporating the new photographic techniques of colour printing were readily apparent. While putting together what would become the first (privately printed) edition of *Peter Rabbit* in 1901, Potter commissioned Carl Hentschel's London firm to produce a colour frontispiece for the book using the new three-colour process. The resulting illustration, depicting Peter Rabbit in bed with his mother ministering camomile tea, offers an immediate contrast with the other illustrations that were appearing in children's books at this date. Whereas these illustrations are typically marked by the stiffness with which they convey character and background, Potter's three-colour frontispiece allowed her work to appear soft and fluid in the way that it meets the eye. This is apparent in the manner, for example, in which the variegated watercolour textures of Mrs Rabbit's brown fur and powder-blue dress are captured by the photographic process. The overall effect produced is one of warmth and reassurance, qualities also emphasised by the glossy clay-surfaced paper required by the three-colour reproduction process. The contrast between Potter's book illustrations and those of her contemporaries, far from being the sort of fine-grained subtleties only apprehended by trained eyes, were immediately apparent to even the youngest of her readers.

Potter's utilisation of this cutting-edge technology for her 'little books', as she described them, offers an indication of both her aesthetic sense and also of her business acumen. In terms of aesthetics, it is easy to understand why she spent so much time (and expense) in working on the printed design of her books. But we also need to recognise the increasingly competitive nature of the children's book market at the start of the new century. Apart from Grant Richards' 'Dumpy Books' which were published from 1897, several other publishers had, by the first years of the decade, launched their own series of small format books for young children: these included J. M. Dent's 'The Bairn Books' (from 1901), Swan Sonnenschein's 'The Oogley Oo Books' (from 1902), Hodder & Stoughton's 'The Little Ones' Library' (from 1902), Nister's 'The Rosebud Series' (from 1902), and Raphael Tuck's 'Children's Gem Library' (from 1902). Before this field became so crowded, Potter had almost certainly been influenced in her decisions regarding the design of *Peter Rabbit* by Helen Bannerman's *The Story of Little Black Sambo*, which had first appeared in Grant Richards' 'Dumpy Books' series in 1899. The small size of Bannerman's book, which was ideal for a child's hand, and its remarkable commercial success, alerted Potter to the potential for her own little book, which had begun life as part of an illustrated letter she had written to the son of a former governess. The publishing firm Frederick Warne recognised the potential of Potter's book to appeal to a young audience but also shared her feeling (in light of the publishing climate for small nursery books outlined above) about the paramount importance of the book's design. Warne therefore supported Potter's decision to have all of the *Peter Rabbit* plates reproduced by the three-colour process, even though this would prove initially costly. The decision to take this gamble on the future success of the book was, however, the right one for publisher and author: the first edition of 8,000 books sold out in advance of its publication, and by the end of 1902 alone there were 28,000 copies in print (Lear 2008: 152).

The remarkable and enduring success of *Peter Rabbit*, and the later 'little books' which she wrote and illustrated, was not predicated entirely upon their visual impact. Their up-to-date appearance clearly caught the eye of readers around the time of their initial publication, but as the *Edinburgh Review* critic cited above argued, the three-colour process quickly became a commonplace in Edwardian book production. The more lasting prominence of Potter's books was instead founded on the unusual harmony she achieved between image and text. To gain a better sense of Potter's achievement here, it is worth briefly examining Bannerman's *The Story of Little Black Sambo* alongside *Peter Rabbit*. In Bannerman's book, the text evidently plays a subordinate role to the pictures, with the words effectively captioning the illustrations:

> And Little Black Sambo went on, and by and by he met another Tiger, and it said to him, 'Little Black Sambo, I'm going to eat you up!' And Little Black Sambo said, 'Oh! Please Mr. Tiger, don't eat me up, and I'll give you my beautiful little Blue Trousers.' So the Tiger said, 'Very well, I won't eat you this time, but you must give me your beautiful little Blue Trousers.' So the Tiger got poor Little Black Sambo's beautiful little Blue Trousers, and went away saying, 'Now I'm the grandest Tiger in the Jungle'. (Bannerman 1899: 20–2)

The simplistic nature of the text, while well judged for a novice reader, is not essential to a child's understanding of a story that is already clearly conveyed by Bannerman's naïve but memorable wood-engraved illustrations. Indeed, a young reader might choose to ignore Bannerman's text with no real impairment to their understanding of the tale. While the general thrust of the *Peter Rabbit* narrative might also be conveyed by the illustrations alone – rabbit enters garden in defiance of mother, is chased by gardener, and eventually returns home with the loss of his jacket – the words play an integral part in creating a balanced and harmonious relationship between all elements of the book.

The specific nature of this relationship is evident in the opening of the narrative. On the left-hand page is an apparently commonplace nature study, in watercolour browns and greens, of an adult rabbit with four young rabbits who are playing among the roots of a large tree. On the right-hand text page, there is the following text:

> Once upon a time there
> were four little Rabbits,
> and their names were –
> > Flopsy,
> > Mopsy,
> > Cotton-tail,
> > and Peter.
> They lived with their Mother
> in a sand-bank, underneath the
> root of a very big fir-tree. (Potter 1902: 9)

While the text layout offers a pattern on the page designed to intrigue novice readers (in a manner reminiscent of Lewis Carroll's 'A Mouse's Tale', in *Alice's Adventures in Wonderland* (1865)), it is the narrator's tone that makes the more lasting impression; Barbara Wall's description of this narrative tone as both 'detached' but also 'reassuring' seems accurately to identify the quality of voice achieved by Potter's narrators throughout her series of 'little books' (1991: 162). The blend of a traditional fairy tale-like opening with the conversational formulation 'and their names were –' suggests a narrator who is at once obeying storytelling convention, but is also prepared to deviate from archaic forms into more modern and potentially surprising pathways. The list of rabbit names immediately confirms this conjunction of the familiar with the fresh; the cute and conventional bunny names (apparently conjured up by an uninspired and possibly reluctant narrator) are spiked by the addition of the final name 'Peter'. This name, incongruous in context, draws the reader's eye back to the facing picture to identify 'Peter' among his fellows, but this rather stock image of rabbits in woodland appears at odds with the potential anthropomorphisation hinted at by this name. Potter instead exploits the potential of the page turn, leading the reader forward into the following page's illustration to satisfy the curiosity piqued by the opening sentence. In this next image, the rebellious Peter is implicitly identified in the foreground of the picture, separated from his siblings and their kindly mother. The space occupied by the page turn also allows Potter to transport the reader from the natural world into an evidently unnatural environment in which rabbits adopt human language, dress, and – to some extent – social characteristics, but still retain key elements of their animal qualities, in particular their subordinate relationship to human beings.

The hybrid human-animal qualities of the creatures depicted in this image are further developed on the accompanying page of text:

> 'Now, my dears,' said old
> Mrs. Rabbit one morn-
> ing, 'you may go into the fields
> or down the lane, but don't go
> into Mr. McGregor's garden:
> your Father had an accident
> there; he was put in a pie by
> Mrs. McGregor.' (Potter 1902: 10)

Apart from generating the tension upon which the book's narrative will turn, this passage also appears to set up the book as a moral fable. Yet it is already evident that the predictable narrative of transgression and then punishment will not follow the established formal conventions. Rather, the deviation of the tale's narrative from that of its more traditional predecessors is inscribed in the apparently macabre conjunction of the words 'accident' and 'pie'. This comically elliptical rendering of Mr Rabbit's fate forcefully underscores the penalties for disobeying Mrs Rabbit's injunction (thus anticipating Peter's moral transgression), while simultaneously undercutting and subverting the seriousness of this moral message. Potter in this passage pays her young reader the compliment of recognising that they are able to understand the disjunction between the surface meaning of Mrs Rabbit's words and the reality to which they allude. Thereafter, Potter invites her readers to interrogate a further gap between the text and the action that seems to be taking place in the accompanying picture. Readers are asked to apply their interpretive faculties on several levels, and in the process they engage in a distinctly active reading experience. The grim space between 'accident' and 'pie' on the second text page serves to launch this dynamic engagement from the outset. Without having to employ cumbersome stage directions, Potter suggests to the child reader that what appears on the surface of things (in terms of words and images) is only the starting point for a truly imaginative engagement with the text.

Potter invites child readers to invest *Peter Rabbit* with their own imaginative responses to what they encounter, yet she skilfully manipulates and directs the ways in which these readings might take place. This sort of directed creative reading is managed via a number of strategies designed to control the pacing of the text; as Margaret Mackey argues, 'the story is shaped around the bursts of text and the delays' (Mackey

1998: 11). We can recognise this manipulation of the reader taking place, for example, in the pages that take us from Peter's initial trespass into the garden until his first encounter with Mr McGregor. The opening of this sequence of image and text conveys (in a single sentence strung over two text pages) Peter's progress as he grazes in a leisurely fashion through the garden's lettuces, French beans and radishes, and then searches for parsley to counteract the effects of his overindulgence. The three lines of text on each of these pages are placed at the centre, thus offering large white text-less spaces, which complement the relative tranquillity of the scene depicted. This calm is immediately disturbed by the image on the following page, which depicts Peter dwarfed by Mr McGregor; the reader, having witnessed the first nine images of the book at rabbit level, now encounters Peter overshadowed by the human-sized Mr McGregor (Potter 1902: 24). A chase narrative then ensues with passages in which Peter breathlessly evades the clutches of Mr McGregor, interspersed with quiet but fraught scenes in which Peter falls into exhausted despair. The ebb and flow of the chase, which realistically evokes the combat between predator and prey, allows Potter to incorporate considerable suspense, tension and reflection into her short narrative. These central passages in the book conclude with Peter's escape from the garden and his subsequent return to the safety of his domestic space. In this ending, the lyrical pace of the tale's opening passages is book-ended, and the conclusion of the moral message is, apparently, delivered. The conditional clause is necessary here, because, although the morality of the book's conclusion is at once simple and easy to interpret (Peter, the disobedient rabbit, lies ill in bed while his more dutiful siblings enjoy their welcome supper of milk and the blackberries), neither the narrator's words nor the accompanying pictures confirm that this meting out of punishment and reward is in any way preordained. The penultimate text page in fact thwarts our anticipation of a neatly conventional 'conduct book' resolution for *Peter Rabbit*:

> I am sorry to say that Peter
> was not very well during the
> evening.
> His mother put him to bed,
> and made some camomile tea;
> and she gave a dose of it to
> Peter!
> 'One table-spoonful to be
> taken at bed-time.' (56)

Here instead of a genuine and recognisable punishment that might underline the penalty for illicit behaviour, the narrator informs us with characteristic understatement that Peter was dosed up only with benign herbal tea. The final lines of this page, in referring to medicine rather than punishment, seem self-consciously to reflect upon Potter's sub-version of the traditional morality tale narrative. As Alison Lurie has argued, 'consciously or not, children know that the author's sympathy and interest are with Peter ... and not ... with obedient, dull little Flopsy, Mopsy, and Cottontail' (1991: 114).

While *Peter Rabbit* is clearly not a radical text in the sense that it sets out directly to provoke a child's disobedience of parental authority (Humphrey Carpenter is quite wrong to identify Potter's work as 'pretty close to a series of immoral tales' (Avery and Briggs 1989: 279)), it is a text which, at the very least, draws attention to the social construction of behavioural rules. In this way, Potter was attempting to liberate her young Edwardian readers from obedient books which called for obedi-ent reading. Her imaginative blending of text and fresh images invites an equally imaginative response from very young readers, who, in the early years of the century, were unlikely to have seen any other books quite like this. Indeed, in its combination of effects, Potter's *Peter Rabbit* has a realistic claim to be the first work to take infant readers seriously as consumers of print culture: Graham Greene went as far as to call Peter Rabbit one of the 'great characters of fiction' (Greene 1970: 176). The immediate popularity of *Peter Rabbit* signalled a ready market for Potter's work, and she published a further fifteen 'little books' with Warne between 1903 and 1910. Although these books remained basi-cally uniform in their production design, their subject matter drew upon a range of literary genres: apart from what might be considered the *Peter Rabbit* sequels (*The Tale of Benjamin Bunny* (1904) and *The Tale of the Flopsy Bunnies* (1909)), these also included the historical fable (*The Tailor of Gloucester* (1903)), the moral fable (*The Tale of Squirrel Nutkin* (1903)), farce comedy (*The Tale of Two Bad Mice* (1904)), the comedy of manners (*The Tale of the Pie and the Patty-Pan* (1905)), tragicomedy (*The Tale of Jemima Puddle-Duck* (1908)), and the sensa-tion novel in miniature (*The Tale of Samuel Whiskers or, The Roly-Poly Pudding* (1908)).

While the novelty of the appearance of Potter's books diminished over the course of the decade, other books for children emerged which further exploited the opportunities for book illustration using innovative colour reproduction techniques. In particular, a number of gift books, lavishly illustrated by artists such as Arthur Rackham and Edmund Dulac, offered a new and distinctive lease of life for classic children's texts: Rackham's Edwardian output included edi-tions of Washington Irving's *Rip Van Winkle* (1905), Barrie's *Peter*

Pan in Kensington Gardens (1906), Carroll's *Alice's Adventures in Wonderland* (1907), *Fairy Tales of the Brothers Grimm* (1909), and Jonathan Swift's *Gulliver's Travels* (1909); Dulac's work in the same period included illustrated editions of *Stories from the Arabian Nights* (1907), and *The Sleeping Beauty and Other Fairy Tales from the Old French* (1910). Rackham, who, as a former insurance clerk, shared a background with many of the writers discussed in the previous chapter, had studied art at evening classes before embarking on his career as a professional illustrator; also in common with those aforementioned ex-clerks and ex-drapers, Rackham took advantage of the burgeoning periodical market by working for titles such as the *Pall Mall Budget* and the *Westminster Budget*. Before his *Rip Van Winkle* edition appeared, he was largely known as a black-and-white artist, but the unique quality of the colour work in this book immediately established his reputation on another footing. The fifty-one colour plates in *Rip Van Winkle*, with their fine line drawing underpinned by a muted palette of watercolour browns, reds and yellows, instigated a signature artistic style which would remain uniformly recognisable over Rackham's long career; his final volume, a posthumously published edition of Grahame's *The Wind in the Willows*, appeared in the United States in 1940. Dulac's work in book illustration, like Rackham's, was highly distinctive, with its rich selection of watercolours selected to complement his typically romantic and often exotic subject matter. Rackham and Dulac's gift books took their place alongside other volumes for children in the Christmas book market, but they were also highly prized by adult collectors, and the high cover price of these works (in Rackham's case, typically forty-two shillings for a deluxe edition, and fifteen shillings for a trade edition) clearly limited their circulation. The *Times Literary Supplement*'s review of *Peter Pan in Kensington Gardens* confirmed that books of this type were 'addressed to the drawing-room rather than to the nursery'. With a clear note of regret, this reviewer argued that:

> it could only be put into little hands under careful supervision, and even then we rather tremble for the fate of its luxurious pages, its tissue fly-leaves, and fluttering prints each half-mounted on a sheet of brown paper in approved collector-fashion. It will remain, we may be pretty sure, 'downstairs'. (Anonymous 1906b: 418)

London art exhibitions typically accompanied the launch of these gift books, and artwork from the featured edition could be bought by wealthy collectors, thus reinforcing the sense of the connoisseur environment surrounding these artist's books. Although Edwardian children were unlikely to get their hands on these highly prized and costly volumes, they would, in time at least, be able to access cheaper editions; Rackham's *Alice's Adventures in Wonderland*, for example, was available in a more modestly priced six-shilling edition in 1907.

It is important to keep in view the wider publishing contexts in which Potter's miniaturist work, and Rackham and Dulac's more epically proportioned artwork, first appeared. Between these polar extremes of the children's publishing market were a growing number of books featuring three-colour process illustrations which were, as the *Bookman* in October 1904 noted, creating 'a revolution in the appearance of gift and prize books for the young . . . [and] thus considerably enhanced their attractiveness by the brightness of the illustration' (Anonymous 1904c: 6). While a number of commentators failed to share this celebratory perspective (the *Edinburgh Review* critic cited at the start of this section decried 'the cheap-popularity and vulgar effrontery' of modern colour-printing (Anonymous 1908e: 229)), the voices of these naysayers had little impact on a publishing culture which increasingly recognised that readers expected three-colour illustrations for particular types of books; by the middle of the decade, a children's book which lacked, at the very least, a three-colour frontispiece, appeared distinctly outmoded. These considerations ensured that by the end of the Edwardian decade, the revolution that Potter had quietly instigated in 1901 had profoundly and permanently changed the look and feel of books designed for child readers.

E. Nesbit's Suburban Modernity

Whether or not E. Nesbit is, as Julia Briggs has claimed, 'the first modern writer for children', she undoubtedly brought something immensely fresh and appealing to this field in the first decade of the twentieth century (Briggs 1987: xi). Like Potter, Nesbit was much influenced by a number of writers for children who had gone before her – in Nesbit's case, these included Lewis Carroll, Juliana Horatia Ewing, Kenneth Grahame and Rudyard Kipling – but she was never content merely to replicate their work. As Julia Briggs argues, Nesbit's references to earlier works are not merely 'glancing allusions'; they offer instead 'an extended examination of a particular literary model that [often] includes elements of parodic reply' (402). In this fashion, Nesbit uses the writing of her predecessors as an inspiration to produce distinctive work that epitomises what we might now consider Edwardian modernity. This quality can be apprehended in a number of different ways in Nesbit's work: in, for example, the characteristic voices of her narrators; the self-conscious reflections in her texts about the process of storytelling; and in the employment of the sorts of ordinary protagonists and unglamorous geographical locations (implicitly counterpointing the more conventionally 'literary' characters and settings used by many of her models) with which her readers would readily identify. As this section will argue, Nesbit created from her borrowings a series of unique and memorable texts, which, in their turn, would go on to influence future generations of children's writers: C. S. Lewis's Narnia Chronicles, for example, were indebted to Nesbit's work, as, more recently, were J. K. Rowling's Harry Potter novels – in an article in Scotland's *Sunday Herald* in 2000, Rowling stated: 'I identify with E Nesbit more than any other writer' (Rowling 2000).

To understand the form that Nesbit's work takes, it is vital to comprehend her relationship with the Edwardian magazine market. Over the period from the late 1890s until 1913, when her final serial for the *Strand Magazine* (*Wet Magic*) was concluded, Nesbit originally published all of her books in instalments in the popular magazines of the day: key works include her stories of the Bastable children, *The Story of the Treasure Seekers* (1899), and *The Wouldbegoods* (1901); her 'Five Children' series of fantastical adventures, *Five Children and It* (1902), *The Phoenix and the Carpet* (1904), and *The Story of the Amulet* (1906); the 'Arden' series of time-travelling novels, *The House of Arden* (1908), and *Harding's Luck* (1909); and a number of stand-alone volumes, invariably featuring a small group of children at play, including *The Railway Children* (1906), *The Enchanted Castle* (1907), and *The Magic City* (1910). The magazines in which her work regularly appeared (including the *Strand*, which became the predominant publisher of her fantastical fiction, the *Illustrated London News*, *Pall Mall Magazine*, *Windsor Magazine* and the *London Magazine*) relied upon stories that complied with recognisable genre formats, including tales of detection, historical romance, fairy and fantasy tales, and family stories. While Nesbit's work certainly conformed to the broad remit of these story categorisations, she also ensured that her submissions would incorporate her own stylistic signature. In this way she effectively built the characteristic and popular Nesbit 'brand' (much as Beatrix Potter had crafted her own distinctive 'brand' identity) thus guaranteeing regular commissions for her writing throughout the period before the Great War. Without this form of market presence, talented individuals might well become lost among the swelling ranks of Edwardian writers and artists. But with a recognisable 'name', they might, like Nesbit, be able to earn £30 per story or episode (as Nesbit did for her *Strand* publications), on top of the royalties they might claim for the book version of their work (Briggs 1987: 218).

We can see the characteristic features of what would become the Nesbit 'brand' already evident in *The Story of the Treasure Seekers*. This collection of loosely connected tales concerning the Bastable children had already appeared in various magazines from 1894, before being collected together in book form in time for the Christmas market of 1899. These stories are narrated by twelve-year-old Oswald Bastable, who describes the ways in which he and his siblings attempted to 'restore the fallen fortunes' of their 'House' (1899: 16). These 'fortunes' have declined because their widowed father's business partner absconded with the money, a traditional plot device across much adult and juvenile Victorian fiction. The genteel poverty in which the children then find themselves provides a platform from which their various misadventures can take place. Although this narrative formula is a familiar one, Nesbit's decision to make Oswald conceal from the reader his identity as the narrator of the tales provides an intriguing and distinctive initial twist. He announces at the outset that:

> It is one of [the Bastable siblings] that tells this story – but I shall not tell you which: only at the very end perhaps I will. While the story is going on you may be trying to guess, only I bet you don't. (15)

This conceit is designed by Nesbit to be quickly seen through by the attentive reader, yet Oswald's dogged perseverance with this deception allows us to witness his youthful self-fashioning from a covert position. What emerges is both richly comic and also revealing in the ways in which it exposes the process of storytelling. Just as Beatrix Potter's books encourage very young readers to think about what lies beneath the surface of her words, Nesbit engineers Oswald's often artless attempts at controlling his public image to deliver an essay on the practicalities of authorship and tale-telling.

These issues are evident at the start of the second chapter of *The Story of the Treasure Seekers*, where Oswald reflects upon what he now perceives as the dullness of his opening chapter:

> It is always dull in books when people talk and talk, and don't do anything, but I was obliged to put it in, or else you wouldn't have understood all the rest. The best part of books is when things are happening. That is the best part of real things too. This is why I shall not tell you in this story about all the days when nothing happened ... of course time goes on – whether you say so or not. So I shall just tell you the nice, interesting parts – and in between you will understand that we had our meals and got up and went to bed, and dull things like that. (Nesbit 1899: 24)

While he is ultimately successful in introducing incident into his text (the demands of the monthly magazine story dictate that Oswald must produce a recognisable tale in his allotted span of words), he also proves easily sidetracked into more quotidian matters. Oswald is particularly vulnerable to these digressions at points in the narrative when he wants the reader to recognise his pre-eminence among his siblings. Far from acknowledging his superiority, however, we instead recognise Oswald as a boastful and vain youth. Readers in this way register his likely unreliability, and are encouraged to interrogate the text to form more reliable interpretations of the people and events that he describes. Implicit questions are generated on a number of related themes: what, for example, do the adults that Oswald encounters really think about his own and his siblings' behaviour?; what is the Bastables' genuine social situation behind Oswald's romantic musings on the fortunes of his fallen 'House'?; and in what ways does Oswald's confident adoption of a role that Briggs describes as 'the complacent Victorian patriarch in embryo' (Avery and Briggs 1989: 246) really play out in the changing social scene evident in the new century? Nesbit's manipulation of Oswald's role across three collections of Bastable stories encouraged child readers to become self-aware about the nature of their roles as readers of texts. Where earlier children's stories perhaps encouraged a passive acceptance of a story's narrative, Nesbit, by contrast, is always inviting active participation from readers in the interpretation of her tales.

A close engagement with readers is equally recognisable in Nesbit's stand-alone fantastical magazine stories that she collected together for *Nine Unlikely Tales for Children* (1901). This bond is typically established at a moment in which the narrator shares a wry reflection with her readers on the inequities of life as experienced by children living in an adult-controlled world. We recognise this form of collusion between narrator and reader in the collection's opening story entitled 'The Cockatoucan or Great Aunt Willoughby'. Here, a young girl named Matilda wearily anticipates a visit to her great-aunt's house in Streatham:

> She would be asked about her lessons, and how many marks she had, and whether she had been a good girl. I can't think why grown-up people don't see how impertinent these questions are. Suppose you were to answer, "I'm top of my class, Auntie, thank you, and I'm very good. And now let's have a little talk about you. Aunt, dear, how much money have you got, and have you been scolding the servants again, or have you tried to be good and patient as a properly brought up aunt should be, eh, dear?"
>
> Try this method with one of your aunts next time she begins asking you questions, and write and tell me what she says. (1901: 7)

This mischievous and playful tone, clearly indebted to Carroll's Alice, is characteristic of the narrative voice Nesbit cultivates across this collection. The position she adopts here is typically that of a youthful-minded adult (the tone of voice suggests a much older sibling, or a young-at-heart aunt) who is still able to relate to the day-to-day life of children. With evident good humour and authority, the narrator gains the reader's trust while suggesting that it is in fact children who are the arbiters of sanity in a largely imbecilic adult world. The main offenders against good sense tend to be maiden aunts and servants – individuals who have power over children while having little empathy with them as fellow human beings. In setting up these bad examples, Nesbit writes fiction which is designed to appeal primarily to children – the innocent victims of this abuse of power – but also to those adults who prided themselves on their enlightened guardianship of the children in their care. The need to appeal to both adult and child audiences was understandably helpful for fiction that first appeared in magazines. Publications of this type might expect their readers to work through the month's offerings indiscriminately, and editors would therefore favour submissions which had broad as well as niche appeal: this breadth of appeal is perhaps best represented by the work of one of Nesbit's literary heroes, F. Anstey, an instalment of whose comic fantasy novel *The Brass Bottle* appeared alongside Nesbit's 'The Cockatoucan' in the *Strand*'s March 1900 edition.

In addition to the careful crafting of an appealing range of narrative voices, Nesbit also developed an intimate bond with her readers by locating her work within those suburban locations, which, as the previous chapter indicated, were increasingly familiar to readers of Edwardian print culture. The specificity of place in her texts suggests that Nesbit (like F. Anstey before her) was playing to a gallery of metropolitan readers, who would enjoy watching the spotlight falling on their otherwise unfashionable neighbourhoods: 'The Cockatoucan' includes references to Brixton, Streatham Common, Camberwell New Road, the Elephant and Castle, New Cross and Islington. The rationale behind Nesbit's use of authentic London locations can be seen to good effect in *The Phoenix and the Carpet*, in which the children's mother buys a carpet for their nursery in the Kentish Town Road, 'not far from the hotel that is called the Bull and Gate' (Nesbit 1904/1976: 17). This authentic and prosaic location counterpoints the tale's magic, which emerges only after the carpet's enchantment becomes apparent: Nesbit's juxtaposition of ordinary and extraordinary is directly acknowledged in *The Story of the Amulet*, when the narrator remarks that 'the parlour in Fitzroy Street was a very flat background to magic happenings' (1906/1996: 28). To make this contrast effective Nesbit needed first to establish in convincing fashion the everyday life of her ordinary, middle-class, villa-dwelling family. She achieves this by offering a snapshot of this life which might be recognised as authentic by readers, whether or not they were familiar with the suburbs of north London:

> Sunday at 18, Camden Terrace, Camden Town, was always a very pretty day. Father always brought home flowers on Saturday, so that the breakfast-table was extra beautiful . . . Then there were always sausages on toast for breakfast, and these are rapture, after six days of Kentish Town Road eggs at fourteen a shilling. (Nesbit 1906/1996: 57)

The wry perspective of the knowing narrator is captured a little later to good effect, when she describes the children's mother being summoned by the unhappy general servant:

> Mother went out into the passage, which is called 'the hall', where the umbrella-stand is, and the picture of the 'Monarch of the Glen' in a yellow shining frame, with brown spots on the Monarch from the damp in the house before last . . . (58)

The combined effect here is to establish a fellowship with readers, who recognised their own lives in these details and presumably welcomed the opportunity to witness the magical transformation of this environment.

Aside from the geographical specificity inscribed in her work, Nesbit also locates her fiction in a present day signposted by up-to-date cultural reference points. Nesbit's insistence that her child characters are potentially interchangeable with her readers ('they were not bad sorts on the whole; in fact, they were rather like you' (21)) is strengthened by the children's first-hand knowledge of the latest 'things'. The children's trip to see *The Water Babies* at the Garrick Theatre relives in fiction an authentic treat enjoyed by numerous readers during the Christmas holidays in 1902: the narrator underlines this connection by arguing that 'I am not going to tell you about the play. As I said before, one can't tell everything, and no doubt you saw "The Water Babies" yourselves' (225). Rather than appearing as an isolated concurrence of real and imagined treats, this trip to the Garrick Theatre appears in Nesbit's work alongside visits to other popular Edwardian places of entertainment, including the Hippodrome, Maskelyne and Cooke's 'Egyptian Hall' in *The Story of the Amulet* (1906/1996: 269, 270), and Madame Tussaud's in *The Railway Children* (1906/1975: 9). While the inclusion of these London venues might appear merely a superficial investment of the contemporary in her work, the blend of fact and fiction was effective in infusing the text with a sense of authenticity and modernity. Nesbit wanted her fictional children to appear 'rather like you', and she therefore needed to build up pictures of lives recognisable to her readers. A clear way in which to achieve this was to fill out her picture with locations and things redolent of the present day. Whether these were the brand names of commercial products (Eiffel Tower Lemonade, Bovril, Waterbury watches), shops (the Army and Navy Stores, Liberty, the Lowther Arcade toysellers), or commercial firms (Phoenix Fire Insurance, Dyer & Hilton house agents, Carter Paterson carriers), the combined effect is of a collage of the sorts of cultural and mercantile life that comprised the landscape of an urban reader's everyday existence.

Over and above Nesbit's compulsive inclusion in her work of the stuff of everyday Edwardian life, it is in her persistent drawing from other writers for children that her writing assumes its more radical sense of modernity. Her protagonists share with their readers a library of favourite books in ways which create a compact. This compact is acknowledged directly in *The Wonderful Garden* (1911), where companionship is established between characters through a shared literary landscape of favoured texts:

> A tide of friendliness swept over the party, and when they found that he had also read *Alice in Wonderland*, *Wild Animals I Have Known* [by Thompson Seton], and *Hereward the Wake* [by Charles Kingsley], as well as E. Nesbit's stories for children in the *Strand Magazine*, they all felt that they had been friends for years. (1911/1933: 21)

But beyond this bonding exercise between characters and readers (and some brazen self-promotion for Nesbit), a more profound understanding of the effects of reading and its relationship with play is also evident. As Marah Gubar has argued, Nesbit's 'child protagonists are enmeshed in and affected by the culture they inhabit' (2010: 43). Their immersion in this culture, Gubar further contends, 'influences but does not entirely constrain them' (129). One suspects that Nesbit would be sympathetic to this interpretation of reading as a potentially two-way process of influence. Rather than simply saturating her stories with intertextual reference points, Nesbit wants to present the act of reading as a potentially dynamic and life-enhancing practice. She invites her readers to consider her own up-to-date stories as part of a plastic world of older texts which exist, not as fixed or static entities, but as part of a continuing dialogue with works yet to come; the current nature of Nesbit's literary references can be detected in, for example, her identification of Anstey's *The Brass Bottle* as an inspiration for the children in *Five Children and It* only months after Anstey's story had itself appeared in the *Strand* (1902/1979: 214).

Nesbit's employment of Kipling's work is particularly revealing in this respect. Kipling is presented as a literary figure whose name not only

evokes awed respect among Nesbit's child characters, but is also designated as a talisman of imagination and play. The first of these qualities
is evident in a passage from *The Story of the Treasure Seekers*, in which
Oswald and his brother encounter a lady poet who is a fellow Kipling
fan: after telling them that she is 'very pleased to meet people who know
their Jungle book', she asks them if they are now off to 'the Zoological
Gardens to look for Bagheera?'. Oswald then registers his approval of
the poetical lady, 'We were pleased, too, to meet some one who knew
the Jungle book' (1899/1958: 51). The language used here invests
Kipling's collection of Indian animal fables (*The Jungle Book* (1894)
and its sequel *The Second Jungle Book* (1895)) with the structural position that the Bible had occupied in an earlier era of more pious children's
texts; the Zoological Gardens in this reimagining becomes a place of
modern secular worship. Elsewhere, this swapping of sacred for secular
authority is reaffirmed when Oswald remarks that the Bastable children
especially admired their Lewisham Road neighbour ('Albert's uncle')
because 'he gave us our Jungle books' (182). The form of worship available to the children through Kipling and his work is realised dynamically
in the opening chapter of *The Wouldbegoods*, in which the Bastables
'play jungle book' (1901/1934: 11). In this 'play', the children adopt the
roles of the book's characters (Oswald typically claims the plum role of
Mowgli) and reimagine their garden in line with the book's setting:

> Of course the shrubbery was to be the jungle, and the lawn under the cedar
> a forest glade, and then they began to collect the things . . . We all thought of
> different things. Of course first we dressed up pillows in the skins of beasts
> and set them about on the grass to look as natural as we could. And then we
> got Pincher [the dog], and rubbed him all over with powdered slate-pencil, to
> make him the right colour for Grey Brother. (1901/1934: 12)

The rest of the chapter comprises an increasingly inventive use of house-
hold items (including prized taxidermy, beer stands, sofa cushions,
copies of *The Times*, Condy's fluid, and Father's mackintosh) to the
point where 'the lawn under the cedar was transformed into a dream of
beauty, what with the stuffed creatures and the paper-tailed things and
the waterfall' (15). If Nesbit's texts do indeed accord Kipling a form of
quasi-divine status, this position is always couched in playful ways that
guard against a more static reverence. The *Jungle Books*, once read by
a group of like-minded, imaginative children like the Bastables, might
become a starting point for play that reached beyond the fixed script of
a written text. The overall effect of Nesbit's dynamic engagement with
other writers and their texts is, as Gubar suggests, 'to break down the
divide between adult writer and child reader by suggesting that both

parties can improvise on other people's stories to produce their own narratives' (Gubar 2010: 132). This opening up of connections and possibilities is at the heart of Nesbit's modernity, making her work stand out from what had gone before and, in the process, suggesting new paths for children's literature in the twentieth century.

Wodehouse and the Modern School Story

P. G. Wodehouse, unlike Beatrix Potter and E. Nesbit, is rarely thought of as an Edwardian writer. Indeed, it comes as a surprise to many readers of Wodehouse's work that his long career as a published author began in the first months of the twentieth century. While Wodehouse's work for children in this period has not, like Potter's *The Tale of Peter Rabbit* and Nesbit's *The Railway Children*, remained in the public eye, its contextual significance deserves wider recognition. Like Potter and Nesbit, Wodehouse entered an established category of literature, in his case the school story, and reworked this genre in ways that would facilitate its remarkable popularity in the twentieth century. The school story that Wodehouse inherited when he published *The Pothunters* in 1902 dated back to the phenomenal success of Thomas Hughes' *Tom Brown's School Days* in 1857, and Frederic W. Farrar's equally popular *Eric, or Little by Little*, which appeared in the following year. Between the 1850s and the start of the twentieth century, the format of school fiction remained generally uniform: its key elements were a demand for the unimpeachable morality of its public-school pupils; a solid underpinning of orthodox religious virtues; and plenty of heroism, typically proved on the sports field. The results of Wodehouse's own attempts to update an already massively popular genre of writing are evident across the seven books of school stories that he published in the Edwardian period: *The Pothunters* was followed by *A Prefect's Uncle* (1903), *Tales of St. Austin's* (1903), *The Gold Bat* (1904), *The Head of Kay's* (1905), *The White Feather* (1907), and *Mike* (1909). In common with Nesbit, almost all of these books were originally published in magazines, and this connection with the periodical press is again a crucial consideration when assessing the significance of Wodehouse's writing. The need for writers working in this environment to connect with their readership in direct and immediate ways evidently dictated the form and content of the material that they produced. Nesbit and Wodehouse's work in this period, therefore, needed self-consciously to declare its modernity and therefore its difference from the children's fiction that had emerged in the Victorian era. Wodehouse, who was writing for magazines targeted towards schoolboys, needed in particular to appeal to readers who would be excited by the prospect of fast motor cars, up-to-date slang, and syncopated jazz rhythms.

The background to Wodehouse's career as a writer of school stories has its roots in his father's decision to block his plans to go to university after he had finished his education at Dulwich College. Wodehouse, at eighteen, was instead ushered into a career in banking, joining the Hongkong and Shanghai Bank in September 1900. He drew extensively upon his banking experience for *Psmith in the City* (1910), and his narrator's rueful remark, 'banks have a habit of swallowing their victims rather abruptly', appears an accurate reflection of his own experience (Wodehouse 1910/1950: 20). As for Bennett and Wells before him, the literary marketplace offered a potential escape route from this decidedly unappealing fate; Wodehouse underlined, in a letter he wrote to his friend Bill Townend in 1949, the favourable conditions under which he had started his literary career:

> How on earth does a young writer of light fiction get going these days? Where can he sell his stories? When you and I were breaking in, we might get turned down by the *Strand* and *Pearson's*, but there was always hope of landing with *Nash's*, the *Story-teller*, the *London*, the *Royal*,. . .the *Pall Mall*, and the *Windsor*, not to mention *Blackwood*, *Cornhill* and *Chambers's* and probably about a dozen more I've forgotten. (Wodehouse 1953: 156)

Wodehouse had the opportunity to publish his way out of the bank, but he had little experience of life to draw on. It was, therefore, out of necessity rather than choice that his early literary ventures were inspired by his time at Dulwich College. Wodehouse was fortunate that when he embarked on his literary career, the school story was enjoying a new wave of popularity, following the success of Kipling's *Stalky & Co.* in 1899. It was also to his distinct advantage that two recently established magazines, *Public School Magazine* and *The Captain* (founded in 1898 and 1899 respectively), were eager to receive copy on school topics from relatively unknown authors. Like Bennett and Wells, Wodehouse was impatient to gain his financial independence, and he was equally tireless in ensuring that he would earn enough from freelance work to enable him to resign from his day job at the earliest opportunity; his literary earnings for 1903, after he had resigned from the bank, totalled over £215, an impressive figure when compared with his weekly income of £3 3s 10d from the bank (McCrum 2004: 61, 43). In January 1906, Wodehouse followed the route of many ambitious young Edwardian writers in securing Pinker as his literary agent; in his letter of approach to Pinker, he proclaimed confidently that he had 'made a sort of corner in public-school stories, and I can always get them taken' (Ratcliffe 2013: 61).

Wodehouse's success as a writer specialising in boys' school fiction was grounded in his close understanding of this genre and his awareness of the limitations of the other material appearing in this field at the time. He was a voracious reader of popular literature while at Dulwich, and paid attention to the form as well as the content of the fiction he encountered. In an article he wrote for *Public School Magazine* in August 1901 entitled 'School Stories', Wodehouse outlined something of a manifesto for his future work in this area. While admiring the work of his predecessors in the field (singling out school story specialists such as Talbot Baines Reed and Andrew Home for particular praise), Wodehouse opined that writers had still largely failed to present 'school life as it is', choosing instead to offer a more formulaic depiction of this existence:

> A time may come [he argued] when a writer shall arise bold enough and independent enough to retail the speech of school as it really is, but that time is not yet . . . Rudyard Kipling went near to it, a gallant pioneer of the Ideal, but even the conversation of Stalky and Co. leaves something unsaid, not much, it is true, but still a something. (Wodehouse 1901: 125)

Wodehouse understood the 'inwardness of school life' (as he described it in his 'School Stories' article) extremely well; crucially too, his knowledge of this life was still very fresh. Unlike many of the other writers of school stories at the time, he was just months away from his own schooldays when he published the first instalment of his school serial *The Pothunters* in *Public School Magazine* in January 1902. While *The Pothunters* displays the predictable weaknesses of the novice writer in terms of plotting and structure, its rendering of dialogue is remarkably adept. Here, for example, a group of boys discuss the demerits of the head boy of their school house:

> 'Yes, he's an awful man,' said Vaughan.
> 'Don't stop,' said the Babe, encouragingly, after a silence had lasted some time. 'It's a treat picking a fellow to pieces like this.'
> 'I don't know if that's your beastly sarcasm, Babe,' said Vaughan, 'but, speaking for self and partner, I don't know how we should get on if we didn't blow off steam occasionally in this style.'
> 'We should probably last out for a week, and then there would be a sharp shriek, a hollow groan, and all that would be left of the Mutual Friend would be a slight discolouration on the study carpet.'
> 'Coupled with an aroma of fresh gore.'
> 'Perhaps that's why he goes off in the afternoons,' suggested the Babe. 'Doesn't want to run any risks.'
> 'Shouldn't wonder.' (1902/1987: 38–9)

Noticeable here is a lightness of touch, a keen judgement of pace, and the ways in which these elements facilitate the text's comedy. We can already recognise the qualities, especially Wodehouse's keen ear for the rhythms of colloquial speech, that he would go on to develop to excellent effect in his later adult fiction. In this passage, rather than resorting lazily to slapstick for comic effect, Wodehouse's comedy emerges from verbal interchanges and skilful word choice.

The use of slang is a key component of Wodehouse's rendering of dialogue, and the inventive use of the demotic was also central to the success of his later work. The very title of his first novel, *The Pothunters* (a distinctive slang term indicating one who competes in sport only for the prize or the reward), immediately set it apart from earlier works in this field, such as *Tom Brown's School Days*, *Eric, or Little by Little*, and Talbot Baines Reed's *The Fifth Form at St. Dominic's* (1881). An *Athenaeum* review of the book confirms its novelty, even if the paper's critic remained unconvinced about its mode of construction: 'We confess to a doubt of the taste or sense of writing a book entirely in juvenile slang'. But even this reviewer was able to recognise that Wodehouse's use of demotic contained something unmistakably fresh: 'slight as it is, there is considerable vivacity in the story' (Anonymous 1902b: 519). His use of slang also offered his work authenticity, a truth-to-life which E. V. Lucas recognised in an originally anonymous *Times Literary Supplement* review of *The Gold Bat* in 1904: 'no writer of school tales has so much vigour and realistic spirit as Mr. P. G. Wodehouse' (Anonymous 1904: 348). While we might be sceptical about the qualification of Lucas (then thirty-six years old) to judge the veracity of schoolboy language, the 'vivacity' and 'vigour' recognised in his and other contemporary reviews points towards the reasons for Wodehouse's success. The evident popularity of his work among its target audience offers tangible proof of his achievement in creating the revolution in realistic literary style that he had proposed in his 'School Stories' article.

Aside from introducing a new era of realism in language and dialogue into the school story, Wodehouse's texts of this period also evince modernity in other significant ways. Like Nesbit, Wodehouse invested his text with up-to-date social and cultural reference points. He refers, for example, to current sporting celebrities throughout his Edwardian writing, and the efforts of his schoolboy characters are regularly compared with these figures. But it is in his incorporation of popular music, in particular ragtime-era jazz, that Wodehouse achieves an especially authentic and effective reflection of contemporary youth culture. In a revealing anticipation of the later impact of rock'n'roll music, Wodehouse identifies the subversive potential of black music in his school settings. In the following scene from *The Head of Kay's*, for example, the disaffected Fenn allows his personal frustrations to emerge during the school concert. Following an encore received for his playing of the 'Moonlight Sonata', he lets rip with a popular 'cakewalk' tune:

> Three runs and half-a-dozen crashes, and there was no further room for doubt. Fenn was playing the 'Coon Band Contest'.
> 'He's gone mad', gasped Kennedy.
> Whether he had or not, it is certain that the gallery had. All the evening they had been stewing in an atmosphere like that of the inner room of a Turkish bath, and they were ready for anything. It needed but a trifle to set them off. The lilt of that unspeakable Yankee melody supplied that trifle. Kay's malcontents, huddled in their seats by the window, were the first to break out. Feet began to stamp in time to the music – softly at first, then more loudly. The wooden dais gave out the sound like a drum . . . Soon three hundred pairs of well-shod feet were rising and falling. (Wodehouse 1986: 34)

Similar acts of teenage rebellion would be played out with comparable results in much later fiction of this ilk, but this episode seems to offer a foundational moment for the literature to come. Wodehouse's proximity to the age of his readers and his own keen understanding of the affecting power of popular music lends this scene a degree of realism, and an energy largely unavailable to older practitioners of the school story. This understanding of the psychology of generational difference and its expression through music was not used to promote any desire for change in the public-school system of the day; as George Orwell later argued, Wodehouse's school stories are 'by no means a satire on the public-school system . . . the "play the game" code of morals is accepted with not many reservations' (Orwell 1998: 55). Rather, Wodehouse's intention was to demonstrate, with verisimilitude, the lives of boys living within (and policing) those apparently restrictive codes of conduct. While his often high-spirited characters kick in healthy ways against the restrictions within which they are bound, they respect a public-school code which valorises sporting prowess over academic achievement, militates against sentimentality and emotionalism, and promotes an unswerving belief in a chivalric code of behaviour. Wodehouse sees nothing incompatible or anachronistic in locating his 'modern' jazz-loving, motor-car riding, and independently minded youths within these traditional contexts. His characters move with the times but also understand the value of tradition in a period of technological and social transformation.

Just as Wodehouse's evocation of modernity was, like Nesbit's, embedded in a world of up-to-date cultural reference points, so his fiction is self-reflexive in terms of its relationship to preceding work in its field. Wodehouse's desire to eradicate caricature in school fiction, and replace it with greater realism in characterisation, is underlined at certain key moments in his texts, when his own characters are defined in opposition to their more stereotypical counterparts. We recognise this in the first meeting in *Mike* between the title character, Mike Jackson, and Psmith; the latter would go on to be one of Wodehouse's most popular comic characters, featuring in a number of his later adult novels. After introducing himself to Mike, Psmith asks his schoolfellow: 'Are you the Bully, the Pride of the School, or the Boy who is Led Astray and takes to Drink in Chapter Sixteen?' and Mike replies: 'The last, for choice . . . but I've only just arrived, so I don't know' (1909/1932: 179). The narrator in *Mike* augments this process of intertextual self-awareness by repeatedly drawing the reader's attention to the gap between the narrative that they are reading and what would happen in an equivalent situation in a more conventional school story. In the following passage from *Mike*, for example, the narrator describes Mike's first cricket match played at his new school:

> In stories of the 'Not Really a Duffer' type, where the nervous new boy, who has been found crying in the boot-room over the photograph of his sister, contrives to get an innings in a game, nobody suspects that he is really a prodigy till he hits the Bully's first ball out of the ground for six. With Mike it was different. (1909/1932: 226–7)

As is the case with Nesbit, this overt recognition of the trappings of earlier fiction does not lead towards a form of writing which sets out to eschew dramatic event (Mike goes on to make an impressive score of 277 not out); instead, and also like Nesbit, Wodehouse assumes he is writing for an intelligent and savvy reader who is quite capable of reading the material to hand against the grain of its fictional predecessors. Building upon his own reading of this genre of fiction, Wodehouse imagines a modern audience that welcomes subtlety, plausibility and playfulness in its reading.

While Wodehouse abandoned the boys' school story after *Mike*, his legacy as a moderniser of this genre of writing is evident in its continuing popularity throughout the twentieth century and beyond. The immediate influence of Wodehouse's work can be detected in the emergence of the *Gem* and the *Magnet*. Frank Richards drew in these papers upon several elements that Wodehouse had introduced to this field (particularly the character comedy), but tailored this material to a social demographic consisting largely, according to Orwell, of 'the sons of shopkeepers, office employees and small business and professional men' (Orwell 1976: 183). These readers lived 'outside the mystic world of quadrangles and house-colours' but were attracted by this alien world and its apparently privileged trappings (182). This glamorisation of the public school for an outside audience seems to have played little part in Wodehouse's original scheme for his stories. His own desire, and something which he appears to have successfully achieved, was to offer his Edwardian readers a form of fiction which spoke directly to them about their lives. In doing this, he recognised, like Nesbit, that the distinction between young readers and their adult counterparts was negligible in terms of their abilities to appreciate intelligent, subtly crafted and relevant fiction.

Chapter Four

Department of Decadence: Sex, Cars and Money

The start of the twentieth century coincided with a series of social revolutions – some tangible and others less substantial. This chapter investigates three key areas which epitomised the revolutionary current of the time: sex, motorcars and money. As Samuel Hynes has noted, the tensions brought about by a new century marked by such decadent keynotes was almost inevitably one in which 'old and new ideas dwelt uneasily together' (Hynes 1968/1991: 5). As this chapter will demonstrate, Edwardian literary culture always attempted to do more than simply reflect the uneasy society from which it emerged. We can see this in the rise of the Edwardian sex novel, discussed in the first section, which in its various manifestations looked to break away from the perceived prudishness that had marked Victorian publishing. The Edwardian reading public clearly had an appetite to consider sexual relations more openly, and many writers and publishers, in apparent defiance of morality campaigners, attempted to satisfy these demands. While the motorcar (discussed in this chapter's second section) now appears an unlikely totem of controversy, literary discussions of the car in its earliest years were almost always contentious. The apparently equal measures of excitement and danger associated with this new form of transport ensured its symbolic association with a coming epoch which seemed marked by uncertainty. In the final section, money, the fundamental source of much Edwardian decadence, is discussed in relation to the new forms of drama that appeared during the era. While contemporary writing focused on sex and motorcars explored the putative cutting-edge of modernity in the new century, the primary issue of money allowed a more fundamental enquiry into the forces driving modern behaviour. Underpinning much of the material discussed in this chapter is the question that C. F. G. Masterman posed in the opening lines of his influential study *The Condition of England* (1909): 'What will the future make of the present?' (1). For Edwardian writers on both moral and progressive literary wings, the issues discussed in this chapter formed the key battlegrounds on which Masterman's question would be contested. The contemporary significance of these key tenets of Edwardian modernity has been gradually erased by the passage of time, and so the following chapter sets out to reinstate their contemporary importance. This process of reinstatement also offers an intriguing platform from which to respond to Masterman's thesis question: what sort of sense can we, living in Masterman's imagined future, make of his radically uncertain Edwardian present?

The Edwardian Sex Novel

The old adage 'sex sells' was evidently true for Edwardian publishers. When Desmond Flower produced his list of bestselling titles for the years between 1830 and 1930, the Edwardian decade's eighteen representatives included a disproportionate number of controversial novels in which sex and its consequences played a central part: these included Victoria Cross's *Anna Lombard* (1901), Lucas Malet's *The History of Sir Richard Calmady* (1901), Frank Danby's *Baccarat* (1904), Robert Hichens' *The Garden of Allah* (1904), W. J. Locke's *The Morals of Marcus Ordeyne* (1905), Elinor Glyn's *Three Weeks* (1907), H. de Vere Stacpoole's *The Blue Lagoon* (1908), and Florence L. Barclay's *The Rosary* (1909) (Flower 1934: 18–20). While the decadent 1890s introduced readers to what we might consider as modern sexual topics, especially via the 'New Woman' novel and its corresponding forms, the Edwardian decade built upon and developed them. As this section will confirm, it is certainly not the case that the Oscar Wilde trials of 1895 brought about a return to standards of mid-Victorian reticence in the publishing industry; John Lane, the publisher of *The Yellow Book*, proved premature in stating that after the trials 'the sex novel was played out' (Springfield 1924: 157). Edwardian writers were almost bound to keep faith with fiction of this type, not simply because of its potential for financial profit, but because contemporary theoretical writing on the topic provided plentiful new angles for discussion: among the most conspicuous figures in this field were Havelock Ellis, who published several volumes on sexual topics during the decade, including *Studies in the Psychology of Sex*, Vol. 1, *Sexual Inversion* (1900); Edward Carpenter, whose pioneering work on homosexuality influenced Edwardian writers such as Fr Rolfe (Baron Corvo), E. M. Forster, and Forrest Reid; Friedrich Nietzsche, a number of whose major works (including *Beyond Good and Evil* in 1907) were translated into English for the first time during the Edwardian decade; and arguably Sigmund Freud, although his *Three Essays on the History of Sexuality* was not translated into English until 1910 (under the title *Three Contributions to the Sexual Theory*).

Against this background, as Peter Keating has noted, the 'sex novel' (or 'sex problem' novel) was a category term 'used indiscriminately and applied by hostile critics to almost any novel which contained a sexual element'. What critics were actually alluding to when employing this term, Keating further suggests, was the period's preoccupation with 'questions of sexual psychology once the constraints of Victorianism had been cast away' (Keating 1991: 208). While it is inadvisable to take on trust Keating's black-and-white reading of the transition between these eras, the mark made by the new trends in sexual psychology was certainly evident in the work of numerous Edwardian writers, including Violet Hunt, Lucas Malet and May Sinclair. These period-specific trends are equally apparent in the popularity throughout the decade of one component of the 'sex novel', the 'marriage problem' novel. After boldly describing writing of this type as 'the dominant subject of Edwardian fiction', Jane Eldridge Miller reinforces this claim:

> By the Edwardian era, the public debate on the marriage problem and on divorce reform made it difficult for marriage to function in the novel simply as a happy ending, or as a positive indicator of personal success and social unity; increasingly, marriage in itself was a *subject* for fiction, and all but the most conventional novelists ceased to treat it as an unproblematic ideal ... there was a general feeling that relations between sexes were breaking down, and it is reflected in the fact that the novels of the period are filled with unhappy marriages; the institution of marriage is relentlessly scrutinized in Edwardian fiction, even in those novels which eventually advocate it. (1994: 44, 45)

Evidence to endorse Eldridge Miller's position is compelling. The sheer number of Edwardian novels that can be bracketed together under the heading 'marriage problem' gives weight to her claims for the topic's primacy: a necessarily selective list of examples of this form might include W. Somerset Maugham's *Mrs Craddock* (1902), Arnold Bennett's *Whom God Hath Joined* (1906), John Galsworthy's *The Man of Property* (1906), May Sinclair's *The Helpmate* (1907), Ada Leverson's *Love's Shadow* (1908), Maurice Hewlett's trilogy of novels, *Halfway House* (1908), *Open Country* (1909) and *Rest Harrow* (1910), and Olivia Shakespear's *Uncle Hilary* (1910). While this section is not primarily concerned with examining the 'marriage problem' novel as a literary phenomenon, several of the 'sex novels' discussed in the following pages might also be classified under this label.

By the end of the decade, there was a perception among moralistic critics such as William Barry that the popularity of the 'sex novel' in its various manifestations had delivered a 'plague of licentious thought' to the era's readers (Barry 1910: 179). This 'plague', as manifested in the new century, might be traced to two novels that appeared within days of each other in November 1900. The extraordinary popularity of these books – Laurence Housman's anonymously published *An Englishwoman's Love-Letters*, and Elinor Glyn's *The Visits of Elizabeth* – alerted writers and publishers alike to the ways in which female sexual desire might be incorporated into literature designed for popular consumption. Although much of the supposedly decadent literature of the 1890s had challenged the boundaries of what was then deemed acceptable in print, Housman's and Glyn's works are distinctive, in that while they incorporate much erotically charged material, they largely escaped the moral censure experienced by earlier counterparts. By carefully controlling the nature of their work and its impact in the marketplace, Housman, Glyn and their publishers produced texts that were (in contrasting ways) deemed suitable for a mainstream adult readership. In this way, *An Englishwoman's Love-Letters*, *The Visits of Elizabeth* and the work that followed in their wake began to redefine the boundaries of what was considered acceptable subject matter for twentieth-century popular publications. The strategies behind the publication of these bestselling novels and the history of their reception point towards the careful packaging and mediation of desire and eroticism for an evidently enthusiastic reading public.

Laurence Housman's *An Englishwoman's Love-Letters* provides an object lesson in the ways in which the literary marketplace at this time was open to manipulation. The book was originally marketed, by its eminently respectable publisher, John Murray, as an authentic cache of love letters, whose female author had died shortly after her lover had broken off their engagement, following his discovery that their relationship was within the 'prohibited degrees'; this term indicates the legal or religious restriction on marriage between blood relatives. Rather like the recently published (in 1897) letters of Elizabeth Barrett Browning (to which they were compared by a number of critics), these love letters evoked the intense passion and poetic sensibility of their writer. Housman's evocation of these qualities can be glimpsed in his 'Englishwoman's' unguarded declarations of desire:

> come to me somehow, dear ghost of all my happiness, and take me in your arms! I ache and ache, not to belong to you. I do: I must. It is only our senses that divide us; and mine are all famished servants waiting for their master … Beloved, in the darkness do you feel my kisses? (Anonymous 1900a: 306)

But rather than focusing on the acceptability or otherwise of the levels of female desire so unambiguously expressed in the letters, early critical responses tended to centre instead on other ethical dimensions. The *Athenaeum*'s review of the book, for example, voiced anxiety at the publication of the private in the public sphere:

> it is difficult to believe that even in this unreticent age, when the interviewer seems to have for the time abolished that dignified reserve as to private life which the generation now thinking of lowering its sails was taught to deem a specially English virtue, people could be found so heartless and tasteless as to publish for the behoof of the circulating library those sacred, and in some cases secret outpourings of a friend's or kinswoman's heart. (Anonymous 1900c: 716)

For those critics who recognised the love letters as an entirely fictional construction, much energy was expended in identifying the book's anonymous author. Prior to Housman's unveiling as author late in 1902, various literary figures were proposed as candidates for this role, including Pearl Craigie (John Oliver Hobbes), Alice Meynell, Elizabeth von Arnim, Edith Wharton and Oscar Wilde. The quality of the writing evident in *An Englishwoman's Love-Letters* encouraged the association of the text with a number of these contemporary writers: the novelist Lucas Malet (the pseudonym used by Charles Kingsley's daughter Mary) was not alone in considering that the book was the work of 'a writer of genius, or something very refreshingly near that' (Anonymous 1901b: 109). Yet while *An Englishwoman's Love-Letters* is certainly uneven, and betrays many signs of its rapid composition, the intensity of focus is impressive. The letters are short and balanced, and the staccato rhythm that they sound draws the reader through the text at pace. Housman's prose moves between breathless declarations of love – 'My own one beloved, my dearest dear! Want me, please want me! I will keep alive for you' (Anonymous 1900a: 304) – into the sort of elegant phrasing and ideas that had made his poetry critically if not popularly acclaimed in the 1890s:

> If I hold my breath for a moment wickedly . . . and try to look at the world with you out of it, I seem to have fallen over a precipice; or, rather, the solid earth has slipped from under my feet, and I am off into vacuum. (1900a: 7)

This channelling of Housman's poetic sensibility, reinforced by liberal references to fine art and high literature (George Meredith is much admired by the 'Englishwoman'), was leavened by the playful, sometimes kittenish, tone of the female subject. Together this blend of qualities produced a portrait of a cultured, bright, mischievous and passionate young woman, with whom readers might readily identify.

This assumed identification with the ultimately tragic 'Englishwoman' is further enhanced by the absence of replies to the letters. In this blank space, readers were able to shape the male interlocutor in any way that they desired. By the time *An Englishwoman's Love-Letters* finally went out of print (due to wartime paper shortages in 1944) it must have appeared a rather quaint relic of a then far-distant era, but on its original publication, it seemed to symbolise a literary world intent on challenging anew the boundaries of decency in print.

Further evidence of the sort of lamentable trend in publishing identified above by the *Athenaeum*'s reviewer was offered with the publication of Elinor Glyn's first novel, *The Visits of Elizabeth*. This novel, which had originally appeared anonymously in serial form in *The World* magazine, also consisted of a collection of letters, this time apparently written by an unchaperoned and precocious seventeen-year-old making her debut in the country house milieu. The structural resemblance between these two one-sided epistolary fictions ensured that Glyn's novel gained widespread publicity on its emergence in the wake of *An Englishwoman's Love-Letters*, and this clearly helped to propel her career as among the bestselling novelists of the Edwardian era: Glyn's later Edwardian works, which included *The Vicissitudes of Evangeline* (1905), *Beyond the Rocks* (1906), *Three Weeks* (1907), *One Night* (1909) and *High Noon* (1910), came to epitomise over-the-counter eroticism for Edwardian readers. But while the two books by Housman and Glyn provide direct access to the often unguarded and intimate thoughts of their female correspondents, the individual collections of letters are couched in contrasting registers: the 'Englishwoman's' tone is serious and poetic, while the keynotes sounded in Elizabeth's letters are those of glib satire and erotic titillation.

Glyn appears to have understood from the outset of her writing career the combination of elements that would prove irresistible to the Edwardian reading public. The letters that make up *The Visits of Elizabeth* take us on a grand tour of fashionable locations (including manor houses, grand hotels, yachts, chateaus and castles), in the glamorous company of high society (lords and ladies, dukes and duchesses, comtes and comtesses, vicomtes and marquises). Glyn peppers her text with descriptions of fashionable clothing, chic shops, haute cuisine, modern pastimes (Bridge is the latest craze), and up-to-the-minute technology. At the centre of this fashionable milieu is the aristocratic Elizabeth, an ingénue, whose letters (all written to her mother) describe her exciting daily life among the upper crust. Glyn's wish to satisfy her readers' craving for diverting and often illicit pleasure is apparent in the many sexualised glimpses of Elizabeth which her letters afford. Full advantage is taken, for example, of those bathing and swimming scenes which license intimate physical descriptions of otherwise concealed bodies: a marquise's bathing-dress we are informed 'was thin enough red silk for us to see how beautifully she is made' (Glyn 1901: 107); Elizabeth's failure to leave behind a wet chemise in the bathroom reveals her habit of bathing *'toute nue'* to a shocked French godmother, who accuses her of 'deplorable immodesty' (145); and she herself is offended when the Vicomte reveals that he has watched her undressing while she was staying in a curtain-less room at a French inn – *'Comme Mlle. est ravissante le soir! un petit ange à son déshabillé! Une si éblouissant chevelure!'* (82–3) – the untranslated French here perhaps offers an additional frisson for an Anglophone reader. A different form of eroticism is evident elsewhere in the novel, when Elizabeth discloses her own growing understanding of how to be an effective manipulator in the debauched game-playing she invariably encounters: her minx-like qualities are to the fore when she confesses that 'it is much better to have two [dance] partners, Mamma, because then one is not left to oneself at all, and they are each trying to be nicer than the other all the time' (157). Indeed, any attempt at character development in the novel is predicated on Elizabeth's increasing ability to control her environment to her advantage. In this way, we witness Elizabeth evolve into a young woman fully able to exploit the passionate male desire she invariably attracts.

Given the relentless if playful eroticism upon which Glyn's book is constructed, it is not surprising that it gained a reputation among Edwardian readers as a spicy novel, for which access by impressionable readers should be restricted; John Buchan's future wife, then Susan Grosvenor (later Tweedsmuir), read *The Visits of Elizabeth* surreptitiously when she was a young woman after what she remembered as 'pointless discussions raging over my head as to whether [she] should be allowed to read' a book so full of 'double meanings' (Tweedsmuir 1966: 44). Although early reviewers agreed that it should not be recommended *virginibus puerisque*, there is little sense in its critical reception that it was considered dangerously immoral. Indeed, perhaps surprisingly, Elizabeth was described in the *Saturday Review* as 'a charming and healthy specimen of the best type of English girlhood' (Anonymous 1900f: 728). A further key feature of the novel's reception is found in a *Pall Mall Gazette* review, which, while acknowledging the book as 'clever', tempers this apparent praise by emphasising its 'malicious kind of cleverness' (Anonymous 1900h: 3). This remark gets to the heart of Glyn's method and perhaps exposes the reasons behind its success. The combination of glamorous locations and Elizabeth's often acerbic comment on its denizens, brings about a distinctly fresh if rebarbative approach to the comedy of manners. The foregrounding of sex in this amalgam clearly encouraged the book's evident cross-gender appeal, which resulted in Duckworth selling 60,000 copies in eleven impressions by June 1901 alone; this information was proudly included in Duckworth's trade advertisement, alongside a proclamation of its status as 'The Book of the Day' (Anonymous 1901a: 712). Glyn was further enriched when *The Visits of Elizabeth* became a hit in the lucrative American market, a success she later exploited with a profitable sequel predictably entitled *Elizabeth Visits America* (1909).

Many later Edwardian novels which focused their attention on sex incorporated elements prominent in the Housman and Glyn texts. Perhaps most readily apparent among these is a willingness to locate fiction in the sort of 'exotic' foreign locations that might provide evocative backdrops for erotic (mis)adventures: an *Edinburgh Review* article published in 1907 wryly suggested that the familiarity of overseas settings in Edwardian fiction of this kind was brought about by 'a desire . . . to avoid the heavy protective duty levied by the British convention on home-made immorality' (Anonymous 1907b: 204). While Housman's *An Englishwoman's Love-Letters* does not directly transport the text's protagonists into its classical Italian settings, it does use this high cultural background to inflame the Englishwoman's ardour. Glyn goes further in exploiting the relaxed social mores apparently encountered abroad (in this case, the French country house milieu) to license the more risqué material in her novel. But a text that emerged in the early months of 1901 took this connection between eroticism and place to altogether new extremes. Victoria Cross's *Anna Lombard* was probably the most highly charged and sensational erotic novel of the decade: it was also one of the bestselling novels of its era, shifting an astonishing six million copies by the 1930s (Cross 1901/2006: vii). Set largely in northern India in the final years of the nineteenth century, it recalls the blighted relationship of Gerald Ethridge, an assistant commissioner in the Indian Civil Service, and the title character, a General's daughter 'just out from England' (6). Gerald, the first-person narrator, having fallen in love with Anna in the novel's opening chapter, is promptly posted to an inhospitable region of Burma for a five-year period. During the time of their separation, Anna becomes the lover of a local Pathan servant, Gaida Kahn, and the main business of the novel is concerned with the complexities of the resulting inter-racial love-triangle. One has the sense when reading *Anna Lombard* that Victoria Cross (Annie Sophie Cory's pseudonym) was testing what the mainstream book market was prepared to allow in terms of sexual subject matter. Cross and her publisher, John Long, were clearly prepared to risk the wrath of moral guardians, in the knowledge that this censure would encourage a rewarding *succès de scandale*.

Cross's background as a novelist had accustomed her to some degree of notoriety before the publication of *Anna Lombard*. Early work published in *The Yellow Book* and in John Lane's 'Keynote' series (*The Woman Who Didn't* (1895) written as Victoria Crosse) began to establish her name among a slew of 1890s writers whose work focused on problems inherent in relationships and marriage. But the eye-catching plot and undisguised erotic material in *Anna Lombard* were clearly designed by Cross to set her apart from the pack. This is evident in a number of set-piece moments in the novel which are calculated to establish the intensity of Gerald's erotic desire for Anna, before redirecting this energy towards the obsessive sexual jealousy he experiences when imagining his love rival. The pivotal episode in this respect sees Gerald, newly returned to Anna's town after his Burmese exile (and having now become engaged to her), deciding to 'steal into her compound' at night to 'gain a few delicious moments with her alone' (Cross 1901/2006: 51). Having equipped himself to play the lover, with his guitar slung across his shoulders, and with his 'heart beating to suffocation', he senses the sound of her breath coming from inside the house while he stands outside her window (52). Gerald's desire to respond to her with a 'joyful cry' of 'Anna' is, however, stifled by another sound from Anna's room, which comes to his ear 'clearer than the last':

> 'Ke khubsurat ho' ('how beautiful thou art'). It was Anna's voice and speaking in Hindustani. Her voice, and yet as I had never heard it. There seemed a deep contralto note in it – a vibration of intense passion. And I stood beneath, immovable, stunned and paralysed. Thick, intense, palpable silence for many seconds, and then again that deep whisper in the air, terribly distinct to my distended ear.
>
> 'Tumko ashik karti hun' ('I love you'), and then two long sighs, and then silence again, so long, so absolute that it seemed to mock all sound as dream. (Crosse 1895: 52)

Any ambiguity about this being a direct rendering of the climax of a sexual encounter is removed by Anna's later frank admission of her physical desire for Gaida Kahn: 'I am only too glad to submit' to a man, she tells Gerald, whose 'touch delights', adding that her body has forced her 'soul to submission' (55). Anna's 'passion' expressed in this carnal desire is, she argues, a form of 'madness' and should not be confused with the purer and sanctified love she feels for Gerald (54). But it is perhaps Anna's unwillingness to give up her visceral desire for Gaida (whom she has secretly married) that make the book's narrative line especially distinctive and challenging: Gerald avers that she 'lived her double life and divided herself between two loves, undisturbed' adding that 'circumstances seemed to lend themselves completely to her wishes' (69). What Cross manages here is an effective subversion of the gender balance evident in the more conventional forms of the love-triangle plot. In place of the man unable to overcome his lustful desires for a physically alluring but unsuitable lover, we have occupying that role instead, a General's daughter, who seemingly epitomised all that was healthy and desirable in English middle-class womanhood.

Cross's desire to extend the limits of what was deemed permissible in mainstream British fiction was not, in the first half of the decade anyway, noticeably matched by the efforts of her contemporaries. Those writers who gained a reputation for dealing with issues related to sex in their work tended to remain relatively decorous when describing acts of physical intimacy and its possible contingencies. Whereas Cross's publisher, John Long, was clearly prepared to support her literary experimentation, other firms preferred not to risk unseemly battles with moral gatekeepers such as the National Vigilance Association (NVA) – an organisation founded in 1885 to protect the public from what was perceived to be the growing tide of vice then besetting the British people. For other publishing firms and writers, glamorous overseas settings were widely employed to licence those descriptions of sexual encounters that might, as the *Edinburgh Review* critic had argued, prove unacceptable if set at home. A case in point here is Robert Hichens' massively successful *The Garden of Allah* (1904), a novel which single-handedly inspired the category of 'desert romance' fiction; this form of writing reached the peak of its popularity in 1919 with the publication of E. M. Hull's international bestseller *The Sheik*, and its subsequent 1921 film version starring Rudolph Valentino. Hichens' novel, set in the Sahara Desert, concerns the ill-fated and improbable love affair between the statuesque English noblewoman, Domini Enfilden, and her angst-ridden Russian lover, Boris Androvsky, an absconding Trappist monk. While the book promises its readers an erotic crescendo to the protracted desert courtship and marriage enacted in its pages, it actually delivers a singularly bathetic climax to this narrative: 'She did not resist him. Still holding her in his arms he blew out the lamp' (Hull 1919: 316). This rare example of economy in prose for the normally prolix Hichens underlines his desire to avoid unduly offending the sensitivity of his readers. Hichens wanted instead to achieve a frisson of erotic excitement which would titillate while not overstepping the line of decency. His approach in *The Garden of Allah* was intriguingly dissected in a review of that novel in the *Speaker*. Here the reviewer, noting that Hichens' previous novel, *The Woman with the Fan* (1904), had drawn 'too bold a picture of fashionable "fastness" to please public opinion', went on to clarify this statement:

> People liked the suggestiveness of the scenes of luxurious depravity, but shook their heads over the dubious moral. But there can be no mistake about the high ethical standard of *The Garden of Allah*. There is a happy absence of unpleasant truths; there is the fervour of feminine 'passion' in moral flood; there is the *chic* feeling of Bond-street *toilettes* and nice up-to-date breeding *vis-à-vis* with the terrible and emancipating radiance of the desert skies. Withal, the book's moral plane is so singularly elevating and the heroine's somewhat irregular attitude is so inspired by altruistically pure motives that the most particular vicaress might put down the book feeling an inward glow of spiritual purification. Mr. Hichens has instinctively comprehended that the pleasing stimulants of 'passion' are drugs not acceptable to the British public unless made up and presented in neat and soluble moral capsules. (Anonymous 1904b: 319)

The final point here acknowledges the Christian morality in the text, a quality that sets *The Garden of Allah* apart from other fiction discussed in this section; the *Speaker*'s reviewer suggesting that the novel would answer 'the spiritual requirements of the most fastidious minds'. The plot of Hichens' novel hinges on the Catholic Domini's decision to return her husband Androvsky to the monastery from which he has absconded. Domini's rationale for acting against the instinct of her heart is dictated by her conviction that indulgence in worldly bliss now, in defiance of Androvsky's holy orders, will result in eternal celestial separation for the couple. (As Claud Cockburn later argued, as late as 1904 readers of popular fiction were reassured by novels which appeared to be 'dealing with the most serious possible ideas' (1972: 45).) The escapist and often forbidden pleasure to which Hichens' readers were exposed was in this way licensed by the payment of a morality tax.

Towards the end of the Edwardian decade, Arnold Bennett (writing under the name Jacob Tonson for his 'Books and Persons' column in the *New Age*) reflected upon the fact that Elinor Glyn's racy novels, which had continued to appear with regularity since *The Visits of Elizabeth*, had largely evaded censorship. This thought was prompted by the publication of Glyn's novel *His Hour* (1910), which Bennett dubbed 'magnificently sexual'. He went on (with characteristic irony) to suggest that 'the source of the deepest gratification to me, Jacob Tonson, is the fact that the Censorship Committee of the United Circulating Libraries, should have allowed this noble, daring, and masterly work to pass freely over their counters' (Bennett 1910a: 41). By contrast, two novels which Bennett considered more temperate in tone and content, Mary Gaunt's *The Uncounted Cost* (1910) and John Trevena's *Bracken* (1910), had recently been banned by library censors: the latter novel, Bennett suggested, contained 'nothing that for sheer brave sexuality can be compared to a score of passages in *His Hour*'. Bennett cites the impressive dedicatee of *His Hour* (Her Imperial Highness the Grand Duchess Vladimir of Russia), suggesting cynically that Trevena had missed a trick in failing to secure the patronage of an equivalently aristocratic figure to guarantee his own '*savoir-vivre*' (Bennett 1910a: 41). In making these arch interventions on the then highly topical issue of literary censorship, Bennett underlined the lack of a centralised regulation of published texts in Britain. While he was not encouraging the introduction of such a regulatory body, Bennett lamented the fact that, in its place, self-appointed moral gatekeepers were often empowered to make *ad hoc* judgements on what they considered to be offending texts. Unlike the stage, for which the Lord Chamberlain had acted as censor of plays since the passing of the Licensing Act in 1737, the publishing profession was largely a self-regulating body at this time, and so, aside from the 1857 Obscene Publications Act (which anyway failed to set out a definition of what might constitute an 'obscene' publication), decisions on inappropriate printed material were generally left for private individuals and committees to decide. It was in this rather uncertain climate, during the first seven years of the decade, that novels such as *Anna Lombard* and Glyn's racy *Three Weeks* circulated with little serious complaint, while James Joyce's *Dubliners* (originally accepted for publication in 1906) was not released because of publisher Grant Richards' anxieties about possible prosecution; the anxieties of his printer were also a central factor here, because under existing law, the printer was directly liable for the material he produced. While more intrepid firms and writers, such as John Long and Victoria Cross, published and waited to be damned, others stuck fearfully to what they perceived as the undrawn line of public decency.

From around 1907, however, the issue of censorship in British publishing became the topic of much more urgent public discussion. The timing of this intensification of debate was prompted to some degree by a perception among critics that the self-regulation of publishing was failing adequately to police the industry. While it is difficult to verify the extent to which print discussions of sexual topics were actually becoming more 'advanced' at this time, both Peter Keating and David Trotter recognise the second half of the decade as a watershed period for novels of this type: Trotter suggests that the 'sex novel' reached its zenith between 1905 and 1914, during which time it appeared especially 'dangerous to the purity groups because it was explicit' (1993/1998: 207–8). Keating also identifies 1905 as the date from which 'literary journalists and moral reformers began drawing attention' to this literary form, but he refines this dating somewhat when arguing that 'throughout 1907 and 1908 the sex-novel consolidated its position' (208, 209). Whether or not 'shameless and shameful fiction' was indeed 'increasing at a rate without example', as 'A Man of Letters' argued in an article entitled 'The Fleshly School of Fiction: A Protest against the Degradation of the Modern Novel' in the *Bookman* in October 1907, accusations of this type created an acute awareness of the likelihood of a growing tide of 'degenerate' literature. The tenor of this debate is well captured in the following doomsday scenario evoked by the 'Man of Letters':

> Dissolution has set in, provoked by the agents of death which cannot thrive except where Heaven's sweet air is shut out and darkness holds rule. Yesterday, Paris almost alone spread the plague. To-day it rages in London. Fashionable publishers keep it in stock; newspapers advertise it in spicy paragraphs; women's clubs and afternoon teas reek with its odours; is it not time to ask whether we want this tainted literature among us, and if not, how we shall get rid of it? (Anonymous 1907c: 25)

Rallying cries such as this, vociferously supported by prominent campaigning groups such as the NVA, looked to identify and then eliminate egregious examples of 'tainted literature'. Among the most prominent of their targets during this period was *The Yoke*, a novel written by Hubert Wales and published in 1907 by John Long. The watchfulness that singled out and successfully halted further publication of Wales' novel in 1908 was a feature of the decade's final years, as the debate regarding literary censorship became increasingly polarised.

While prosecutions of mainstream publishers for issuing indecent literature in Britain were rare, the spectre of the trials and imprisonment of Henry Vizetelly in 1889 for publishing English translations of Émile Zola's work were still, in the Edwardian period, relatively fresh in the collective memory. The NVA had been behind the Vizetelly prosecution, and was also at the forefront of subsequent Edwardian morality campaigns. But in the case of *The Yoke* prosecution, it was the *Academy* rather than the NVA which initially identified it as an indecent novel, and went on to attack it in a sustained campaign. Only when this campaign appeared to be stalling in its aim to bring about the banning of the book did the NVA take over the initiative and carry out its own successful prosecution. It is clear from an examination of numerous inflammatory editorial articles that appeared in the *Academy* on the topic of 'undesirable books' during 1908 that the paper's editor, Lord Alfred Douglas (Oscar Wilde's former lover), initially targeted the publisher, John Long, before training his focus upon specific novels issued by this firm; although the editorial articles in the *Academy* were unsigned, they were almost certainly written by Douglas himself, with the probable cooperation of T. W. H. Crosland, his pugnacious sub-editor. Douglas originally picked his fight with John Long after the *Academy* had received for review two other 'indecent' books from that publisher: Victoria Cross's *Five Nights* (1908) and Cosmo Hamilton's *Keepers of the House* (1908). Unusual in the *Academy* article was its willingness to identify specific examples of what it called 'wicked and unregenerate' literature. Earlier protests against degenerate books (such as that outlined by the *Bookman*'s 'A Man of Letters' in 'The Fleshly School of Fiction' article) had carefully avoided naming names in an effort, one assumes, to prevent increasing the sales of exemplary titles. But an *Academy* article entitled 'Broad and Long' in the 30 May edition of the periodical was evidently designed to draw up battle lines between moral and immoral parties in more specific terms. The extent to which the *Academy* under Douglas's stewardship wanted to raise the stakes in this matter can be gauged from the article's following proposition:

> We believe that if the police made a raid on Mr. Long's premises and confis-cated such copies of [Cross's *Five Nights*] as they might happen to find there they would be well within their function. Twenty years ago they would have done it, and, so far as we are aware, the law about these things has not been changed in those twenty years. (Anonymous 1908a: 832)

Although this article included the name of Hubert Wales, among others of John Long's 'elegant pornographers', no novel of his was singled out at this stage. Instead Douglas focused on Cross's novel to justify his righteous indignation:

> there is probably not a single page [of that novel] which we could print *in extenso* in these columns ... Miss Cross deliberately overrides all the basic conventions with regard to the relationship between man and woman, and she does it in the most brazen, unblushing, and impudent manner. (Anonymous 1908a: 832)

Cross's gender clearly compounded the felony for the near-hysterical Douglas.

Given the vehemence of this attack against *Five Nights*, it is perhaps surprising that it was *The Yoke* (a novel originally published in January 1907), rather than Cross's work, that was singled out for more sustained attack by the *Academy* from August 1908. But although the timing of the attack was surprising, *The Yoke*'s content made it a prime target for the attention of moralistic critics once it had appeared on the radar. Wales's novel is centrally concerned with the sex drive and the need to ensure that this drive, rather than being suppressed, is satisfied in a healthy way. Society as it is currently ordered, the novel suggests, drives young men towards the use of prostitutes in order to relieve their urgent sexual needs: the dire consequences of this method of relief are meted upon one of the novel's characters who dies after becoming infected with venereal disease following sex with a prostitute. While Samuel Hynes correctly identifies the emergence in June 1908 of a one-shilling 'popular' edition of *The Yoke* as a primary reason for its belated prosecution, his suggestion that the cheaper edition was considered more harmful by campaigners because of its broader potential readership among 'the young and the impressionable poor' appears less convincing (Hynes 1968/1991: 291). A more probable reason for scapegoating *The Yoke* was that the novel's shilling edition arrived in the *Academy*'s office for review shortly after the initial warning was issued to John Long about his 'indecent' publications, and its appearance reignited that earlier challenge. It was therefore an accident of timing rather than a more considered class-based rationale that placed Wales' novel at the forefront of the *Academy*'s campaign, and the NVA's subsequent prosecution. Yet once *The Yoke* had appeared on the *Academy*'s radar, the proposal of action against the novel was immediately and vehemently instigated. The *Academy* took a predictably high-handed position in relation to the novel's content, and after quoting passages of various Acts of Parliament (which the paper's solicitor had suggested might be applied to an 'indecent publication'), the following question was posed: 'Does Mr Wales's book fall properly under the head of an indecent or obscene work?' Having answered this question in the affirmative, the article continued:

> We believe that a jury of intelligent men would agree with us, and we do not believe that either Mr. Wales or Mr. Long could find a member of the Bar who would be willing to stand up in court and read out aloud [*The Yoke*] and contend that it was decent. We shall not sully these pages with a résumé of the vile tale Mr. Wales unfolds. We will only say of it that if it means anything at all it means unthinkable and unspeakable things. (Anonymous 1908b: 227)

The article's threatening tone is underlined by its conclusion, unambiguously setting out the paper's demands:

> If the book is withdrawn there is an end of the matter; if it is not withdrawn Mr. Long is not unlikely to hear from us again. We do not propose to be mealy-mouthed about such scandals, and if the need arises we shall not hesitate to take off the gloves. (Anonymous 1908b: 227)

Although Douglas and the *Academy* decided not to pursue this matter through the courts, the NVA readily stepped in on their behalf, and the paper was able to report the successful prosecution of *The Yoke* in their 19 December edition. John Long, having been summoned for selling, publishing and uttering 'a certain indecent, lewd, wicked, scandalous, obscene libel' containing 'divers lewd, impure, gross and obscene matters', undertook to discontinue the novel's publication, and the magistrate ordered the destruction of warehoused copies of the book. But as Douglas quickly recognised, this was only a pyrrhic victory for the NVA. While *The Yoke* was banned from further publication, Long was not (as had happened to Vizetelly following his initial trial) obliged to desist from issuing titles with similar subject matter. As Douglas noted, there was 'nothing to prevent [Long] from publishing at any moment an even fouler book than "The Yoke," if he can find one'; and, as Douglas further repined:

> it is plain that all [Long] has to do is to procure Mr. Wales to supply him with a new masterpiece, and to go on publishing it for all he is worth until the National Vigilance Society wakes up again, which will probably not be before the end of another twelvemonth. (Anonymous 1908b: 227)

The significance of Douglas's intemperate reflections for the wider Edwardian censorship debate are evident here. While the successful prosecution of *The Yoke* might have appeared a triumph for morality campaigners, and was certainly promoted in this way by the NVA, it was only with the institution of a centralised official censor of printed material that this isolated victory might be translated into a more programmatic control of literary publishing. But without government appetite to tighten up the laws controlling fiction in this way, successful actions against legitimate publishers were likely to remain symbolic, rather than more broadly significant.

While the freedom of Edwardian mainstream literature to discuss sex and sex relations continued to be circumscribed by perceptions of what was acceptable in print, there is little real sense that the moral campaigns of the decade succeeded in reining in the desires of Cross, Wales and Wells (whose *Ann Veronica* had caused moral panic in some quarters in 1909) to write with at least some degree of freedom on this topic. In this respect, it is difficult to argue with Hynes' conclusions that morality crusaders 'were at war with the twentieth century, and it was a war that could not be won'. But Hynes' additional claim that 'moral improvement movements' such as the NVA 'won many skirmishes and, like the Boers, succeeded in harassing for years the enemy that they could not defeat', can equally and instructively be recast (Hynes 1968/1991: 280). We might instead consider Cross, Wales and Wells as representing the guerrilla combatants of the literary world, largely fighting from cover in defence of the right to express themselves with freedom in their work. While 'sex novel' writers such as Glyn skirmished more openly and in more overtly commercial ways, others adopted ethical positions to justify their warfare on behalf of the new century's potential freedoms. The often hysterical interventions of the forces ranged on the moral side of this argument were ultimately counter-productive to their cause. In describing individual, and often serious-minded works of fiction, as 'tainted', 'pornographic' and 'poisonous', self-appointed moral guardians, such as Douglas in the *Academy* and Wells' antagonist John St Loe Strachey in the *Spectator*, made it all too easy for their targets to appear measured and reasonable in counter-attack. Neither the bulk of Edwardian readers nor the Edwardian establishment at large appears to have had a serious appetite for the sort of new moral fundamentalism demanded by the purity wing of the debate. While the banning of D. H. Lawrence's *The Rainbow* in 1915 and James Joyce's *Ulysses* in 1922 confirms that individual works were still vulnerable to suppression as the century progressed, the actions of campaigning editors, the NVA and library committees were ultimately unable to prevent such liberated figures as Anna Lombard or Ann Veronica from making themselves heard.

The Emergence of the Motorcar

Although motorcars began to appear on British roads at the end of the nineteenth century, the concept of motoring only came of age during the early years of the new century. Like the sex literature discussed in the previous section, Edwardian writing on this new technological marvel engaged with a topic that was exciting, provocative and endlessly divisive. It is difficult from a twenty-first-century perspective to reconstruct a sense of the car's ability to polarise public opinion, but its apparent capacity to manipulate time and space was almost bound to inspire reactions which ranged from wide-eyed wonder to fear and dread. And, unlike other forms of new Edwardian technology such as the wireless, cinema and aeroplane, the growing prevalence of the motorcar after 1900 meant it was almost impossible to avoid; the frequent appearance of motorcars in the pages of *Punch* from 1900 indexes its relentless incursion onto the roads of Britain and into the pages of its literary culture. A knowledge of the ways in which this shock of the new was incorporated into Edwardian literature complicates the notion that Edwardian writers, in common with those Georgian poets who followed, were wholly resistant to the sort of change epitomised by the coming of the machine. Edwardians were, in fact, fascinated with speed and power, even when this fascination was underpinned by apprehension. It is, perhaps, especially among those writers who denounced the blight of motor transport that we can best gauge the dangerous and seductive appeal of this increasingly ubiquitous machine. Their anxiety betrayed an insistent sense that, far from being just another passing technological fad, the motorcar would transform all our lives for good. This knowledge ensured that it rapidly became a vital topic of discussion across all forms of Edwardian literary culture.

The rapid shift of the motorcar in public consciousness, from the sort of fantastical projection that might be encountered in an H. G. Wells novel to a position of general familiarity, can be traced via parliamentary legislation and registration statistics. Only a short period before the start of the new century, the Locomotives on Highways Act (1896) had increased their maximum speed limit to 14mph, and abolished the old red flag rule; the latter legislation had obliged mechanised vehicles to be preceded by a flag-waving pedestrian. Although this legislation began to liberate early motorcars from the strict controls which initially governed them, they remained a rare sight in Britain until after 1900, when the production of new vehicles began steadily to increase; the first national registration figures indicate that there were already roughly 8,500 private cars by 1904, with this figure nearly doubling within a year, and then nearly doubling again to 32,500 by 1907. By the end of the decade (when there were 53,000 registered cars among a total of 143,000 general motor vehicles in use), it is reasonable to assume that the vast majority of British people had seen a motorcar, even if they had not actually travelled in one (Plowden 1973: 482). L. P. Hartley's autobiographical novel, *The Shrimp and the Anemone* (1944), evokes the arrival of the motorcar in a Norfolk seaside town in the summer of 1905. When the novel's central character, a small boy named Eustace, is briefly missing from his home, the family servant expresses anxiety about the possible cause of his disappearance: 'we were afraid he might have been run over by one of those motor-car things. I saw another yesterday, that makes four in a fortnight' (Hartley 1944/1971: 80). By this date, as Hartley's text suggests, the novelty value of the car in provincial Britain was rapidly passing as the motorist became an established presence on its roads.

In the earlier years of the century, when the sight of a car on the road was still a newsworthy event, much curiosity was generated about the physical sensation of motor travel. This form of transport, the general public seemed instinctively to grasp, would offer a very different experience for travellers from that of earlier mechanised vehicles such as the railway train or bicycle. Readers of the February 1902 edition of *Harper's* magazine had this supposition confirmed in an article that offered a vivid introduction to the physical and metaphysical repercussions of motoring at speed. Here, Maurice Maeterlinck, the Belgian playwright and essayist, reflected on the sense of transformation that would engulf an individual when travelling fast in what he called 'the marvellous beast':

> A great desire comes over us to be alone in Space with this unknown animal that dates but from yesterday; we burn to discover what it is in itself, what it grants and what it withholds, what obedience it will offer to its strange master, and what new lesson the new horizon may teach us, wherein we shall be plunged to the very soul by a force that, issuing now, and for the first time, from the exhaustless reservoir of undisciplined forces, permits us in one day to absorb as much landscape and sky, as mighty a spectacle, as in former days would have been granted to us in the course of an entire life. (Maeterlinck 1902: 397)

To a readership still speculating about the long-term viability of motorcars, which were in 1902 prohibitively expensive and notoriously unreliable (in Kipling's 1902 story, 'Steam Tactics', the narrator's steam car breaks down (Kipling 1904: 177–210); Act Two of Shaw's *Man and Superman* (1903) opens with a broken-down car occupying the centre of the stage (47)), Maeterlinck brushed aside practical difficulties while forcing readers to engage their latent sense of wonder. This quality would become active, he proclaimed, for all those who were prepared to submit to the motorcar's marvellous capacity to conquer time and space. The seductive quality of speed, the key component in this conquest, is exposed by Maeterlinck in its raw and insistent appeal:

> I conquer the plains, which bow down before me. Slowly do I turn the mysterious 'advance ignition' handle, and regulate as well as I can the admission of the petrol. The pace grows faster and faster: the delirious wheels send forth a shrill and eager cry. And at first the road comes moving towards me like a bride waving palms, rhythmically keeping time to some melody of gladness. But soon it grows frantic, springs forward, and throws itself madly upon me, rushing under the car like a furious torrent, whose foam dashes over my face; it drowns me beneath its waves; it blinds me with its breath. Oh, that wonderful breath! (Maeterlinck 1902: 398)

Noticeable here is the way in which Maeterlinck conveys to readers the sensation of speed by animating the nature around the onrushing car. As Sara Danius argues, Maeterlinck's description of the roadside atmosphere flying past the car creates an exhilarating procession in which 'it is not the car but nature that acquires agency' (Classen 2005: 413). Danius helpfully connects early attempts such as these to render the feeling of rapid motorcar movement to the spectacle of early cinema: she cites the French writer Octave Mirbeau's 1907 motoring 'novel', *La 628-E 8* (the title refers to the licence plate of a car involved in a European tour), as an example of a text in which 'the world emerges as a film' through the introduction of a 'succession of moving images' (Mirbeau 1907: 414). Taking into account the parallel emergence of the moving image with that of the car, it seems logical that one new form of revolutionary technology should be employed to help readers understand another. There is certainly a sense in Maeterlinck's prose of the need to find new and dramatic ways in which to jolt readers into some comprehension of the motorcar's potential to act as an agent of perspectival and philosophical liberation.

Here, some seven years before Marinetti placed the car and 'the beauty of speed' at the centre of his Manifesto of Futurism (stating 'we intend to hymn man at the steering wheel, the ideal axis of which intersects the earth, itself hurled ahead in its own race along the path of its orbit'), we can already see the roots of this influential Modernist art movement taking hold (Rainey et al. 2009: 51). For the largely mainstream readers of *Harper's* in 1902, their introduction to the motorcar heralded the symbolic start of the new century, one in which the full potential of the machine age might be unlocked. But Maeterlinck's remarkable celebration of speed and evocation of the potential of the machine to conquer space and time, perhaps understandably, gained a mixed reception from Edwardian commentators. A diary piece in the *Academy* mockingly quoted from Maeterlinck's article, before suggesting that it would now be 'interesting to have [his] interpretations of a steam-roller, and alarm-clock, and a penny-in-the-slot weighing-machine' (Anonymous 1902c: 104). Elsewhere, however, the significance and implications of Maeterlinck's words were registered in more serious ways, and this recognition often came from unexpected sources. While Edward Thomas might now be considered the high priest of early Georgian ruralism, he was sensitive to the broader implications of Maeterlinck's writing on the motorcar, going as far as to suggest that it had managed 'to reconcile science and poetry'. Thomas further argued that readers should 'applaud this essay' because of the reassurance that it offered that 'mechanical inventions do not destroy adventure and romance' (Thomas 1911: 1, 2). In the ensuing twentieth-century machine age, Thomas suggested, new ways of thinking about adventure and romance might evolve alongside such 'marvellous' mechanical beasts as that conjured to life in Maeterlinck's vivid prose. Kipling, an early motoring enthusiast, offers evidence of the ways in which the motorcar might facilitate romance in his story 'They', which first appeared in book form in *Traffics and Discoveries* (1904). This story depicts a motorist driving across the Sussex Downs ('snapping forward of a lever, I let the county flow under my wheels' (Kipling 1904: 303)), before becoming disoriented and stumbling upon an ancient house. In the grounds of this house the motoring narrator encounters what he later realises are the ghosts of dead children. The motorcar's ability to cover large swathes of remote Sussex countryside convincingly sets up the portal through which this fairy-tale-like encounter can take place. Far from being the enemy of romance, in Kipling's story the motorcar becomes its facilitator.

The potential marriage of adventure and romance in the motorcar is something that Edwardian writing beyond Kipling appeared enthusiastic to promote. Long before the publication of Marinetti's Manifesto of Futurism, British popular writers were celebrating their own sense of an exhilarating technology-driven modernity. Elinor Glyn, in *The Visits of Elizabeth* (one of the 'sex' novels discussed in the previous section), was by 1900 promoting the motorcar as an agent of decadent pleasure. It is in France, very much the cradle of the motorcar's technical development, that Elizabeth first experiences this new and dynamic force:

> It is lovely motor-carring; you get quite used to the noise and smell, and you fly along so, it takes your breath away; even with your hat tied on with a big veil, you have rather the feeling you have got to screw up your eyebrows to keep it from blowing away. We seemed to be no time in doing the ten miles. (Glyn 1900/1901: 132)

While Glyn employs the car as a totem of life spent in the lap of the sophisticated glamour of high society, she is also anticipating Maeterlinck's (and later Marinetti's) sense of the raw appeal of the speeding motorcar. 'Motor-carring', as she terms it here, might be distinctly uncomfortable, with noise and smell assailing nose and ears, but it's also clearly breathtaking, in both senses of that expression. Like Maeterlinck, Glyn's narrator implies that the discomfort contingent on motor travel is something that only the dull and unimaginative would fixate upon. For those readers who considered themselves advanced, the experience of 'motor-carring' was evidently an essential one. The motorcar's glamorous presence in writing such as Glyn's helped to establish its appeal for a generation keen to associate themselves with all things modern.

These qualities are also much evident in C. N. and A. M. Williamson's *The Lightning Conductor: The Strange Adventures of a Motor-Car* (1902), a novel published in the same year as Maeterlinck's article. The Williamsons, a rare husband-and-wife novel-writing team, recognised the potential for novels based on the motorcar to appeal to progressive-minded Edwardian readers of romance; the Williamsons' novel was singled out by one critic as an example of the 'successful adaptation of romance to modern requirements' (Anonymous 1902a: 308). The titles of their Edwardian novels, including *My Friend the Chauffeur* (1905), *The Car of Destiny* (1906), *The Botor Chaperon* (1907) (this time featuring a motor-boat), and *The Motor Maid* (1909), indicate their success in blending these literary elements. *The Lightning Conductor*, which is clearly indebted to Glyn's methods and materials, offers a hybrid of romance and travel narrative through a collection of letters written by the principal characters. These letters trace a journey through France and Italy undertaken by a beautiful American heiress and her chauffeur, who is actually an English gentleman under cover. On their trip, freed by the motorcar from being tied down to a time-table, they have ample opportunity to experience and convey to their interlocutors the compelling sensation of rapid motor travel. Here, for example, the disguised chauffeur, Jack Winston, describes what it feels like to encounter an oncoming car while motoring through southern France:

> We met no other vehicles; we seemed to have the world to ourselves; but once, far along the road, we spied a black dot which seemed to come towards us at incredible speed, growing larger as it came. In less time than it takes to write we saw that it was an enormous racing automobile, probably undergo-ing a test of speed. We were running at our highest pace, perhaps forty-five miles an hour; the thing approaching us was coming at seventy or more. You may imagine the rush of air as we passed each other. One glimpse we had of a masked automobilist like a figure of Death in an Albert Dürer cartoon, or the familiar of a Vehmgericht, and then we were gasping in the vortex of air caused by the speed of the gigantic car. Almost before we could turn our heads it was a black dot again on the horizon. Perhaps it was the great Fournier himself. (Williamson and Williamson 1902/n.d.: 176)

The growing and then receding black dot, an image once again reminis-cent of early cinema, communicates the unfamiliar perspectival shift that would be experienced by a car's driver and passengers. This apparently fantastical sight is grounded in real life by the introduction of two telling details: the identification of Henri Fournier, an early celebrity of motor racing, as a likely candidate for the 'masked automobilist'; and the speed of the onrushing racing car estimated at 'seventy or more'. Readers of the novel would probably be aware that Fournier had broken the land speed record for the mile in 1902 (with a then-astonishing speed of 76mph) and the knowledge of this fact is clearly intended to animate the fiction by grounding it in fact.

Also noticeable in the Williamsons' account of the speeding car is the proximity of death. The masked driver is imagined here as the 'figure of Death', marching inexorably on while leaving the observer in a 'vortex of air'. Other early accounts of motoring in British literature foregrounded the connections between speed and death, with the potential for death seemingly adding to the thrill of the ride. G. Stewart Bowles' 1903 poem 'The Song of the Wheel', which originally appeared in *Car Magazine*, offers a celebration of the raw and dangerous power generated by the car. The lyric voice of this verse is articulated by the motorcar itself:

> Fire in the Heart of me, moving and chattering,
> Youth in each part of me, slender and strong,
> Death at the foot of me, rending and shattering,
> Light and tremendous I bear you along;
> Up to the brow where the levels go wearily,
> Down to the vale where the gravels give speed,
> Holding it, moulding it, scolding it cheerily,
> Slave to your purpose and sign of your need. (Young 1904: 310)

While Stewart Bowles' jaunty rhymes were designed to entertain a coterie readership of motorists, they also identified a key battleground that had emerged around the motorcar by this time. The image here of the motorcar as agent of a Nietzschean 'Superman', one whose animated machine is capable of wielding the power of life and death, was also commonly invoked by those protesting against the motor age. C. F. G. Masterman, in his 1909 study *The Condition of England*, lamented that the actions of

> a section of the motoring classes . . . in their annexation of the highways and their indifference to common traditions stands almost alone as an example of wealth's intolerable arrogances, and has certainly excited more resentment amongst the common people than any extravagance of pleasure or political reaction. (Masterman 1909/1910: 65)

Long before Masterman's withering judgement on motoring arrogance, Marie Corelli, the bestselling novelist, outlined an equivalent position (albeit in a very different register) in her 1902 story entitled 'The Devil's Motor: A Fantasy'. This tale was designed to counter what Corelli dubbed the 'inane dullness and melancholy stupidity of "society" as it exists in this present gloriously-progressive Motor-Era' (Corelli 1902: 3). Her quasi-Biblical fantasy imagines the Devil piloting a monstrous car, which destroys all in its wake:

> mingling with the grinding roar of its wheels came other sounds . . . yells and shrieks and groans of torture, – the screams of the suffering, the sobs of the dying, – and as the Fiend drove on with swiftly quickening speed, men and women and little children were trampled down one upon another and

killed in their thousands, and the Car was splashed thick with human blood. (Corelli 1902: 145–6)

Corelli's abhorrence of the veneration of speed in the modern era is underlined when the Devil-motorist screams out his rallying cry: 'Progress and Speed! ... Rush on, world, with me! – Rush on!' (146). G. K. Chesterton, in an article which appeared in the *Illustrated London News* in 1910, echoed Corelli's sense of the wrongheadedness of those who saw progress as synonymous with the modern machine. Looking back from the end of the Edwardian decade, Chesterton returned to the motorcar's original prophet, Maeterlinck, for his own sober assessment of its place in modern society: 'Maeterlinck may go perpetually swifter and smoother in his modern motor car through throngs of modern, timid, and evasive men. But there will be a frightful clash and collision when he first runs into a child' (Chesterton 1910: 4). By the time this article appeared, a number of children had indeed been killed in motor accidents and these deaths received widespread media coverage, which encouraged further waves of literary protest: a fatal accident in April 1905, in which a child was killed by a chauffeur-driven car belonging to Hildebrand Harmsworth (the brother of Alfred Harmsworth, proprietor of the *Daily Mail* and the *Daily Mirror*), became a national *cause célèbre* (Plowden 1973: 51).

Considerations of the destructive power of the car were much in view when perhaps the most famous motorist in Edwardian literature, Mr Toad, appeared in Kenneth Grahame's *The Wind in the Willows* in 1908. The first appearance of a motorcar in this novel results in the smashing of the picturesque gipsy caravan in which Rat, Mole and Toad are making a leisurely tour of the countryside. In the prelude to this crash, Grahame carefully describes the movement of the approaching car in ways which mirror several of those motoring passages quoted above:

> Glancing back, they saw a small cloud of dust, with a dark centre of energy, advancing on them at incredible speed, while from out of the dust a faint 'poop-poop!' wailed like an uneasy animal in pain. Hardly regarding it, they turned to resume their conversation, when in an instant (as it seemed) the peaceful scene was changed, and a blast of wind and a whirl of sound that made them jump for the nearest ditch, it was on them! The 'poop-poop' rang with a brazen shout in their ears, they had a moment's glimpse of an interior of glittering plate-glass and rich morocco, and the magnificent motor-car, immense, breath-snatching, passionate, with its pilot tense and hugging his wheel, possessed all earth and air for the fraction of a second, flung an enveloping cloud of dust that blinded and enwrapped them utterly, and then dwindled to a speck in the far distance, changed back into a droning bee once more. (Grahame 1908: 19)

But unlike those texts which looked to celebrate the exhilaration of motorcar travel, Grahame's focal point here is its capacity for pain and destruction. The horse, startled by this uncanny apparition, backs the gipsy caravan to which it is harnessed into a ditch, where it is smashed to matchwood. Although Grahame invites readers to side with Rat in his cursing of the motorist and his passengers – 'You villains' he shouts shaking his fists, 'You scoundrels, you highwaymen, you – you – road-hogs! I'll have the law on you!' – Toad's articulation of the remarkable effects that the car has upon him complicates this simple taking of sides:

> [Rat and Mole] found [Toad] in a sort of trance . . . "Glorious, stirring sight!" murmured Toad . . . "The poetry of motion! The *real* way to travel! The *only* way to travel! Here to-day – in next week to-morrow! Villages skipped, towns and cities jumped – always somebody else's horizon! O bliss! O poop-poop! O my! O my! . . . And to think I never *knew*! . . . All those wasted years that lie behind me, I never knew, never even *dreamt*! But *now* – but now that I know, now that I fully realize! . . . What dust-clouds shall spring up behind me as I speed on my reckless way! What carts I shall fling carelessly into the ditch in the wake of my magnificent onset! (20)

All the energy in this scene is invested in Toad, who infectiously registers his wonder at the 'stirring sight'. Grahame, judging this scene from his own standpoint (that of a man approaching his fifties) probably under-estimated the extent to which Toad's beguilement might be shared by a younger generation of Edwardians. Rather than mourning the loss of the horse-drawn caravan and quiet country lane, youthful proto-futurists would understandably side with Toad when presented with his arresting vision of the world to come.

E. M. Forster, in his 1910 novel *Howards End*, appeared, like Grahame, to assume that readers would instinctively side with the ancient pastoral tradition in opposition to vulgar machine-age moder-nity. Here, the motor-loving capitalist Henry Wilcox occupies the role of Toad when clashing with the cultured intellectual Margaret Schlegel, who inhabits the structural position of Rat. On a 'motor-drive' ('a form of felicity' we are told that Margaret 'detested') from London to Wilcox's house in the country, Howards End, he remarks to her that 'The motor's come to stay . . . One must get about. There's a pretty church – oh, you aren't sharp enough. Well, look out, if the road worries you – right outward at the scenery' (Forster 1910/1989: 198). The novel's narrator then describes the effect on Margaret's eye of landscape viewed from a speeding motorcar: 'It heaved and merged like porridge. Presently it congealed. They had arrived' (199). While this passage satirises the wide-eyed lyricism of Maeterlinck's view from the motorcar, another scene in *Howards End* attacks the arrogant and destructive capacity of the 'Superman' motorist. Here Margaret is passenger in a car which apparently strikes a dog, causing its young owner to leave her roadside cottage and scream wildly at the motor party. Margaret's instinctive and compassionate reaction is to return to the scene to help in some way, but even after jumping from the moving car she is prevented from attending the site of the crash by her future stepson, Charles, who sees the killing of a mere pet as something that a wealthy motorist might resolve simply by writing a cheque: the fact that the crushed pet turns out to be 'only a rotten cat' rather than a dog makes this incident even more insignificant in the eyes of Charles and his male companions. The typically Forsterian summary of this incident divides the organic 'real' world of the compassionate Margaret from the superficial and meaningless world of the unfeeling Wilcoxes: 'They had no part with the earth and its emotions. They were dust, and a stink, and cosmopolitan chatter, and the girl whose cat had been killed had lived more deeply than they' (213). For Forster, the motorcar offered an eloquent symbol of one side of a schism, well established by 1910, between a modern world in which 'telegrams and anger count' (41), and an older worthwhile existence, rooted in land and tradition. Henry Wilcox's confidence in asserting that 'the motor's come to stay' suggests the extent to which *Howards End* was designed in part as a lament for the old ways crushed by 1910 under the motorcar's unstoppable wheel. The opening in the following year of Henry Ford's first European factory in Trafford Park, Manchester, seems to confirm the truth of Wilcox's confident assertion.

This position was already anticipated in a 1903 review of a translation of Nietzsche's *The Dawn of Day* which appeared in the *Athenaeum*: 'To disregard [Nietzsche] is like disregarding the motor-car because you prefer your carriage and pair. He is a new force, like electricity in its modern development' (Anonymous 1903a: 298). This pragmatic connection between radical new forces recognises the ways in which the inevitability of the motorcar era was immediately understood and indeed welcomed by many of those who lacked Forster's nostalgia for a prelapsarian Britain. Unsentimental writers such as George Bernard Shaw were quick to recognise the wider social repercussions that might accompany this unstoppable new force. In his play *Man and Superman* (1903), Shaw depicts, in the role of Henry Straker, the chauffeur, the potential power of the working-class engineer in modern society. As his wealthy employer, Jack Tanner, remarks, 'He positively likes the car to break down because it brings out my gentlemanly helplessness and his workmanlike skill and resource' (Shaw 1903/1928: 50–1). For Tanner, the Polytechnic-educated Straker is the embodiment of 'a very momentous social phenomenon'; while 'literary and cultured persons' had widely proclaimed the phenomenon 'of the New Woman whenever some unusually old fashioned female came along', Tanner avers that they had consistently failed to notice 'the advent of the New Man' (51). The growing centrality of the machine in the twentieth century promised 'New Men' such as Straker a vital share in the coming evolution of society. In Shaw's play, this transformation of society is already upon us, with Tanner claiming in an only partly tongue-in-cheek remark, that he is 'slave' to his chauffeur and his car (48). This truth is reinforced by a female member of Tanner's class, who confirms the chauffeur's indispensability: 'We are dependent on our motor cars; and our motor cars are dependent on him; so of course we are dependent on him' (147). In a prefatory letter published with the play text, Shaw acknowledged that the character of Straker, while apparently indebted to J. M. Barrie's shipwrecked butler Crichton in *The Admirable Crichton* (1902) (discussed in the next section) was more directly inspired by H. G. Wells' writing on 'the efficient engineering class'; according to Shaw, this was a class which Wells hoped would 'finally sweep the jabberers out of the way of civilisation' (Shaw 1903/1928: xxvii). Wells had discussed the significance of what he called this 'growing class' in his non-fiction work *Anticipations* (1901), noting that the coming technological era with its prevalent 'motor-cars, photographic and phonographic apparatus' would require a population of 'repairers, "accessory" dealers and working engineers'. As Wells presciently argued, this cohort, with its 'necessary intelligence and numbers' would 'play a very conspicuous part in the social development of the twentieth century' (Wells 1901/1902: 56, 57).

From a twenty-first-century perspective, it is possible to recognise the ways in which the motorcar and other new technologies of the Edwardian era would make a profound impact on the ensuing century. Although the centrality of the motorcar to everyday life is something we largely take for granted, many commentators in its early years saw it only as a harbinger of destruction and desolation. Criticism of this kind far outlasted the early 1900s, as an article written in 1924 by Virginia Woolf testifies. This article, which appeared in *Nation and Athenaeum* entitled 'The Cheapening of Motor-Cars', echoed Kenneth Grahame in bemoaning the ruin of the country road. Claiming that it was 'already almost impossible to take one's pleasure walking', Woolf goes on to remark that the English road had become 'black as cinders, smooth as oilcloth, shaven of wild flowers, straightened of corners, a mere racing-track for the convenience of a population seemingly in perpetual and frantic haste not to be late for dinner' (Woolf 1988: 440). But in a diary entry less than three years later, in August 1927, Woolf suggests a *volte face* on this issue. Having bought a motorcar with the profits from *To the Lighthouse* (a second-hand Singer costing £275), Woolf quickly abandoned her original resistance to this form of transport: 'Soon we [she and Leonard Woolf] shall look back on our pre-motor days as we do now at our days in the caves' (Woolf 1980: 151). So, some twenty years after Mr Toad recognised 'all those wasted years' before he had encountered the wonderful motorcar, Woolf appears to have shared his transformation. Indeed, the majority of the Edwardian motor-phobics discussed in this section either willingly or more reluctantly accepted the convenience of motor travel: Marie Corelli, for example, made her own *volte face* on this issue when she bought her first motorcar, a Daimler, in 1910. To turn one's back on the motorcar from this time onwards became a sign of eccentricity in the same way that to refuse air travel would signify oddity for a later generation of travellers. Like it or not, by the end of the Edwardian decade, the motorcar really had, to borrow Henry Wilcox's formulation, 'come to stay'.

New Drama and Money

The question of money and its role in British society at the start of the twentieth century is at the heart of much of the material already discussed in this chapter. While such popular writers as Elinor Glyn celebrated the abundant freedoms and pleasures afforded by wealth in this exciting new epoch, more conservative voices decried the corrosive influence of money on modern life and morals. The start of the new century seemed an apposite moment to re-evaluate the role of money in society, especially in the decade's drama. This section will focus on a number of Edwardian plays which took advantage of the period's new theatrical initiatives to investigate this pressing issue. It is particularly appropriate to use drama as a way to examine this topic because what appeared on the Edwardian stage was, to a large extent, dictated by financial imperatives. From the content of plays, to the internal and external design of buildings in which they were performed, Edwardian commercial theatre was governed by the perceived taste of an affluent but culturally conservative audience; even the conventional eight o'clock curtain time for evening performances was chosen to allow theatregoers to take early dinner before the play began. In this atmosphere, as Ian Clarke argues, 'the dominant social tone of the theatre [was] a correlative of the furnishing and fitting of the more expensive parts of the house' (Clarke 1989: 5). Edwardian theatre followed Victorian precedent with light social comedies, which showcased fashionable society, elegant costumes and luxurious backdrops. Although some popular dramatists of the period did confront social issues in their work, this material was strictly controlled, to ensure that little offence was taken by a polite and respectable audience. One example of a play of this type is Arthur Wing Pinero's *His House in Order* (1906), which ran for an impressive 428 performances at St James's Theatre in London. While this play criticised the hypocrisy of its establishment characters, Pinero's comedy was engineered to ensure that it contained nothing likely to disturb an enjoyable evening out; Pinero's success in this respect can be measured by the £78,000 taken during the play's long London run (Clarke 1989: 19). Edwardian theatre was extremely lucrative for dramatists, producers and actors in tune with their audience, and in this climate, safe and unchallenging productions were guaranteed a handsome return on an investment.

While the majority of Edwardian drama was uninspiringly bland, certain popular plays managed to combine diverting entertainment with thought-provoking themes. J. M. Barrie's *The Admirable Crichton* (1902) and *Peter Pan* (1904), for example, blended amusement and spectacle with underlying commentary on the iniquitous organisation of present-day society. In *The Admirable Crichton*, for example, the practical and resourceful butler, Crichton, takes control when shipwrecked on a desert island with his wealthy employer's family. Here, in an environment in which inherited money and rank can offer no inalienable guarantee of survival, Crichton holds the key to the family's continued existence. Barrie dramatises the ways in which 'Nature', a key concept in the play, dictates a new meritocratic social structure in which the servant can become the master. But the final Act of the play, in which Crichton resumes his customary subordinate role following the rescue of the party from the island, underlines the injustice embedded in Edwardian social relations. The intelligent daughter of the house, Lady Mary Lasenby, confirms what has been evident throughout the play, when at the final curtain she tells Crichton 'you are the best man among us'. His clear-sighted rejoinder, 'on an island, my lady, perhaps; but in England, no' (Barrie 1999: 71), equally registers the changeless nature of a feudal society where individual worth is subordinated by entitlement. Although this ending might suggest a pessimistic assessment of the immutable state of society at the opening of the new century, the intellectual context in which the play emerged offers an alternative interpretation. Taken together with Shaw's depiction of the chauffeur Straker in *Man and Superman*, Barrie's Crichton endorses Wells' prediction of the inevitable rise of the technologically savvy 'New Man'; we witness this, for example, in the way in which Crichton's pre-eminence on the island is consolidated by the remarkable engineering projects that he designs and implements. Viewed in this way, Barrie's play illustrates the unsustainable nature of the old order and heralds its replacement by ability rather than rank. But it would be wrong to interpret *The Admirable Crichton* as a play which seeks primarily to press home a radical polemical agenda. Barrie constructed the script to appeal both to those audiences broadly sympathetic to the idea of an impending social revolution, alongside those who simply enjoyed the escapist entertainment of the play's topsy-turvydom.

The same might be said of Barrie's *Peter Pan*, its popularity undiminished since it opened in December 1904. Its political critique has largely been overlooked in latter-day pantomime productions, but the original play script made plain Barrie's disquiet at the profound effects of modern working practices on domestic family life. The Darling family, as witnessed in the play's opening Act, struggle to live a respectable middle-class life on their breadwinner father's modest earnings as an office clerk. The setting for this Act, the nursery of a shabby genteel house in Bloomsbury, is only kept together by Mrs Darling and the resourceful 'scrapings of her purse' (Barrie 1999: 87). Although Barrie's establishment of the Darlings' relative poverty is intentionally comic rather than tragic in tone (Nana, the family's Newfoundland dog, is pressed into service, because they 'could not afford to have a nurse' (88)), the invidious effects of keeping up appearances on a clerk's modest salary are plainly realised. The most profound consequence of this struggle is seen in Mr Darling, whose cowardliness and confusion about the role he should take up in relation to his children leaves him a comically pathetic figure; his weakness is illustrated particularly in his childlike need for reassurance – 'nobody coddles me. Oh dear no. I am only the breadwinner, why should I be coddled? Why, why why?' (95). But behind the comical failure who emerges from the play's opening Act, Mr Darling is (according to the stage directions) 'really a good man as breadwinners go' (90). Moreover, his liberation into the world of imagination in the 'Never Land' scenes (the actor playing Mr Darling conventionally doubles with the pirate Captain Hook) suggests an alternative and more spirited existence for him, one at variance with that of the hard-pressed drudge we encounter in the first and final Acts of the play. Set against Mr Darling's uncertain masculinity and effete wage-slavery, Peter Pan's world of perpetual play appears an enviable if unsustainable alternative. Peter himself confronts this choice of diverging destinies with Mrs Darling after she has offered to adopt him in the play's final Scene:

Peter: Would you send me to school?
Mrs Darling: (*obligingly*) Yes.
Peter: And then to an office?
Mrs Darling: I suppose so.
Peter: Soon I should be a man?
Mrs Darling: Very soon.
Peter: (*passionately*) I don't want to go to school and learn solemn things. No one is going to catch me, lady, and make me a man. I want always to be a little boy and to have fun. (Barrie 1999: 151)

The inevitable linkage here between manhood and the need to support domestic responsibilities by earning money in an uninspiring occupation makes Peter's decision to fly away a readily understandable act of resistance to modern life.

Issues such as this were addressed much more explicitly by the 'New Drama' that emerged in those repertory seasons offered at the Court, the Savoy and the Duke of York's theatres in London between 1904 and 1910. These seasons revitalised drama in Britain by providing a platform for new work largely free of the pressing need for long runs and contingent profit. Their key dramatists, George Bernard Shaw, Harley Granville Barker and John Galsworthy, were able to incorporate ideas and dramatic modes that the commercial theatre was reluctant to touch. The roots of this new movement in twentieth-century British theatre can be found in a number of play-producing societies, including the Independent Theatre Society (1891), the New Century Theatre (1897), and the Stage Society (1899). These societies staged short runs of work, moving between theatres as space to stage individual productions became available. By contrast, the repertory seasons associated with specific management teams offered a fixed location and a uniform company of actors for the plays that they staged. The most significant of these repertory seasons were those offered between 1904 and 1907 under the management of J. E. Vedrenne and Granville Barker at the Court Theatre. Among the plays that first appeared in the matinee performances presented during these seasons were Shaw's *John Bull's Other Island* (premiered 1904), *Man and Superman* (1905), *Major Barbara* (1905), and the *Doctor's Dilemma* (1906); new plays by novice playwrights, including Granville Barker's *The Voysey Inheritance* (1905), St John Hankin's *The Return of the Prodigal* (1905), Galsworthy's *The Silver Box* (1906), John Masefield's *The Campden Wonder* (1907) and Elizabeth Robins' suffrage play *Votes for Women!* (1907); and drama by major modern European playwrights including Henrik Ibsen, Gerhart Hauptmann, Arthur Schnitzler and Maurice Maeterlinck. The wider influence of the Court's initiative can be recognised in the establishment of repertory theatres specialising in 'New Drama' in a number of British cities, including Manchester (1907), Glasgow (1909), Liverpool (1911) and Birmingham (1913); these were all anticipated by Dublin's Abbey Theatre, which first opened in 1904. The fanning-out of the repertory movement beyond the metropolitan centre ensured a wider audience for new work that, according to Desmond MacCarthy's 1907 assessment of the Court's recent seasons, was marked by 'a critical, dissenting attitude towards contemporary codes of morality' (MacCarthy 1907: 15).

This willingness to take aim against the hypocrisy underlying modern codes of morality is central to St John Hankin's comedy *The Return of the Prodigal*, first staged at the Court in September 1905. It draws upon the well-known Biblical parable, in this case relocated to Chedleigh Court, the Gloucestershire country home of Samuel Jackson, a wealthy cloth manufacturer. The play begins with the return from Australia of Jackson's scapegrace son Eustace, a prodigal who has run through the £1,000 provided for him by his father. Unlike the Biblical story, no redemptive feast awaits the son following his reappearance, relationships in this modern transposition being governed by money and self-interest rather than familial love. This prodigal son, who honestly admits that he has no talent for any form of useful employment, looks instead to coin his potential to embarrass his family; a threat to install himself in the local workhouse is designed to undermine the air of respectability carefully controlled by the Jackson family. Eustace's father and brother prove perfect candidates for blackmail; Samuel Jackson, hoping for a seat as a Conservative MP, wants to prevent the politically sensitive news of his son's abject poverty coming to light; and Eustace's brother Henry is similarly concerned that public knowledge of his destitute sibling will upset his forthcoming marriage to a baronet's daughter. In this climate, the prodigal cuts through the family's veneer of decorum to spell out to them his true worth as a son and brother:

> Your sensible course is to destroy me. But you daren't do that. Social convention won't allow you; the law would make a fuss . . . You want me to go to Australia, where you'll never hear of me again, where in fact I shall be dead to you. (Weales 1962: 133)

The bargain fixing the prodigal's expedient disappearance is settled with an annual allowance to him of £300, which will be paid quarterly to prevent the funds running out too quickly. While Eustace recognises his actions as shamelessly exploitative, he also sees an equivalence between his immoral behaviour and that of his unscrupulous father, who blithely exploits his own workforce. This outline of the play indicates the reasons why contemporary reviews registered its freshness in contrast with the standard dramatic fare of the day: the *Academy*, for example, following an affirmative assessment of the play, suggested that 'the "average" play-goer, probably, would not stand Mr. Hankin's directness' (Anonymous 1905a: 1010). Apart from its uncharacteristic candour, Hankin's play also contrasted with much Edwardian drama in lacking sentimentality, avoiding traditional morality, failing to offer much in the way of love interest, and deliberately eschewing the conventional need for a sympathetic central character: the *Academy* reviewer also noted that the 'average play-goer' would 'complain that he was not allowed to sympathise with any one of the chief actors in the drama' (1905a: 1010). Whereas Eustace might in the hands of other contemporary playwrights have elicited the audience's amused pity, Hankin's script prevents an actor manipulating the role in this way. The play has a serious core and an integrity that makes it stand apart from the standard social comedies of the period, even though Hankin's characters and scenes are drawn from the same social milieu as these more conventional offerings. Hankin's decision to employ familiar settings and characters for his altogether more biting satire throws into relief the relatively insipid work of his Edwardian playwriting peers.

John Galsworthy's comedy *The Silver Box*, which appeared in the Court's 1906 programme, offers a number of correspondences with Hankin's play, notably in showing the ways in which money can be employed by the wealthy to manipulate individuals and institutions. Here, as in *The Return of the Prodigal*, a rich father buys off his wastrel son by exercising the power of his money. But Galsworthy's play, unlike Hankin's, incorporates working-class characters and settings. The socially polarised scenes in *The Silver Box* allow Galsworthy a direct comparison between his haves and have-nots to focus the central theme of 'one law for the rich, another for the poor'; Galsworthy argued that this was the case 'not because society wills it so', but instead 'through the mechanical wide-branching power of money' (Marrot 1935: 330). The play concludes with a trial scene, during which an unemployed working-class man, Jones, stands accused of stealing a silver cigarette box and a lady's purse from the home of John Barthwick, a wealthy member of parliament. The purse taken by the drunken Jones had already been stolen earlier that evening by Jack, Barthwick's equally drunken son; the latter's motivation was to 'score' off a woman who, we assume, had spurned his advances (Galsworthy 1909: 24). But while both acts of robbery might equally be classified as theft, the rich man's son has his crime erased when his father pays the purse's owner £8 to settle what euphemistically he describes as 'this claim'; concluding the bargain, Barthwick senior tells the woman, 'I need make no comment

– no thanks are necessary' (25, 26). By contrast, Jones has no ability to pay off his 'victim' and the magistrate who judges his case sentences him to one month's imprisonment with hard labour (88). The courtroom scene in which Jones is severely admonished for his drink-induced crime also incorporates Jack, whose guilty presence provides a physical reminder of the hypocrisy enacted by a supposedly blind justice. Jones, after shouting to the magistrate that it was only Jack's *'money* got *'im* off'*, finishes his protest with the single word *'Justice!'* (89). This dramatic moment, generated by the normally inarticulate Jones, is followed by the symbolic shutting behind him of the 'prisoner's door', and the departure of Jack Barthwick with a 'swagger' through a separate exit to freedom. Galsworthy's symbolism, a consistent element in his dramatic work, underscores the clear-cut nature of morality in *The Silver Box*, and leaves the audience under no illusion about the play's political message.

Granville Barker's own contribution to the Court's 1905 season, *The Voysey Inheritance*, once again foregrounds a father-and-son relationship in which money corrupts familial love. In this case, the son, Edward Voysey, discovers that his apparently respectable solicitor father has been embezzling his clients' money. Edward, a solicitor in his father's firm, has his youthful idealism shattered at the moment of this discovery, leaving him unable to comprehend his father's capacity for immoral behaviour: Edward's innocent reaction following his discovery of the crime, 'It's not right', is countered by his father's matter-of-fact pragmatism, 'why is it so hard for a man to see beyond the letter of the law!' (Barker 1987: 91). The corruption of Edward's once clear-cut sense of right and wrong is exacerbated when he discovers that his grandfather had long ago instigated the practice of embezzling clients' cash, thus setting in train the Voysey 'inheritance'. This becomes Edward's own legacy when his father suddenly dies leaving him to face the play's key moral dilemma: should he come clean and bring public disgrace on the family firm, or should he attempt to replace the missing money by legitimate means and in the process make good the crimes perpetrated by his father and grandfather? Granville Barker engineers this moral problem in ways that implicate various members of the Voysey family alongside distinguished clients and employees of the firm. As each of these interested parties is encountered, Edward realises that the seemingly simple question of right and wrong is complicated by an individual's vested financial interests. Edward's artistic brother Hugh addresses this issue with him directly when he remarks, 'what do we know about right and wrong? Let's say legal and illegal. You're so down on the governor [Voysey senior] because he has trespassed against the etiquette of your own profession' (125). Elsewhere, highly respectable clients of the firm representing key elements of the British establishment are little interested in the ways in which their dividends are sourced as long as they are paid on time. Scant notice, for example, is taken by the vicar, Colpus, of the need to protect the firm's more vulnerable clients in the event of its exposure and collapse: as in *The Return of the Prodigal*, Christian charity appears superseded in Edwardian Britain by personal investment and security. Edward's decision to continue the deception while attempting to put matters right represents his own acceptance and employment of the kind of specious logic against which he had earlier railed. The play's deliberately inconclusive ending, in which the question of Edward's destiny (along with that of the firm) is left unresolved, leaves the audience (unlike Galsworthy's *The Silver Box*) with no clearly defined moral message. What is evident is that Edward's loss of innocence and idealism leaves him better able to navigate his way through the murky Edwardian waters. Alice Maitland, who becomes his fiancée at the play's end, endorses Edward's *realpolitik*, telling him that 'it's your own wicked nature coming out at last. That's what we've been waiting for ... that's what we want. That's you' (Barker 1987: 157). Thus toughened, Edward can craft a fresh morality which is suitably tailored to the modern society in which he must operate. Without this ability to evolve, the play's ending suggests, individuals such as Edward are doomed to obscurity and extinction, their inherited moral standards proven irrelevant in the present day.

Bernard Shaw's *Major Barbara* (1905) is also focused on money and family relations, but here the localised implications of these matters are consistently in dialogue with their wider public and political significance. The play opens with the return of the millionaire arms manufacturer, Andrew Undershaft, to his family home after a long period of estrangement. Although his son Stephen deplores the notion of drawing on his father's sullied cash ('I would die sooner than ask him for another penny'), Undershaft's wife, Lady Britomart, takes a more pragmatic approach to the need for money: 'it is not a question of taking money from him or not: it is simply a question of how much' (Shaw 1905/1960: 60). This issue gains broader significance in the interplay between Undershaft and his daughter, the Major Barbara of the play's title. Barbara, an officer in the Salvation Army, is appalled when Undershaft's tainted money is readily accepted by her own commanding officer, Mrs Baines, whose reasoning is articulated in the following terms: 'Who would have thought that any good could have come out of war and drink? And yet their profits are brought today to the feet of salvation to do its blessed work' (109). By contrast, Barbara upholds the Salvation

Army's core Christian principles and resigns her commission on the spot, pinning her badge of office on her father with the words 'It's not much for £5000, is it?' (110). But Barbara, like Edward Voysey, follows her loss of idealism with a new pragmatism that manifests itself towards the close of the play's final Act. The location for this Act, Undershaft's arms manufactory and its impressive accompanying model town, confirm for visiting members of his family the capacity that Undershaft's money has for creation as well as destruction: Cusins, soon to be Barbara's husband, has his tongue only partially in his cheek when he describes the utopian town built by arms money as 'perfect! wonderful! real! It only needs a cathedral to be a heavenly city instead of a hellish one' (129). In this location, Barbara declares her need to be of use in society and, with this in mind, endorses Cusins' decision to succeed Undershaft as head of the arms firm. From this powerful platform, Barbara will no longer work with the 'weak souls in starved bodies' that she encountered in the Salvation Army shelter, but instead with:

> fullfed, quarrelsome, snobbish, uppish creatures, all standing on their little rights and dignities, and thinking that my father ought to be greatly obliged to them for making so much money for him – and so he ought. That is where salvation is really wanted. (Shaw 1905/1960: 152)

Having seen through the innocent hypocrisy of the Salvation Army and its fetishisation of the redeemed poor, Barbara is ready to work along-side apparently antipathetic forces to achieve her cherished goals. Even in her controversial final lines in the play (she drags at her mother's skirts while begging for a marital home in the model town), Barbara suggests her newfound chameleon-like ability to inhabit an unfamiliar role (in this case that of the infantilised child) if this will enable her to reach a worthwhile goal. Both *Major Barbara* and *The Voysey Inheritance* in this way demonstrate their young and initially narrowly idealistic characters in the process of becoming effective political players. For Barbara and Edward, their initially simple conceptions of right and wrong are broken down and remade in ways that allow them to operate in a contemporary world governed by self-interest and driven by money.

This position is also adopted by the title character of Cicely Hamilton's *Diana of Dobson's*, which was first performed at the Kingsway Theatre in 1908 during Lena Ashwell's tenure there as actor-manager. Hamilton's play opens with a stark critique of the shop girls who share a dormitory above a large London drapery emporium. One of these girls, Diana, who unexpectedly inherits £300 from a distant cousin, decides to discount the wise council of her fellow-workers, who advocate the prudent investment of this legacy. Instead, Diana invites her colleagues to ask themselves if they have 'ever grasped what money really is? It's power! Power to do what you like, to go where you like, to say what you like' (Hamilton 1908/2003: 87). She elects to exercise this power by enjoying 'a month of everything that money can buy me – and there are very few things that money can't buy – precious few' (88). The contrast Hamilton establishes between the death-in-life wage-slavery evident at Dobson's and the luxury Diana enjoys during her month in a Swiss mountain hotel is reminiscent of the similar examination of diverging options for existence established in *Peter Pan*; both Barrie and Hamilton employ hyperbolic methods to emphasise the diminished quality of life lived by individuals such as Diana and Mr Darling under modern capitalism. Hamilton does not invite her audience to criticise Diana's irresponsibility (and her later deception in posing as a wealthy widow in the Swiss hotel); she instead depicts her actions in a wholly sympathetic light. Like that of Edward Voysey and Major Barbara, Diana's behaviour is seemingly licensed by the tenor of an age in which existing notions of right and wrong are rendered meaningless. Elizabeth Robins' suffrage play, *Votes for Women!*, first performed in the Court's 1907 season, takes this redrawing of the boundaries of right and wrong to an entirely new level. Here, Vida Levering, abandoned while pregnant by the promising Conservative politician Geoffrey Stoner, decides to use the threat of his exposure and ensuing disgrace as a bargaining chip to promote the cause of female suffrage. Vida's readiness to employ her aborted baby as a tool of persuasion to ensure that Stoner publicly endorses appropriate political reform indicates the extent to which 'New Drama' might license the gloves to be removed.

The final major repertory season in the Edwardian era, the American impresario Charles Frohman's 1910 programme at the Duke of York's Theatre, included two major new comedies which continued and, in certain respects, extended the themes and staging innovations discussed elsewhere in this section. Granville Barker's *The Madras House* and Shaw's *Misalliance* are both centrally concerned with the effect of money on modern families; in particular, those whose livelihoods depend on commercial organisations. The world of trade, so unfashionable on the Edwardian stage (other than in the field of musical comedy), provides the setting from which the key intellectual ideas emerge in these plays: in *The Madras House*, the affairs of a number of individuals connected with a large drapery shop take centre stage, and in *Misalliance*, the family and home of a self-made man, John Tarleton of Tarleton's Underwear, provides a similarly central element. Both plays, in line with much other 'New Drama', sacrifice plot for free-ranging discussion, and both are therefore challenging to summarise in a limited space. But Philip Madras in *The Madras House* helpfully identifies the keynotes of that play in its earliest stages, when he poses a rhetorical question to his friend: 'what are the two most important things in a man's character? His attitude towards money and his attitude towards women' (Barker 1910/1977: 5). The play proceeds to demonstrate the ways in which a social cross-section of women experience lives that are determined and controlled by moneyed men. In the play's first Act, the six Huxtable sisters, who live in the comfortable middle-class family home of their linen draper father, are effectively bound in bored captivity. Unable to enter the world of work, which is deemed an undignified option for the daughters of a well-off businessman, they are consigned to a future in which marriage is the only realistic option for escape. The boredom of their empty lives is brilliantly underscored by Granville Barker's decision to include in his script the repeated phrases of conventional welcome, salutation and solicitation: a whole page of the play script, for example, is taken up by the ritual of saying 'good-bye' (34–5). The lives of the female drapers (as witnessed in the play's second Act) are similarly circumscribed and, like Cicely Hamilton, Granville Barker looks in particular to expose the inequity of the living-in system; this was a familiar element of the lives of many unmarried staff members, who were expected to reside in the retail establishments in which they worked. Elsewhere in the play, the existence of female fashion models is seen to be little different from that of automatons; indeed, one member of staff acknowledges that 'time and money' had been given to 'elaborating a mechanical moving figure to take' their place, but that these prototypes had so far proved unreliable (Barker 1910/1977: 89). Throughout this play, women from across class divides are seen to exist as mere chattels, expected to play a docile role in work and home environments devised for the comfort and satisfaction of men.

The Madras House of the title, an upmarket Bond Street fashion store, brings the servility of modern women into sharp focus by depicting the poorer women at work and the richer women shopping. This epitome of modern capitalism exists, according to Mr State (the American millionaire who is in the process of taking over the business), to offer women a much-needed sense of purpose: for the woman who 'sits at the Parlour window of her Provincial Villa pensively gazing through the Laurel bushes ... [or] a Duchess in Mayfair or a doctor's wife in the suburbs of Leicester', the fashion house offers a chance to 'Dazzle and Conquer' (Barker 1910/1977: 88). For the capitalist proprietor who facilitates this service, the fashion business offers quite separate opportunities: State argues that women who shop represent 'in bulk . . . one of the greatest Money Spending Machines the world has ever seen" (88). Philip Madras, whose decision to support the selling of this profitable family business to Mr State is underpinned by his disillusionment with the effects of modern capitalism, decides instead to embark on a more ethical path. His decision to work for the County Council on a modest 'thousand a year' offers a practical first step towards this change. As he tells his wife at the play's conclusion, 'that's how these great spiritual revolutions work out in practice, to begin with' (137).

By contrast with Granville Barker's brand of serious-minded comedy, Shaw's *Misalliance* refuses to incorporate the important themes it discusses with any evident earnestness. But Shaw's free-wheeling and insistently satirical approach to matters of social concern allows him to examine them in a fresh and often unexpected light. One brief exchange in the play, for example, suggests the ways in which Shaw's own work was in dialogue with that of many other Edwardian repertory drama-tists. This occurs when a young couple discuss their proposed marriage with the putative bride's father. Rather than the would-be groom, Percival, asking Mr Tarleton for his daughter's hand in marriage, the daughter, Hypatia, instead asks her father to 'buy the brute for me' (Shaw 1949: 189). When Tarleton probes Percival's motives, suggesting that 'It's purely a question of money with you, is it?', the response he receives offers an unvarnished truth: 'Practically yes: it turns on that' (190). As with other plays discussed in this section, the wider signifi-cance of this romantic union becomes compressed into a simple financial bargain ready to be completed: Tarleton, another father whose business concerns apparently eclipse his capacity for paternal love, asks that his daughter be taken 'off my hands for fifteen hundred a year: that's all that concerns me', while wishing his future son-in-law the 'joy of your bargain' (192). Unlike Granville Barker's hopeful ending to *The Madras House*, Shaw's relentlessly comic mode offers no potential solution to the fixing of a 'post-romantic' Britain. Instead, the ending of his play reminds us of the open-ended nature of any discussion embedded within a seemingly enclosed play. When Tarleton stumbles over his words before suggesting that 'I suppose theres nothing more to be said', Shaw offers a comically ironic reflection on his own prolix style of dramatic discussion; his daughter Hypatia's response, which provides the play's final line, 'Thank goodness!', parodies the position of Shaw's many critics (Shaw 1949: 199). But this rejoinder to the political complacency of the well-made play also underlines the authentic and pressing nature of the issues covered by the play. Like the elliptical 'Yes . . . ' which concludes *The Madras House*, the imperilled state of a money-fixated

Edwardian society was unlikely to be resolved by a few hours in the theatre, but in common with Granville Barker's oblique punctuation points, the ideas aired there might just creep beyond the closing curtain (137).

Chapter Five

Department of Internal Affairs: England and the Countryside

Writing in 1909, C. F. G. Masterman, in his study *The Condition of England*, recognised the pressing question of the day: '"Contemporary England" – its origins, its varying elements of good and evil, its purposes, its future drift – is a study demanding a lifetime's investigation by a man of genius' (Masterman 1909/1910: 9). Although this statement implies that the task was primarily one for political and sociological commentators, Masterman was acutely aware of the role that creative writers might play in carrying out these vital investigations. To this end he argued that:

> the popular writers of fiction, especially those who from a direct experience of some particular class of society – the industrial peoples, the tramp, the village life, the shop assistant, the country house – can provide under the form of fiction something in the nature of a personal testimony. (9)

This chapter responds to and extends Masterman's thesis in examining the ways in which Edwardian England was imagined by its novelists, poets and topographical writers. Following the Anglo-Boer War, and with society seemingly in a state of flux, writers looked in various ways to understand what sort of England might be emerging in the new century. Edwardian poets were especially preoccupied with this issue, and the first section of the chapter traces the contested notions of England and Englishness that appeared in Edwardian verse. While the characteristic mode of the era's poetry is pastoral and nostalgic, writers such as Kipling defined a model of England that might provide a rallying cry to stimulate the defence of a battered and vulnerable post-war nation.

The second section of the chapter traces the ways in which topographical writers repackaged England for a largely armchair urban audience. Here, the myths and traditions of a predominantly rural England are foregrounded in ways designed to preserve in print a land then seemingly in imminent danger of extinction. The coming of the motorcar, and the expansion of the suburbs, while providing a growing readership for nature and topographical writing, also signalled the death of the English countryside for pessimistic commentators. The chapter's final section examines one of those key classes of Englishness that Masterman identified: the country house. The symbolic resonance of the country house is confirmed by the prevalence of such buildings in the era's fiction; as Jefferson Hunter argues in his study of Edwardian fiction, 'the imagination of the decade was invested in landed property' (Hunter 1982: 189). In making this investment, the novelists examined in this section (Galsworthy, Forster, Grahame and Wells) used country houses to explore the question of England's inheritance. Nervousness about the possibility of there being anything of England to inherit perhaps stands behind all of the work examined in this chapter. In the period between the Anglo-Boer War and the Great War, as Wells' condition-of-England novel *Tono-Bungay* makes clear, this nervousness appeared increasingly justified.

Edwardian Poetry and England

Of all the Edwardian period's main literary forms, poetry has perhaps become the most disparaged by critics of subsequent generations. When weighed against the decadent and symbolist poets who preceded them, and the modernist poets who followed on, Edwardian writers of verse are typically judged as at best, insubstantial, and at worst, as characterised by Robert Conquest, 'deplorable' (Millard 1991: 5): even the long-unfashionable Georgian poets of the post-1910 period have to some extent been rediscovered and re-evaluated. But Kenneth Millard's *Edwardian Poetry* (1991) remains to date the only monograph focused on this topic, and the era's verse, as embodied in the work of representative Edwardian poets such as Alfred Austin, Laurence Binyon, Henry Newbolt, Alfred Noyes, Stephen Phillips and William Watson, remains neglected by critics. This neglect, however, has not extended to the work of Thomas Hardy, Rudyard Kipling and W. B. Yeats, all poets working in this period but rarely designated as 'Edwardian'. The reason why an illumination of the work of more characteristically Edwardian poets is worthwhile is hinted at in Derek Hudson's judgement that while this period is 'not, in general, notable for poetry, yet care and enthusiasm were lavished both on the writing and reading of verse of all kinds' (Nowell-Smith 1964: 308). Although this may appear to be the faintest of praise for the period's poetry, Hudson does point towards the significance of poetry as a literary form in its Edwardian context: verse, while greatly diminished in popularity since its Victorian heyday, still enjoyed a high profile and healthy sales in the decade after 1900. The issues of England and Englishness around which this chapter is organised provide a useful opportunity to understand something of the nature of Edwardian poetry through the lens of one of its key thematic preoccupations. Although we might consider England and the pastoral scene as the special province of the later Georgian poets, the Edwardians – who in many cases were subsumed into the Georgian school via Edward Marsh's *Georgian Poetry* anthologies – evidently anticipated and prepared much of this ground. In the process, they constructed an enduring and distinctive 'England' which was drawn with particular attention to rural place and its relationship to the past.

Part of the image problem suffered by Edwardian poetry over the last hundred years can be blamed on a decision made four years before the start of the twentieth century. The appointment of Alfred Austin as Poet Laureate in 1896 (following the death of Alfred, Lord Tennyson in 1892) meant that the official poet of the ensuing period was an individual whose name has since become a byword for bad verse. Austin, an upper-middle-class Tory imperialist, was clearly considered a safe pair of hands by the establishment during an era in which better public poets (such as Kipling and Watson) were deemed less reliable as writers of patriotic verse to order. The drawback for those members of the establishment who had chosen Austin as Poet Laureate, however, was that his poetry invariably played into the hands of satirical critics, such as the *Punch* cartoonist Linley Sambourne, who dubbed him 'Alfred the Little' (Sambourne 1896: 14). Austin's verse, sampled at random, invariably reveals infelicitous rhymes and clichéd images – such as the following, which greeted the denizens of Mafeking on their relief from siege in May 1900:

> As pressed the foe more near,
> Only with naked spear,
> Ne'er knowing what to fear,
> Parley, or blench meant,
> Forward through shot and shell,
> While still the foremost fell,
> They with resistless yell
> Stormed his intrenchment. (Austin 1900: 6)

Austin's attitude towards England was uncomplicatedly expressed in the final lines of this Mafeking poem in which he stated that the deeds of the defenders would swell 'the splendid page/ of England's Story!' For Austin, 'England' was a fundamental article of faith, which would (according to another of his Anglo-Boer War poems which also originally appeared in *The Times*) always 'uphold repudiated Right' and 'bring to end insufferable wrong' ('The Mercy of the Mighty', *The Times*, 24 September 1900, 6). Austin's unwillingness to review this fixed position in the face of shifting historical circumstances is signalled in a later poetic offering which opens with the defiant statement, 'Let the world change, I shall not change' ('CLXXXVI', Crowell 1955: 191). While this solid dependability was useful for an establishment which wanted to ensure that their official poetic spokesman would remain politically on-side, it did little for their credibility with a less jingoistic and more artistically discerning public.

Austin's intransigent loyalty towards his country was not replicated among others of those leading public poets who had emerged during the period of high imperialism at the tail end of the nineteenth century. The Edwardian public verse of Newbolt, Watson and, indeed, Kipling, typically demonstrates, to varying degrees, their shifting stance towards ideas of England and empire in the wake of the Anglo-Boer War. While the 1890s verse of Newbolt, for example, appears to symbolise the imperial adventure as a game played by healthy sportsmen for unquestionably noble rewards (his 1892 poem 'Vitaï Lampada', with its repeated refrain '"Play up! play up! and play the game!"' provides a lasting reminder of Newbolt's role as cheerleader for empire (Newbolt n.d.: 131)), his postwar poetry often affects a more restrained and less heroic mien. This shift in attitude is evident in his 1901 poem 'Commemoration', which, although returning to the English public-school scene that had inspired 'Vitaï Lampada', views this prospect now from a sombre and reflective position:

> And the School passed; and I saw
>   the living and dead
>   Set in their seats again,
> And I longed to hear them speak of
>   the word that was said,
>   But I knew that I longed in vain.
> And they stretched forth their hands,
>   and the wind of the spirit
>   took them
> Lightly as drifted leaves on an endless
>   plain. (Newbolt n.d.: 162)

In this lyric poem, set during a wartime Commemoration Day at his beloved Clifton College, Newbolt contemplates the school's youthful pupils from his standpoint of age and experience: the poem gains additional poignancy from a note Newbolt appended to his poem 'Clifton

Chapel' (also included in his *Collected Poems, 1897–1907*), which informs us that 'of the three hundred Cliftonians who served in the war in South Africa, thirty were killed in action and fourteen died of wounds or fever' (266). Taking this remarkable rate of attrition into account, the rapid shift in tone of Newbolt's poetry from the rousing cheer of the 1890s to the quietly reflective mood of the new century is hardly surprising. The love of school and its ethos remains in 'Commemoration', but this love is now tempered by a sense of the potentially deadly outcome of playing 'the game'. In the gap between the ancient peace of the Chapel, with sunlight falling on its granite pillars, and the restless dreaming of the naïve youth assembled on that day, there seems a profound melancholy. The inability of individuals to 'listen' to the truths communicated by the antique wisdom of place appears beyond the reach of the poet to address; the gap between youth and age is unbridgeable. Repose and reflection, Newbolt's lyric suggests, are gifts granted only after our eyes are opened by experience, and this experience, as the poem's contexts confirm, is often hard won.

William Watson's pre-war poetry, unlike Newbolt's, had already extensively demonstrated his desire to use his verse as a tool to criticise foreign policy carried out in England's name: during the 1880s and 1890s he had made effective use of the sonnet form to attack British foreign policy in Sudan and Armenia. Given this track record, it was unsurprising that Watson should feature as among the most prominent of those poets whose work was critical of British conduct during the war in South Africa. His sense of the wrong-headedness of the conflict is outlined in 'The Enemy', the opening poem of his 1903 collection *For England*, in which he recognises that the historically heroic qualities of the English have now been assumed by their wrongly demonised Boer adversaries:

> They fought as noblest Englishmen did use
> To fight, for freedom; and no Briton he,
> Who to such valour in a desperate field
> A knightly salutation can refuse. (Watson 1903: 18)

This poem, and others in this collection, suggest that misguided imperialism – an imperialism organised for financial gain rather than for altruistic reasons – has robbed England of its cherished attributes of nobility and fair play, and that these qualities are now in the hands of an unsophisticated enemy, who, while apparently 'Unskilled in Letters' and 'Ignorant of empire', are nonetheless rich in qualities of more unassailable value (17). For Watson, the charge of 'anti-patriotism' that came with his outspoken stance on British foreign policy was a troubling one (as he admitted in the dedicatory letter that opened his *For England* volume, to suffer this charge 'without impatience is difficult' (6)), but he stoutly defended his position in his poem 'On Being Styled "Pro-Boer"': 'Friend, call me what you will: no jot care I:/ I that shall stand for England till I die' (20). The England for which Watson stands firm had – far from crushing weaker foes in the way of her rapacious appetite for gain – historically supported the insipient nationalism of other countries, while also proudly opening its own doors to the dispossessed of the world: these admirable qualities are attested in the poem's nostalgic lament for:

> The England that rejoiced to see
> Hellas unbound, Italy one and free;
> The England that had tears for Poland's
>   doom,
> And in her heart for all the world made
>   room. (Watson 1903: 20)

By bravely acting as a defender of liberty, England had established herself above 'all living lands' in the prized qualities of 'Justice', 'Mercy', and 'Love' (21). The historical contexts in which these virtues were enshrined provide for Watson a characteristic way of establishing the contrast between a traditionally gallant England and its latter-day tarnished counterpart; the use of Simon de Montfort, for example, riding 'Fate on Evesham field' in the collection's title poem, 'For England', implicitly establishes a disparity between a noble individual determined to fight and die in 'the steep fight of Liberty', and his tainted, profit-hunting, modern inheritors (46).

In Watson's work, the retreat from a dishonourable and avaricious imperial present into the splendid historical past typically involves a specificity of focus on people and place. This manoeuvre is of great significance for Edwardian poetry more generally, as it increasingly takes account of – and seeks remedy in – the importance of grounding England in the specific qualities of its historical and geographic heritage. In Watson's most celebrated public poem of the Edwardian era, 'Ode on the Day of the Coronation of King Edward the Seventh', he carefully mixes his celebration of the King's Coronation with a 'phantasmal tread' (15) that is rooted in an evocatively archaic location:

> Deira [ancient Northumberland] with her sea-face to the morn,
> And Cumbria sunset-gazing; moist Divnaint, [Devon]
> A realm of coombs and tors; old greatnesses
> From Dee to Severn, where the bards were
>   born. (Watson 1902: 25–6)

The conventional timelessness of this ancient English landscape is then called into question by the poem's final section. Here, Watson delivered a warning to the new King's subjects, informing them of the peril in which the nation finds itself at the start of the new reign. In dwelling complacently upon past achievements, and being 'slow' to 'take the world arriving', he suggested, we 'forget/ How perilous are the stature and port that so/ Invite the arrows, how unslumbering all/ The hates that watch and crawl' (35). The example of ancient England should therefore inspire us to action rather than repose, and this action must complement the land by being 'Of high and singular election, set/ Benignant on the mitigated sea' (36). Watson's contention here was that English history communicated via the eloquence of place and time must surely enlighten those who are alert enough to observe. And, as Watson further avers, the proud history and land branded under the reverential name of 'England' should speak eloquently to young and old alike. Similar ideas are at work in Hardy's epic verse drama *The Dynasts* (1904–8), set in the period of the Napoleonic Wars. While the Wessex setting of the opening of the poem's First Act might suggest partisan nostalgia (the choral figure named 'Spirit of the Years' notes the way in which 'the martial mood stirs England's humblest hearts' (12)), the unfolding drama is in fact, as Jane Bownas has claimed, 'no partisan patriotic work in which only the English are singled out as heroes' (66). In fact, *The Dynasts*, like Watson's poetry, demands that the reader draw parallels between historical wars and more recent imperial conflicts.

A similar sense of warning and anxiety about the vulnerability of a precious England in and immediately after the South African War period is found in abundance in Kipling's Edwardian verse. Kipling, like Watson, was an outspoken critic of British policy during the war and he used a number of the poems in his only volume of new verse to be published during the decade, *The Five Nations* (1903), to warn his readers about the imminent threat to the country's safety. Among the best known of these is 'The Islanders', with its warnings about the deleterious effects on national security of an increasingly sport-obsessed nation:

> With the flannelled fools at the wicket or the
> muddied oafs at the goals
> Given to strong delusion, wholly believing a lie,
> Ye saw that the land lay fenceless, and ye let the
> months go by. (Kipling 1903: 135–6)

In his poem 'The Dykes', Kipling expands further on these issues via the familiar image of the nation's sea defences:

These are the dykes our fathers made: we have
never known a breach.
Time and again has the gale blown by and we were
not afraid;
Now we come only to look at the dykes – at the
dykes our fathers made. (24)

In Kipling's poem, the precious homesteads sheltering behind the dykes are vulnerable to a hostile sea: 'Coming, like stallions they paw with their hooves,/ going they snatch with their teeth,/ Til the bents and the furze and the sand are/ dragged out, and the old-time wattles beneath!' (25). The dynamic animation of the sea here offers an unmistakeable connection with other more substantial, but equally rapacious, human foes; implicitly here those European powers sharpening knives in the wake of Britain's perceived military weakness. The poem's dark final stanza, which suggests a future in which the poet's warning has not been heeded and the dykes lie in ruins, imagines a once-inviolable England now humbled: 'the peace is gone and the profit is gone, and the/ old sure day withdrawn . . . / That our own houses show as strange when we come/ back in the dawn!' (27). For Kipling, the conventional image of an unchanging English landscape is literarily erased here in an effort to shock a complacent and decadent people into defensive action. Like the melodramatically apocalyptic warnings that darkened Watson's 'Coronation' ode (with its imminent threat from the 'march' of 'yonder . . . nations full of eyes' (Watson 1902: 34)), Kipling clearly considered that the dramatic means he employed here were amply justified by the seriousness of the ends he predicted.

The overtly polemical and often hard-hitting poems that characterise *The Five Nations* are, however, counterpointed in that volume by 'Sussex', an affectionate tribute to Kipling's recently adopted county. In this poem, Kipling looks beyond the embattled and crumbling defences of the country left unrepaired by an inattentive people and concentrates instead upon the quintessential qualities of the English landscape that lies beyond. In this way, Kipling implicitly communicates what might actually be at stake if the dykes were breached and Englishness eradicated. And by way of contrast with the raw and confrontational approach he typically adopts elsewhere in *The Five Nations*, he couches this poem in tones that are gentle and companionable. This approach is particularly fitting for his personal appreciation of the ancient English county of Sussex, a place, as this section will suggest, that became a touchstone of England and Englishness for many Edwardian writers. Its vulnerable location on the coastline of southern England, its then relatively rural character, and no doubt also its proximity to the metropolis, are the likely reasons why Sussex achieved its prominent artistic and symbolic profile at this time. Kipling's own move to 'Bateman's', a seventeenth-century Sussex house, during 1902 meant that he was at the forefront of this adoption of the county as a geographical location capable of standing for England; his writing of 'Sussex' in the year of this move confirms the immediate impact that the county had on him at the start of a residency there which would continue until his death in 1936. The first lines of 'Sussex' suggest a decisive move from his macro vision of a monolithic 'England' to its synecdochal association with a single element of that country's geography: 'God gave all men all earth to love,/ But since our hearts are small,/ Ordained for each one spot should prove/ Beloved over all' (Kipling 1903: 69). While the spot singled out in the poem encompasses a large and diverse county, it is at the same time a repository for small-scale and undemonstrative qualities that should be recognised and cherished as the very best of England. Although Sussex cannot, Kipling argues, offer the magnificent or sublime in terms of landscape, the unpretentiousness of its nature should present no barrier to veneration: 'We have no waters to delight/ Our broad and brook-less vales – / Only the dewpond on the height/ Unfed, that never fails' (71). Like the uncelebrated but constant dewpond, Sussex rivers, such as the gently crawling Rother and 'wide-bankèd Ouse', are contrasted with positive emphasis against their more illustrious counterparts, the Thames and Tweed. Similarly and centrally, the 'blunt, bow headed, whale-backed Downs' (the Sussex hills which provide the spine of the poem) may lack the 'tender-hearted garden crowns' of more picturesque hillscapes, but their 'gnarled and writhen thorn' provide a perfect foil for the simplicity and dependability of their 'Bare slopes' (70). Elsewhere in the poem, the quietness and tranquillity of the Sussex scene that Kipling evokes is complemented by the features left behind by earlier human residents: a harmony is evident between the natural landscape and the artificial traces made by man and inscribed in such sights as its ancient barrows which exist alongside 'little, lost, Down churches', the chalk carving of 'the Long Man of Wilmington', and the dolphin weather vane at 'windy' Piddinghoe church (70, 72, 73). This happy combination of the natural and the man-made is crowned in the poem's keynote in which Kipling introduces the triumvirate of 'Memory, Use, and Love' as the dynamic qualities which make the Sussex landscape 'live'. The past of fond 'Memory' and the present of continuing 'Use' are united by the sense of 'Love' that is so much at the heart of the poem's warm and affectionate tones.

Kipling's evident affection for Sussex as expressed in this poem seemingly acts as a counterblast to G. K. Chesterton's claim in his essay collection *Heretics* (1905) that '[Kipling] admires England, but he does not love her'. Using this essay (entitled 'On Mr. Rudyard Kipling and making the World Small') to attack Kipling's militarism, Chesterton argued that his fellow writer 'admires England because she is strong, not because she is English' (47). Chesterton's own relationship to his country, on the other hand, was expressed in ways which posit him as part of the very fabric of its land. This intimate bond which he claimed for himself was contrasted with what he identified as Kipling's more detached and strategic admiration for his country: for Chesterton, Kipling 'knows England as an intelligent English gentleman knows Venice ... but he does not belong to it'. Chesterton claims that this 'belonging' is vital because, 'the moment we are rooted in a place, the place vanishes. We live like a tree with the whole strength of the universe' (49).

The stories Kipling wrote for children in the ensuing period, *Puck of Pook's Hill* (1906) and *Rewards and Fairies* (1910), presumably allayed at least some of Chesterton's doubts about the nature of Kipling's relationship to England. In these stories, and the poems which introduce them, further evidence is offered of Kipling's increasingly keen rapport with England's land and its history. In 'Puck's Song', for example, while Kipling's preoccupation with militarism is still evident in the 'Old wars' he identifies via key players in those conflicts – King Philip, Harold, Alfred and Caesar – these earlier battles are traced dimly against a more lasting natural background. Puck notes in his song that the guns that 'smote King Philip's fleet' have left behind only a 'dimpled track that runs,/ All hollow through the wheat'. Furthermore, the Roman 'Legion's camping-place' can only be traced 'after rain' in the outlines of their 'mound and ditch and wall'; and the 'stilly woods of oak,/ And the dread ditch beside' remind the lyric speaker, Puck, of the place 'where the Saxons broke,/ On the day that Harold died' (Kipling 1906/1987: 41). So while these aides-mémoires can be identified only by a knowing eye, the land on which they are traced has a permanence and sustaining power that is evident to all. Kipling's palpable affection for and connection with the Sussex landscape is foregrounded elsewhere in this poem by his depictions of 'our little mill that clacks/ So busy by the brook', and 'our pastures wide and lone,/ Where the red oxen browse': the use of the possessive 'our' here seemingly confirms Kipling's fellowship with Chesterton as being a part of the scene he defines rather than a more detached observer of its features (40). But Kipling's aim here goes beyond a celebration of the enduringly pastoral qualities of the scene he defines. In the final stanzas of the poem, although 'Trackway and Camp' are largely erased, the importance of this fading history is reinscribed: 'Old Wars, old Peace, old Arts that cease,/ And so was England born!'

> She is not any common Earth,
> Water or wood or air,
> But Merlin's Isle of Gramarye,
> Where you and I will fare. (Kipling 1906/1987: 42)

The landscape is made magical by engagement with the historical and mythical narratives for which it has provided a stage through time. Although the traces of the players on this stage might have been almost erased over passing years, these remnants were nonetheless vital for Kipling in offering his vision of the complex but inspiring interrelationship between English land and its history. The organising principle behind his poems and stories in *Puck of Pook's Hill* suggests that while the English countryside is animated by its history, this history in its turn is brought to life and has its significance established for us by our encounters with the water, wood and air in which it took place. So for Kipling, the didactic example of English history could never be fully subsumed beneath an account of the picturesque, tranquil and lasting pastoral scene. Actors in the landscape (the substantial, and the ethereal like Merlin and Puck) are always at work in Kipling's texts in the service of the bigger truths that he looks to convey.

Kipling's prefatory poem to *Rewards and Fairies*, 'A Charm', drew in the focus of his earlier poems even further to define the very soil of England as the mystical agent of its greatness and health: 'Take of English earth as much/ As either hand may rightly clutch . . . Lay that earth upon thy heart,/ And thy sickness shall depart!' (Kipling 1910: ix). In this poem also, Kipling moved away from the great men evoked in 'Puck's Song' and imagined instead 'the mere uncounted folk/ Of whose life and death is none/ Report or lamentation' (1910: viii).

The yeoman stock of England, emerging from and returning to the English soil, also provide a key part of the English imaginings of Chesterton and Hilaire Belloc. While much of Chesterton's verse on the topic (including his much-anthologised 'The Rolling English Road') was first published after 1910, Belloc's Edwardian poetry provides an indication of their collective musings on England and Englishness. In Belloc's own verse these reflections typically offer Falstaffian celebrations of the satisfaction of appetite available to the simple Englishman in the country inn: the refrain in 'Drinking Dirge' for example, proclaims 'I put my pleasure in a pint of ale' (Belloc 1981: 52); while in 'West Sussex Drinking Song', Belloc celebrates the merry pleasure available at a village pub, the 'Washington Inn': 'The Tipple's abroad and the night is young,/ The door's ajar and the Barrel is sprung' (53). These lyrics of hedonistic pleasure are reined in for 'The South Country', in which Belloc provides a nostalgic meditation on his beloved Sussex; this poem, like 'Drinking

Dirge' and 'West Sussex Drinking Song', appeared in his collection *Verses* (1910). In this poem, like Kipling's 'Sussex' (which it anticipated, being originally written in 1901), Belloc located an essential England in a single county. But what sets Belloc's vision of the south country apart from Kipling's is his much more personal sense of identification with the Sussex people. While the landscape is duly praised in ways that echo Kipling's own lines (for Belloc, the Downs are equally 'So noble and so bare' (Belloc 1910: 7)), it is the poem's celebration of fellowship with the men of Sussex that really sets 'The South Country' apart from 'Sussex'. And the fellowship and communion that Belloc singles out in his poem are, unlike the more mystic connections to yeoman stock that Kipling evokes in 'A Charm', predicated on individual companionship and kindness. Belloc's lyric places him squarely in the frame of the poem, alongside the Sussex men who 'Shall sit and drink with me' (Belloc 1910: 8). These simple men, shepherds and ploughmen who 'watch the stars from silent folds,/ [and] stiffly plough the field' (8), are, according to Belloc, pre-eminent: as 'the kindest and most wise' (7) of people, they symbolise all that is deemed best about the English character. An imagined reconnection with these 'men that were boys when I was a boy' is complete by the poem's close, in which, in a thatched house newly built by the sea, the poet sits with his companions and sings 'Sussex songs' and hears 'the story of Sussex told' (8). Belloc's happy withdrawal to the simple life provides the most striking contrast between his own and Kipling's Sussex meditations. Whereas Kipling, even in his most pastoral mood, looks to inspire action from his dynamic evocation of history in place, Belloc is content here to retire into the nostalgic memory of a vanishing England. The unrealistic nature of the longings that Belloc evokes (plans for building the thatched house are prefaced by the old saw 'If I ever become a rich man') ensure that his nostalgic vision is underpinned by a sense of the improbability of recovering the scene that he evokes (Belloc 1910: 8).

The general tendency of the later Edwardian poetry that attempted to define 'England' was to follow the Chesterton/Belloc path of nostalgic pastoral rather than taking up Kipling's more overtly political conceptualisation of this theme. Although exceptions to this general trend do exist (in particular, among those patriotic poems published in 1905 to celebrate the centenary of Nelson's victory at Trafalgar, such as Austin's 'Wardens of the Wave', Newbolt's 'Trafalgar Day' and Alfred Noyes' 'Nelson's Year' (Noyes 1925: 246)), the image of England that figures in most subsequent Edwardian poetry is that of a timeless repository of rural peace. It follows that a 'real' England found among the hills and villages is often identified in opposition to its adulterated city counterpart. We can see this characterisation of a healthy and ageless England taking place in the work of W. H. Davies, the 'supertramp' poet. While much of his Edwardian verse is focused on his vagrant existence, poems such as 'A Happy Life', found in his volume *Nature Poems and Others* (1908), convey the pleasure of honest country life to a presumably urban readership:

> O what a life is this I lead,
> Far from the hum of human greed;
> Where Crows, like merchants dressed in black,
> Go leisurely to work and back;
> [...]
> Lord, who would live in towns with men,
> And hear the hum of human greed –
> With such a life as this to lead. (Davies 1908: 26–7)

A similar theme is conveyed in Laurence Binyon's poem 'The Escape', which appeared in his *London Visions* (1908). Here, a boy and girl escape from 'London's roaring sea' to where 'the city ends,/ And looks on Thames's stream,/ That under Surrey willows bends/ And floats into a dream'. The countryside into which the children disappear is graced by the 'Odours of dimly flowering June', a 'starry stillness deep', a 'cock [that] crows loud, and bright', and 'The morning star' that 'shines in the pond' by the 'village green' (Binyon 1908: 36–40). A more sophisticated articulation of this scenario can be found in Walter de la Mare's 'England' (taken from his *Poems* (1906)) which begins 'No lovelier hills than thine have laid/ My tired thoughts to rest:/ No peace of lovelier valleys made/ Like peace within my breast.' But even de la Mare succumbs to cliché in his second stanza which imagines an idealised England from abroad as providing a 'refuge green and cool/ And tranquil as a dream' (48). This narrowing of England into a series of safe, familiar and Romantic-leaning rural tropes looks forward to the most characteristic elements of what we have come to perceive as Georgian poetry: a school which David Perkins argues was characterised by a 'traditional and popular style', that was also 'easy, smooth, and perspicuous' (Perkins 1976: 226).

Perkins further suggests that the Georgians 'repudiated the noisier side of Edwardian verse' that they found in the work of writers such as Alfred Noyes (226). But Noyes' 'A Song of England', which appeared in his *Poems* (1904), complicates this distinction between Edwardian and Georgian with its fusion of the pastoral and the public: on one hand it offers a patriotic celebration of England (echoing Watson's verse in its vaunting of the chivalrous men who 'live and love and die/ for England'), while on the other hand firmly grounding itself in the 'ferny glades' and 'leafy lanes of England'. In this way, 'A Song of England' perhaps acts as bridge between the earlier public poetry which waved a flag for an indefinable but unassailable 'England', and its later counterparts which identified an ahistorical model England in the benign countryside. Although Noyes' evocation of rural England offers many of the platitudes found elsewhere in that pastoral verse (the May Queen is crowned here 'With stars of frosty blossom in a merry morris-ring'), the poem's energy helps to negate its more hackneyed elements; this liveliness is, for example, captured in the 'rainbow-coloured sea-spray that every wave can fling/ Against the cliffs of England' (Noyes 1904: 14–16). The success of the poem in surmounting the pitfalls so often met by verse of this kind is registered in a *Speaker* review, which argued that 'A Song of England' offered:

> not the patriotism that depends on mere size or noise, on the spilling of blood or the subjection of men. It is the feeling of a man who loves his country, not because he has been laboriously drilled and beflagged into making an ostentation of love for her, but because the love is a part of his very being, and he could no more help having it than he could stop his heart from beating by clenching his fist. (Anonymous 1904c: 270)

In this way, Noyes' 'A Song of England' offers a channel between the versions of England that appeared in verse in the Edwardian decade. It achieves this by simultaneously inspiring patriotic feelings through its flag-waving, while also grounding its sense of England in the particular and the personal. While it is doubtful that Noyes, one of the most popular of all the Edwardian poets, satisfied both Belloc and Kipling camps with his hybrid song of England, it does perhaps suggest that that these factions were less divided on this issue than might initially seem apparent.

England in Prose Nonfiction

The association of England with its rural heartlands in the wake of the Anglo-Boer War as witnessed in the era's poetry is also abundantly evident in the prose nonfiction of the Edwardian period. In the period's topographical writing, for example, we can see the countryside – typically centred on individual counties – being packaged for a domestic readership keen to discover its own native land in the company of expert guides. Among the most popular writing in this category were those county-by-county volumes published by Macmillan in a series entitled *Highways and Byways*. Although the origins of the series belong to the previous decade (beginning with a volume by Arthur H. Norway devoted to Devon and Cornwall (1897)), the Edwardian period was the one in which the reputation of *Highways and Byways* became fully established: the counties and districts added between 1901 and 1910 include *East Anglia* (1901), *Lake District* (1901), *London* (1902), *Hertfordshire* (1902), *Sussex* (1904), *Oxford and the Cotswolds* (1905), *Derbyshire* (1905), *Berkshire* (1906), *Dorset* (1906), *Kent* (1907), *Hampshire* (1908), *Surrey* (1908), *Middlesex* (1909), *Buckinghamshire* (1910), and *Cambridge and Ely* (1910). The content of the individual texts clearly depended on the personal interests of their authors (in many cases, established writers of the day), but each volume typically foregrounded literary quotation and historical facts about the villages and towns of their designated counties; E. V. Lucas's Sussex volume, for example, included a great deal of poetry, as might be expected from the compiler of the extraordinarily successful and much imitated verse anthology *The Open Road* (1899). Another major series of contemporary publications focused on the counties of England were the *Victoria County History* volumes, which appeared regularly from 1900. The founding general editor of this series, Arthur Doubleday, intended to create an encyclopaedic resource covering every town and village in England. The popularity of literary topography, evident from the success of these county-based series, also inspired A&C Black's 'Pilgrimage' series, which reorganised English geography around its associations with individual popular writers. These volumes, like the *Highways and Byways* series, were profusely illustrated and included titles such as *The Hardy Country* (1904), *The Dickens Country* (1905), *The Thackeray Country* (1905), and *The* [R. D.] *Blackmore Country* (1906). This redrawing of the Ordnance Survey map to plot literary landmarks was also the rationale behind William Sharp's *Literary Geography* (1904), a collection described by Lewis Melville in the *Bookman* as offering a 'sort of Baedeker for the cultured' (Melville 1904: 127); Sharp's collection of author 'countries' added writers such as George Meredith, George Eliot and the Brontë sisters to the existing literary map. Unlike more traditional guidebooks, which offered practical information to the traveller, these cultural guides established an imaginary England, which, like the pastoral poetry of the period, was designed for an urban audience who wanted their country served up to them in refined form. This being the case, the idealised nation that emerges via these cultural Baedekers was greeted by a readership that was wholly complicit in this Edwardian process of mythical mapmaking.

A further dimension of this reinvention of England is witnessed in the widespread popularity of gardening books in the era. The cultivation of a garden plot allowed urban dwellers to create and nurture a small piece of pastoral England on their doorstep. While Gertrude Jekyll's Edwardian garden texts such as *Home and Garden* (1900), *Roses for English Gardens* (1902) and *Some English Gardens* (1904) now form a part of the canon of literary work in this field, these revered texts represent only a fraction of the wide range of garden books published during the decade. These works included 'celebrity' gardening books, written by such familiar figures as novelists H. Rider Haggard (*A Gardener's Year* (1905)), Eden Phillpotts (*My Garden* (1906)), and the Poet Laureate Alfred Austin, whose second series of *The Garden That I Love* appeared in 1907. It is also important to note the proliferation of Edwardian garden books targeted towards urban gardeners: among the many works designed for an evidently growing and enthusiastic cohort of readers were F. M. Wells' *The Suburban Garden* (1901), Mrs Leslie Williams' *A Garden in the Suburbs* (1901), and H. M. Swanwick's *The Small Town Garden* (1907). This desire to connect with nature while living in the urban areas can also be recognised in the practical realisation of Ebenezer Howard's Garden City theories in the development (from 1903) of Letchworth Garden City in Hertfordshire. Howard's ideas, as outlined in his *Garden Cities of To-morrow* (1902), offered a vision of city planning integrated with parkland, thus ensuring that urban dwellers would always live in close proximity to open green spaces. While only one other British city was built to the Garden City plan (Welwyn Garden City, also in Hertfordshire and founded in 1920), the Garden Suburb movement – which developed 'green' suburbs on the outskirts of existing cities – proved a practical and popular alternative to Howard's more ambitious plan. Among the best known of the more modest suburban developments was Hampstead Garden Suburb, which was founded in 1906 by the social reformer Henrietta Barnett.

For those readers who fantasised about leaving urban life behind completely, much-discussed and self-explanatory Edwardian concepts such as the 'Back-to-the-Land' movement and the 'Simple Life' proved enticing propositions: the former movement, according to Fiona MacCarthy, reached its zenith in the spring of 1902, while the latter appears to have peaked slightly later around 1905 (1981: 15). While a desire to renounce sophisticated city pleasures and return to rural simplicity can be found in the most ancient forms of literature, these ideas were newly resonant in the context of the Edwardian period's increasing distrust of urbanism. The ready market for literature addressing the desire for rural escape is indicated by the publication in 1905 of *Letters on the Simple Life*, a collection penned by notable writers (including Marie Corelli and Arthur Conan Doyle) that had originally appeared in the *Daily Graphic*. One review of this book (Corelli et al. 1905), which described its subject matter as 'this burning subject', suggested that the perceived decadence of the present day had made this publication timely: 'Almost everybody deplores the tendency of the age towards luxury, and, of course, a number refer to Rome and her downfall' (Anonymous 1905b: 178). The extent to which this perception had taken root among the general public by the middle of the decade is indicated by a number of books published in 1905 under titles such as *How to Live the Simple Life* (by Calvin Pater), *Quakerism and the Simple Life* (by Rufus Matthew Jones) and *Country Cottages: How to Build, Buy and Fit Them Up* (published under the pseudonym 'Home Counties'). Further manifestations of this desire to escape from a latter-day Imperial Rome and return to an older and more healthy way of life can be witnessed in the revival of English folk traditions, including morris dancing and folk music: the Edwardian revival of the former can be traced back to Cecil Sharp's chance encounter with the Headington Quarry morris dancers in 1899, and was given further stimulus by the publication of his *The Morris Book* (1907); Sharp was also a key figure behind the renaissance of English folk music, and his highly influential *English Folk Songs, Some Conclusions* (which emerged in the same year as *The Morris Book*) was compiled from the songs he had collected in rural England – initially in Somerset – from 1903. In advance of the publication of Sharp's volumes, performances of folk song and morris dancing were given to popular acclaim at the Queen's Hall in London. This bringing of the country into the heart of the city provided, according to one review, 'the jaded modern, who believes that there can be nothing unsophisticated in this twentieth century [with] a reminder that the world is really still quite young' (Anonymous 1907d: 201). The willingness expressed here to accept the authenticity of a revived folk tradition reflects the wider desire to preserve a precious but apparently vanishing England. The nostalgic yearning for an England centred on village and hedgerow, and identified in its purest form by the Edwardian pastoral poetry defined above, clearly inspired the urgency with which Edwardians went about registering, recording and (in Sharp's case) actively reviving a disappearing scene. The fact that this 'authentic' England had never existed in the first place failed to trouble the majority of writers and readers. An England replete with morris dancers and maypoles provided a comforting reassurance of ancient and wholesome stability, which might be set against perceptions of a decadent and corrupt society in the period following the war in South Africa.

The particularities of this pastoral reinvention of England provide a revealing index of Edwardian social and political anxieties: as Martin

J. Wiener has suggested in relation to this period, 'attitudes towards cities and countryside are frequently a key to attitudes towards much else' (1982: 51). This is especially the case when the imagined England that appeared in topographical writing was at its most romanticised and self-indulgent. A prime example of writing of this kind can be found in Alfred Austin's *Haunts of Ancient Peace* (1902), a celebration and reaffirmation of England and Englishness in the wake of a bruising war. Austin's text was organised around a horse-drawn carriage journey taken by three old friends, one of whom, Lamia, declares at the outset of the trip a 'wish to see *Old* England, or so much of it as is left' (19). This notion of an '*Old* England' that is vanishing is conceived by Lamia in opposition to the things (implicitly epitomising *New* England) that should be avoided on the trip: these include:

> paper mills with the newest machinery for turning the pages of yesterday's immortal works into fresh paper on which to print the equally enduring works of to-morrow . . . tubular bridges, whatever they may happen to be, the latest thing in motor-cars, model farms, and elementary schools conducted on an entirely novel system. (Austin 1902: 20)

Instead of encountering these unwelcome reminders of a blighted modernity, Lamia hopes that their journey will reconnect the travellers with better things: 'I confess I crave for the urbanity of the Past, for feminine serviceableness, for washing-days, home-made-jams, lavender bags, recitation of Gray's *Elegy*, and morning and evening prayers'. Readers were invited to contrast the civilised and companionable *Old* England evoked in these entities with their present-day life of 'ungraceful hurry and worry, perpetual post-man's knocks, an intermittent shower of telegrams, reply not paid, dithyrambic vulgarity or life-not-worth-living lamentations, and individual infallibility accompanied by universal incredulity' (Austin 1902: 21). The revolt expressed here against modern life directly echoes and anticipates that evinced in E. M. Forster's *Howards End*. Here the Schlegel sisters' critique of the modern life is focused on individuals such as the Wilcox family who, Margaret Schlegel claims, live 'a life in which telegrams and anger count' (Forster 1910/1989: 41).

Far from this urban world of blighted modernity, the countryside in Austin's work provides a putative vision of hope for the nation's future, and this vision is communicated directly by the book's narrator in the following passage:

> One cannot well drive about England with one's eyes open, without observing indication after indication of the strong, independent individuality of the English character, which may yet prove our best safeguard against that

exotic 'Collectivism' of which we hear so much. The very landscape, its shapeless fields, its irregular hedgerows, its winding and wayward roads, its accidental copses, its arbitrariness of form and feature, are a silent but living protest against uniformity and preconceived or mechanical views of life. Who divided these fields? Who marked out these roads? No one did. They divided and marked out themselves just as strong characters divide and sever themselves from others, settle their own boundaries, and define irregularly their own place and position. (Austin 1902: 23)

This organic growth of the country, the book's narrator argues, might indicate 'waste, from the economist's point of view', but this 'unthriftiness [is] part of our masculinity', part of a national character which 'feels it can afford to be heedless of trifles and details, and in any case will on no account be reduced to slavish formality'. Austin completed this revealing manifesto by extrapolating a romantic justification for imperialism from the pleasing irregularity of the fields and 'lanes that meander and zigzag': 'Like the Poet, England was born, not made, and has grown in its own lavish, wide-spreading fashion' (24). The faith Austin espoused in a national character that is masculine, thriftless and untameable provided a direct contrast with the peaceful femininity of the country scene depicted elsewhere in his text. Austin was at pains in the book's conclusion to underline the latter impression in affirming our debt to a 'silent Past' which laid the glorious foundations for the 'orderly and law-respecting England we know to-day' (178–9). The tranquillity necessary to preserve these qualities had been secured, he informed his readers, by the 'world-wide Imperial Peace that had lately been concluded' following the end of the Anglo-Boer War. In the wake of the 'thanksgiving Ceremonials' for the war's end and the 'beginning of a new Reign', the travellers reflect upon 'a land of peace, that seemed to have been there for all time, and as though it would for all time endure' (178). This 'land of ancient peace', with its 'rustic inns, rectories and alms-houses, honest and not ill-paid labour, happy-looking cottages ... kindly and contented people' represents an 'old' but 'ever youthful' England (184). Few readers, surely, can have accepted at face value the vision of countryside as the sort of utopian paradise that appears in Austin's text, but it is equally clear that the public welcomed this brand of idyllic writing. While the constitution of the market for literary material of this kind is difficult to identify with any degree of certainty, a review of *Haunts of Ancient Peace*, which appeared in the Methodist publication, *The London Quarterly Review*, sheds some light on this question; following much direct quotation taken approvingly from the text under review, the anonymous critic concluded that 'it is good to move amid such scenes even if one is chained to one's fireside, and Mr.

Austin is the ideal guide for such a pilgrimage' (Anonymous 1903c, 183). This fireside readership, one assumes, shared Austin's conservative and nostalgic leanings and felt comforted and reassured by the ancient peace that he invested in his text. These qualities, allied to a clear nationalistic, and even at times a jingoistic agenda ('of all lands, England is the most delightful to roam about in' (184)), ensure that Austin's text provides an eloquent if indirect testimony of the preoccupations and anxieties of the political and social contexts from which it emerged. This nationalistic imperative was equally at work in the opening chapter of P. H. Ditchfield's *The Charm of the English Village* (1908), in which he argued that:

> No country in the world can boast of possessing rural homes and villages which have half the charm and picturesqueness of our English cottages and hamlets. Wander where you will, in Italy or Switzerland, France or Germany, and when you return home you will be bound to confess that in no foreign land have you seen a village which for beauty and interest can compare with the scattered hamlets of our English land. (1)

Blinkered nationalism of this kind constitutes a significant element of Edwardian topographical writing.

The pervasive nature of the pastoral reinvention of the English country scene is also revealed in the work of writers whose political agenda was much less transparent than that of Austin. Ford Madox Hueffer, for example, appears remarkably close to Austin and Ditchfield in the following observations made in his 1907 text *The Spirit of the People: An Analysis of the English Mind*:

> nowhere in the world, so much as in England, do you find the spirit of the home of ancient peace: nowhere in the occidental world will you find turf that so invites you to lie down and muse, sunshine so mellow and innocuous, shade so deep or rooks so tranquil in their voices. (1907: 50)

While Hueffer's interpretation of his own version of the 'ancient peace' to be found in rural England might, out of context, appear parodic, the impressions of the rural scene he offers here are actually delivered straightforwardly. But this idealised image of a serene and nurturing countryside was tempered elsewhere in Hueffer's Edwardian writing by his acknowledgement of the reader's likely response to literary images such as these. This is evident in the opening chapter of *The Heart of the Country* (1906), in which he discussed the psychological benefits that a town-dwelling readership might derive by imagining themselves in the succour-giving countryside. This sort of projection, Hueffer argues, might take the form of a journey that leads the reader into an idyllic rural destination. While destinations of this type are typically identi-fied, Hueffer suggests, under a variety of different names – 'Eldorados ... Happy Hunting Grounds, Lands flowing with Milk and Honey, Avalons, or mere Tom Tiddler's Grounds' – they collectively provide 'the spot that each of us hopes to reach, to which all of our strivings tend, towards which all our roads lead'. Whether in 'labourers' cottages, in omnibuses, in tall offices, we discuss each plan that shall bring us one step nearer' to our personal Eden (Hueffer 1906: 4). For Edwardian town dwellers, Hueffer suggested, these places are most commonly associated with the 'Heart of the Country', a spot that rises as a 'green mirage' between the urban seeker and 'his workaday world' (7). The tendency of Edwardian writers to populate this 'green mirage' with people, buildings, and also more abstract qualities that caricature and idealise the authentic rural scene was seemingly conditioned by their recognition of the urban reader's fundamental ignorance of country matters; the separation between town and country, increasingly evident at the opening of the twentieth century, meant that inaccuracies in rural writing were less and less likely to disturb readers. Hueffer freely acknowledged that the sorts of impressions of the country that he and his fellow topographical writers conveyed were typically focused on an imaginatively reconstructed entity, which might be designated '"the country," in inverted commas'. This phenomenon had emerged because 'the majority of self-conscious humanity – the majority, at least, of those who read books ... regard unbuilt-upon land from [the] outside' (18). Furthermore, "the country", he continued, is an essentially middle-class construction, existing 'for a more or less lettered, more or less educated, more or less easily circumstanced town class' (23). The countryman, for his part, 'will certainly not read "Nature books"' (91), his experience of country remaining 'a more pagan enjoyment than any of the towns-men, who get much of their pleasure out of books' (89). A review of *The Heart of the Country* in the *Saturday Review* endorsed Hueffer's impres-sion regarding the readers of nature writing:

> The supply of country-literature is a response to the demand of the street-bred people: it is not the dweller among the hedgerows who wants to be told the colour of starlings' eggs or to read in strange phonetics a version of the talk he hears every day. (Anonymous 1906c: 728)

For the townsman-reader, Hueffer argued, the 'catalogue of rural sights and sounds' provided in these books would '"waft an odour" of the country into the atmosphere of fog and gaslight' (Hueffer 1906: 90). In this way, the jaded urban palate would be cleansed, the city pollution being gently fanned away by fresher air.

Given this pressing desire for the retailing of an atmospheric and idealised depiction of the English countryside for an urban readership, we
can perhaps understand why Hueffer's impressions of the rural scene at
times come so close to those of Austin and Ditchfield. Hueffer's more
sophisticated literary product, while actively acknowledging the process
of idealisation taking place in his pastoral prose, still sought to satisfy
the reader's desire to encounter 'the country'. He managed this without
sentimentalism, his narrative perspective instead adopting the stance of
a clear-eyed outsider long resident in the country. The knowing depictions Hueffer offers of key players in the country scene (such as field
workers, tenant farmers, landowners, carriers and tramps) build up a
picture of 'the country' that is at once accurate (these individuals do
indeed form the cast of rural life), but at the same time informal and
anecdotal. A sense of Hueffer's method of approach here can be recognised in his discussion of Carew the tramp, a rural character with whom
he claimed personal association. This tramp was given particularity ('he
was the son of a Guardsman and a prostitute' who claimed he had been
'bred up as a tooth-comb maker'), but he also stood as a representative
of a more mythical class of people; Carew is a 'good tramp', an 'artist',
a 'man who loves the road for its own sake: he has not other ambitions than shade from the sun, long grass, and eternal autumn weather'
(Hueffer 1906: 41). Elsewhere, Hueffer introduced a humble female cot-
tager called Meary, an individual he claims to have cared for 'more than
for any friend I have ever made before or since'. While again offering
several small details about Meary's life which impart to her a patina of
fine-grained realism, Hueffer equally connects her to a broader symbolic
realm: 'her memory seems to make sacred and to typify all those patient
and good-humoured toilers of the fields that, for me, are the heart of the
country' (110).

In this way more generally, Hueffer attempts to satisfy the town-
dweller's need for country 'colour', while also offering a frank assessment of the condition of (rural) England. Even though this means that
the ideal and the real are offered up together in close proximity, Hueffer
manages deftly to handle these seemingly contradictory elements. His
stated approach to his material (organised, as stated in his prefatory
'Author's Advertisement', around 'no particular sermon' and 'no particular message' (Hueffer 1906: xiii)), facilitated this fluid movement
from the particular to the general, from the idyllic to the often trenchant
critique. This latter quality can be registered in Hueffer's often prescient
speculations on the future of the countryside: he recognised, for example,
that 'the whole population of field workers is simply throwing down its
tools; it is making no struggle for existence; it is simply going away in

silence, without a protest' (130), to be replaced by mechanisation and the 'advance of the applied sciences' (198). But rather than fatally undermining the pleasing images of a pastoral utopia evinced elsewhere in his text, Hueffer seamlessly incorporates the inevitability of change into the urban reader's Edenic field of vision: 'If it be the fate of the country to be turned into one vast territory of pleasure parks eventually, we shall accept the pleasure park as the standard, just as now, upon the whole, we accept the small farm' (215). Seen in this light, the pastoral version of England retailed by Edwardian writers becomes a powerful enough conception to supersede its more authentic rural counterpart.

An understanding of the ways in which the countryside was reimagined in the Edwardian period would be incomplete without some knowledge of the role played by Edward Thomas, perhaps the foremost country writer of the period. Thomas was a distinctive product of the opportunities opened up for new writers in the new century, in that he was able to establish himself as a journalist with an increasing specialisation in poetry, nature and topographical writing during a boom time for work of this kind. A measure of the scale of this boom can be gauged from the amount of reviewing work Thomas took on between November 1900 and July 1914. These criticisms, preserved in the volumes of newspaper cuttings that Thomas collected, include reviews of about 1,200 books, amounting to just over one million words (Grimble 2004: 123). The publications in which these reviews appeared also indicate the breadth of the reviewing market available for an energetic young writer of the period: these include his regular work for the *Bookman* and for the *Daily Chronicle* and *Daily Post* newspapers, and more intermittent work for the *Nation, Athenaeum, Academy,* the *English Review, Literature* and the *Morning Post.* Work of this kind arguably made Thomas into the leading expert of his day on contemporary pastoral writing and he clearly employed this expertise in developing his own work in the field. After publishing *Horae Solitariae,* a collection of essays focused on rural topics in 1902, Thomas then produced topographical volumes on *Oxford* (1903), *Beautiful Wales* (1905), *The Heart of England* (1906), and *The South Country* (1909); in addition he edited a popular anthology of poetry entitled *The Pocket Book of Poems and Songs for the Open Air* (1907) and a biography (in 1909) of his hero, the Victorian nature writer Richard Jefferies. As a jobbing reviewer, Thomas presumably spent much time during this the period considering his own potential readership and identifying material that would appeal to this market. His admiring review of Hueffer's *The Heart of the Country* demonstrates a sharp-eyed alertness to this marketplace: 'to make a book as intimate and comprehensive as this, we should have to combine parts of fully half a dozen books, and those the best that have been written about the country in recent years' (Thomas 1906: 111). Thomas's pre-eminent expertise in this field indicated that few writers were better equipped in his day to make that judgement.

Thomas's own studies of Edwardian England, *The Heart of England* and *The South Country*, suggest his personal success in bringing together a combination of elements from other contemporary works. Taking *The Heart of England* as an example, and examining it alongside Hueffer's *The Heart of the Country* reveals how Thomas manages to engineer his writing of the English pastoral to maximise its appeal for an urban readership in search of a 'green mirage'. In the opening chapter, 'Leaving Town', Thomas employs a strategy recognisable from Hueffer's text: that of playing to the town-dweller's fantasy of walking away from the city and towards the pleasant land beyond. The newly built suburban streets through which the narrator walks (past, one imagines, the houses of Thomas's most avid readers) retain remnants of the countryside they have subsumed: the new street names, for example, almost mockingly commemorate those 'little villages known to me, [and] streams and hills now buried by houses' (Thomas 1906/1982: 11). While entering the sanctuary of the countryside, Thomas offers a number of short chapters intended to evoke this rural world via just the sort of 'opalescent effect' that he had previously recognised in Hueffer's *Heart of the Country*, in his review of that work (11): the titles of these chapters include 'Garland Day', 'Meadowland', 'An Old Farm', 'A Decorated Church', and 'The Walnut Tree'. But a chapter entitled 'One Green Field' perhaps offers the clearest impression of Thomas's method at work here. Over its five pages, this chapter provides a distillation of Edwardian nature writing in ways designed to transport urban readers directly into their imaginative English Eden with economy and precision. It begins with the narrator's meditation on the elusiveness of lasting happiness in his daily life, a failing which the text implies is a growing part of human experience in modern times. A consolatory 'shadow' of this quality is offered in an imaginative vision of 'a little idle field in a sternly luxuriant country'. This 'little field' is then transposed from a generic concept into something defined in more detailed and tangible terms: 'It is but five grassy acres, and yet as the stile admitting you to it makes you pause – to taste the blackberries or to see how far the bryony has twined – you salute it in a little while as a thing of character' (Thomas 1906/1982: 85). The concentration on sensual language here is developed in a cluster of related images that run over the ensuing pages; these evoke sounds such as 'the gush of water over a dam', linnets which 'sprinkle a song like audible sunlight', and a single thrush singing with 'blitheness' on the 'holly crest'; resonant visual images, including swallows that 'embroider the twilight air', a fox hunt which 'gloriously decants itself among the knolls', and blue rooks which 'unsheathe themselves heavily from the branches'; and country air, that 'blows gently, laden with all the brown and golden savours of Wales and Devon and Wiltshire and Surrey' and which delivers 'scent [that] lifts the upper lip so that you snuff deeply as a dog snuffs' (86, 87, 88). The blend here of an imaginative world alongside abundant (and accurately identified) flora and fauna creates a text perfectly engineered to satisfy the demands of its readership.

In this engineering of his text, Thomas placed Hueffer's 'opalescent effect' alongside the poetic language and resonance found in the Edwardian pastoral poets (the blithely singing thrush has echoes of Thomas Hardy's 'The Darkling Thrush', whose 'voice outburst among/ The bleak twigs overhead/ In a full-hearted evensong/ Of joy illimited (Hardy 1903: 170)). More straightforwardly in terms of its literary debt, Thomas concludes with a gesture towards the field's human history. In these images, the influence of Kipling is strongly felt tracing the presence of man against the natural landscape:

> But the field itself – was there a great house here once and is it dead and yet vocal? Are its undulations and rude edges all that remain of an old wood? Or was there a battle here, and is the turf alive with death? Certainly there is death somewhere speaking eloquently to mortal men. (Thomas 1906/1982: 88)

Although this palimpsestic landscape was not employed for overtly political reasons in the style of Kipling, its use in Thomas's text complements the urban reader's presumed desire to figure in the field's past. The great house, the old wood and the battleground have been introduced here to license the comforting fantasy of a residual memory pulling the reader back to a more uncomplicated time when happiness was sustainable. Like so much else in Edwardian writing of this type, the English countryside is designed to console and fortify its armchair reader, before he or she returns once more to urban reality.

Country House Fiction and the Condition of England

The fiction that emerged alongside these poetic and non-fictional representations of Edwardian England typically employed the figure of the country house as a symbol of the nation's past and its possible future. In these texts, the country house and its residents stood for an England caught in transition between an antique world of stasis and tradition, and an evolving modern world in which custom and heritage appeared little valued. The new democratic imperatives promised by the Liberal landslide election victory of 1906 seemed to provoke a particular literary emphasis on the question of England's future; the revival of the 'Condition of England' novel in the second half of the Edwardian decade, fifty years after its original incarnation, was in direct response to speculation about the likely shape of the nation in the wake of Liberal government reforms. The novels which fall into this category – among them Galsworthy's *The Country House* (1907), Wells' *Tono-Bungay* (1909), and Forster's *Howards End* (1910) – typically address the question that Lionel Trilling argued was at the heart of the latter of these works, 'who shall inherit England?' (Trilling 1965: 118). While these, and the other works of fiction discussed here, came to very different conclusions about the probable identity of England's inheritors, they were broadly in agreement about the demise of the old country house order. With varying degrees of reservation, all of these novels recognised that the old models of Victorian rural hierarchies were untenable in the new century. These texts, therefore, have a double focus: on the one hand they provide an epitaph for what C. F. G. Masterman in *The Condition of England* described as 'the passing of a race of men' in the countryside (1909/1910: 191); while on the other hand they imagine the probable constitution of England's future custodians. Although these projections were centred on provincial locations, the country house's symbolic role as a ship of state ensured that the health of the local community and that of the nation at large were inextricably linked. For this reason, the fates of Galsworthy's 'Worsted Skeynes', Wells's 'Bladesover', and Forster's 'Howards End' have a significance that goes well beyond the boundaries of the villages for which these houses provide a hub of order and tradition.

This sense of the urgency and centrality of the inheritance of England question is foregrounded in Galsworthy's *The Country House*, a novel which heralded the late Edwardian literary preoccupation with these buildings. In this text, Galsworthy imagines his titular country house, Worsted Skeynes, as a relic of England's feudal past seemingly dislocated from the modern era. Its owner, Horace Pendyce, a self-proclaimed 'Tory Communist', sought to crush any individualism in his tenants, considering this quality the 'vice' which had 'ruined England' (6). Pendyce's inability to perceive the needs of others implicitly condemns him to imminent extinction, via the narrator's evolutionary perspective:

> Mr. Pendyce thought this life the one right life; those who lived it the only right people. He considered it a *duty* to live this life, with its simple, healthy,

yet luxurious curriculum, surrounded by creatures bred for his own devour-
ing, surrounded as it were, by a sea of soup! (Galsworthy 1907/1919: 10)

Although Pendyce evidently lacks much in the way of self-awareness or
introspection, he is intelligent enough to recognise the likelihood of his
own – and his class's – probable demise: as he remarks, 'The country
is changing . . . changing every day. Country houses are not what they
were . . . If *we* go, the whole thing goes' (9). But Galsworthy's novel is
less sure-footed in defining who will inherit Worsted Skeynes when the
process of evolution finally extinguishes Pendyce. Likely contenders are
represented by individuals such as, at one end of the scale, the financial
magnate Thomas Brandwhite (of Brown and Brandwhite), who already
owned 'two places in the country, and a yacht' (11); his appearance as
a guest at Pendyce's shooting-party supper table confirms the narrator's
knowing judgement that he 'had a position in the financial world which
could not well be ignored' (11). At the other end of the scale of possible
inheritors, although viewed less distinctly, are a social cohort who, in
Pendyce's view, 'go on existing by the million in the towns, preying on
each other' and who typically live a 'suburban life . . . in little rows of
slate-roofed houses so lamentably similar that no man of individual taste
could bear to see them' (10).

Galsworthy's idea of who will eventually supplant Pendyce and take
control of this piece of England is complicated by the sense, remarked
upon by several of the novel's critics, that he finds it difficult in the final
chapters to consign Pendyce's England to history. John Batchelor points
to several passages in which Pendyce's wife Margery is evaluated by the
novel's narrator and found to be too precious to be washed away with
the forthcoming tide (196–7). In this process of evaluation she becomes
emblematic of an England that needs to be cherished and preserved: her
'gentle soul', we are told, 'unused to action [and] shrinking from vio-
lence', has a 'strength [which] was the gift of ages'; furthermore, the narrator continues, Margery Pendyce possesses an indefinable '*something*',
a quality which represents 'her country's civilisation, its very soul, the
meaning of it all – gentleness, balance' (214). While the opening of *The
Country House* anticipates the eradication of the old order represented
by Pendyce and his superannuated cronies, with the introduction of
his wife into the narrative, the letting-go of the past becomes more
complicated. So complicated, in fact, that Galsworthy ends the novel
with the old order relatively unchanged; although Pendyce is somewhat
chastened following his wife's disobedient departure to comfort the
couple's erring son, he and his boorish Rector are both preserved in a
dignified garden tableau on the novel's final page. Batchelor's suggestion

that the end of the novel represents a 'muddle', brought about because Galsworthy's chosen topic had forced him to 'write disapprovingly about things that he actually loved' (197), seems close to the mark. For Galsworthy, it appears, the glory of a timeless English landscape, a scene much admired in his text, could only be properly understood, nurtured and protected by people like Margery Pendyce, who truly belonged to its soil; the Chestertonian sense of the word 'belonging' is foregrounded once more here. The business magnates and the suburbans, groups who emphatically do not *belong* in this way, could never truly fill this role, and so we are thrown back upon an existing, if somewhat humbled, old order complete with all of its inherent faults. In creating this faint-hearted conclusion to a novel which appeared much more radically oriented at its outset, Galsworthy seemed to be eking out the last moments of winter light on what he tacitly acknowledged was a vanishing world.

Forster, like Galsworthy, was also reluctant to give up his rather more modest fictional country house, Howards End, to the creeping forces of modernity that provide an insistent presence in the novel. But while Forster shared Galsworthy's desire to preserve tradition in the face of its seemingly inevitable eradication, he managed this act of retention in a more measured and thought-provoking way. Forster also ensured that his own country-house novel was much more wide-ranging in its political perspective than Galsworthy's; while *The Country House* gestured towards a broader 'condition of England' resonance, the rural outpost of Worsted Skeynes remained largely detached from the outside world. The more outward-focused perspective adopted in *Howards End* was achieved through Forster's employment of three symbolic social groupings in the novel. These groups, all possible inheritors of twentieth-century England, represent key component parts of Edwardian society: they comprise the Schlegel sisters, cultured and intellectual individuals of independent minds and income; the Wilcoxes, wealthy representatives of the modern world of business and finance; and Leonard Bast, a culturally aspiring first-generation clerk who exists 'at the extreme verge of gentility', in close proximity to 'the abyss' (Forster 1910/1989: 58). Also representing a vital part of Edwardian society, but one detached from these modern constituents, is Ruth Wilcox, a figure who, like Margery Pendyce, represents an ideal of fellowship with nature and tradition. Forster invests her with ethereal qualities that ensure she forms a component part of the landscape from which she emerges; we register this on her first appearance in the novel, when she comes 'trailing noiselessly over the lawn' with a 'wisp of hay in her hands' (36). Her Ceres-like quality is further emphasised in the succeeding passage, which augments this symbolic resonance:

She seemed to belong not to the young people and their motor, but to the house, and to the tree that overshadowed it. One knew that she worshipped the past, and that the instinctive wisdom the past can alone bestow had descended upon her – that wisdom to which we give the clumsy name of aristocracy. High-born she might not be. But assuredly she cared about her ancestors, and let them help her. (36)

With her instinctive wisdom, innate nobility and, crucially, the sense that she *belongs* to her environment, Ruth Wilcox offers the perfect complement to the house and its surroundings. Far from the dislocation from the land evident in the characterisation of her husband and children (members of the Wilcox social grouping), she provides a vital continuum with earlier generations who were attuned to, and formed by, their natural environment.

But in killing Ruth Wilcox off in the first half of the novel, Forster was obliged to plot out the future for Howards End in an era of uncertainty. This projection of the house's (and arguably England's) destiny anticipates and answers Trilling's question of national inheritance – albeit through various improbable manipulations of the narrative. The resulting final scene of the novel offers what amounts to a coalition of the text's three social groups in occupation at Howards End: the now-crippled financier Mr Wilcox, his second wife Margaret Schlegel, and Leonard Bast's illegitimate son, whose mother is Helen Schlegel. It is difficult to make sense of this valedictory moment in the novel, unless we recognise it as an emblematic scenario rather than a more realistic one. Seen in this way, what appears is an England whose future prosperity is fused together by three distinct elements: the business world of Mr Wilcox is united with (and tempered by) the decadent intellectual and cultural class of the Schlegels, which in its turn has merged with Leonard Bast's latent English yeoman stock. This fusion of qualities allows the physical health of the nation to be rejuvenated while simultaneously underwritten by the financial prosperity which the text has argued elsewhere is the key to survival in modern life: '"More and more", Margaret Schlegel argues, "do I refuse to draw my income and sneer at those who guarantee it"' (178). But the apparent optimism of the novel's harmonious ending is undercut by its own insistence on the probable obliteration of Howards End and the traditional England that it represents. Shortly before the text ends, Helen reminds us that just beyond the boundaries of Howards End, the 'red rust' of London is inexorably 'creeping' (329). Her sister Margaret, while attempting to articulate her faith in the survival of the notion of England represented by Ruth Wilcox, also reveals her doubts about the likelihood of this survival: while announcing that she still believes 'very early morning in the garden . . . that our house is the future as well as the past', she also confesses that modernity's 'craze for motion' seems unlikely to be supplanted by a more measured civilisation that will 'rest on the earth' – 'All signs are against it now' (329).

Like Forster, Kenneth Grahame in *The Wind in the Willows* also concludes with a middle class coalition in charge, this time centred on Toad Hall, the novel's symbolic country house. But Grahame's conservatism inspires a more assured blueprint for England's future than that provided by Forster's hesitant liberalism. While Grahame's use of animal characters make their correspondence to human actors somewhat imprecise, his method of anthropomorphisation provides reliable clues to the relative social standings of Toad, Rat, Badger and Mole: Mr Toad, the owner of Toad Hall, is a dissolute and spendthrift landowner; Rat represents the cultured and comfortable rural middle class; Badger evokes a solid and dependable country yeomanry crucially connected to an ancient past; and Mole is depicted, like Leonard Bast, as a member of the burgeoning suburban lower-middle class, a social caste which was evidently of keen and growing interest to Edwardian 'Condition of England' writers. In *The Wind in the Willows*' opening chapter, Rat and Mole are living an idyllic riverbank existence (as characterised by their joyful 'messing about in boats' (4)), yet this enviable Eden is clearly under threat; echoing Horace Pendyce's words on the fragility of current-day country-house life, Rat describes the riverbank as 'so crowded nowadays that many people are moving away altogether. O no, it isn't what it used to be, at all'. The threats here are posed on the one hand by relatively benign riverbank trippers (reimagined as 'otters, kingfishers, dabchicks, [and] moorhens' (5)), and, on the other hand, and more threateningly, by an underclass of stoats and weasels who live in the neighbouring 'Wild Wood'. But a more pressing threat to the pastoral tranquillity enjoyed by Grahame's characters comes from within their own community rather than from outside its boundaries; in Toad's hedonism and inconstancy we perceive a more immediate danger to the stability of the riverbank's currently happy ecology. With a degenerate figure such as the motorcar-loving Toad in charge of Toad Hall, this seat of government for England in microcosm is left open to attack from the revolutionary forces by which it is surrounded. When the stoats and the weasels duly seize Toad Hall (during Toad's imprisonment for stealing a car and 'driving [it] to the public danger' (68)), it is only through the resourcefulness and bravery of Badger, Rat and Mole that Toad is reinstated in his Hall. But this reinstatement does not lead to a simple restoration of existing rural governance in the ways implied at the conclusion of Galsworthy's *The Country House*. Here instead, while Toad remains symbolically set up in his Hall as the community's figurehead, the *actual* power in this community is now firmly in the paws of the respectable middle classes, as represented by Badger and company. Toad's earlier bombastic nature is shattered in the wake of his re-establishment in Toad Hall, where, like a defeated dictator, he is forced to acknowledge publicly the incoming regime's authority: 'Badger was the mastermind', he declares, while 'the Mole and the Water Rat bore the brunt of the fighting'; by contrast, he confesses, 'I merely served in the ranks and did little or nothing' (Grahame 1908/1999: 148). While the 'altered Toad' (149) of the book's climax now appears a diminished and redundant figure, Mole, by contrast, emerges comprehensively transformed from the petit-bourgeois drudge imagined on the novel's opening page. The sage-like Badger's warm endorsement of Mole's worth clarifies his potential role in the new constitution: 'I perceive you have more sense in your little finger than some other animals have in the whole of their fat bodies. You have managed excellently, and I begin to have great hopes of you. Good Mole! Clever Mole!' (137). Like Masterman, who, in *The Condition of England*, recognised 'the latent power of those enormous suburban peoples which are practically the product of the past half century, and have so greatly increased, even in the last decade' (Masterman 1909/1910: 69), Grahame acknowledges the probable significance of this class in any future reformation of England. Grahame's Mole (like Forster's Bast) may not be directly in charge at the end of the novel, but he has certainly shifted his position from the margins to the centre of government in time for the text's conclusion.

Wells' Edwardian fiction is also typically focused on the social significance of the Mole-like little man. At the conclusion of *The History of Mr. Polly* (1910), for example, Alfred Polly, a suicidal draper, having discovered that he has the capacity to change his apparently pre-ordained existence, establishes himself in the Potwell Inn, his own idyllic mode of country house. Similarly, in *Tono-Bungay* (1909), the novel's narrator, George Ponderevo, confounds the life which seems mapped out for him by his lowly heritage to become a notable figure in Edwardian society. Wells constructs *Tono-Bungay* in ways that make explicit its 'Condition of England' status, employing in the process a series of country houses to help think through his ideas regarding the nation's past and potential future. The first and most significant of these houses, Bladesover, allows Wells to consider the England that its citizens had inherited from the nineteenth century. The 'Bladesover system', outlined at the opening section of the novel, is one that the younger George had unquestioningly accepted (when living in Bladesover as the child of its housekeeper) as 'a little working model . . . of the whole world' (Wells 1909/1994: 7). Echoing Horace Pendyce's vision of country house feudalism, George recalls Bladesover as representing a 'closed and complete social system' in which 'gentlefolks' were assured of their own 'primary necessity in the scheme of things' (8). In a manner that also echoes the opening of Galsworthy's novel, *Tono-Bungay* begins with its own epitaph for this anti-democratic conceit:

> There are many people in England today upon whom it has not yet dawned. There are times when I doubt whether any but a very inconsiderable minority of English people realize how extensively this ostensible order has even now passed away. The great houses stand in the parks still, the country cottages cluster respectfully on their borders ... the English countryside ... persists obstinately in looking what it was ... The hand of change rests on it all, unfelt, unseen; resting for awhile, as it were half reluctantly, before it grips and ends the thing for ever. One frost and the whole face of things will be bare, links snap, patience end, our fine foliage of pretences lie glowing in the mire. (8–9)

While Wells – through Ponderevo – registers the widespread influence of the old country-house regime, he, unlike Galsworthy, has little compunction in delivering the fatal blow to bring about its demise. But neither does Wells see any reason to celebrate the present generation of country-house custodians who have taken the place of Pendyce and his ilk. These new incumbents are dominated by Edwardian plutocrats, whose wealth has allowed them to buy up the countryside and its houses by the yard; this group are typified by Galsworthy's Thomas Brandwhite and *Tono-Bungay*'s Sir Ruben Lichtenstein, the Jewish magnate who leases Bladesover along with its furniture. These new-monied men have the wealth and power which allows them to buy the ready-made status represented by country houses, but their significance for the 'England' of these novels goes little beyond that. Wells' characteristically robust view on this issue suggests, through his narrator, that the changing of the country-house guard simply replaces the 'large dullness of the old gentry' with 'a smaller but more enterprising and intensely undignified variety of stupidity'. A small conciliation here is that the rule of the plutocrat offers merely a passing 'phase in the broad slow decay of the great social organism of England', rather than anything more significant (Wells 1909/1994: 55). The possibility of reversing this 'slow decay' provides the novel's central question, but as George himself admits at the outset, any English renaissance remains a distant prospect: 'the new England of our children's children is still a riddle to me' (9).

In an attempt to work this riddle out, Wells focuses his attention on the history of the rise and fall of Ponderevo's uncle Teddy, the success of whose fake patent medicine 'Tono-Bungay' (which gives the novel its title) illustrates the temporality and fragility of the present Edwardian commercial world. The image of the country house is again crucial for Wells in registering the extent to which a successful fantasist like Teddy can now wield the power to buy up England on a whim. Before building his ultimate folly palace, Crest Hill, Teddy has bought (or 'shopped' according to George's idiomatic expression (Wells 1909/1994: 222)) Lady Grove, a genuine and beautiful historic country house that he initially intends to use as a base from which to reinvigorate English traditions '"on Mod'un lines"' (229). This modernisation of the 'old English spirit' will draw upon 'traditional' folk customs, which, as discussed earlier in this chapter, were currently being embraced by an eager Edwardian public – Teddy's plans involve the inevitable erection of a maypole as a centrepiece for 'merrymakings. Lads and lasses dancing on the village green. Harvest Home. Fairings. Yule Log – all the rest of it' (228). Teddy is as untroubled by the inauthenticity of this version of 'old England' as he is about the inefficacy of his patent medicine; he sees the country as a once-popular commercial line now in need of repackaging: 'We got to Buck-Up the country. The English country is a going concern still . . . Only it wants fresh capital, fresh ideas, and fresh methods' (229). Although Teddy's desire to 'Buck-Up' the country is not underpinned by the romantic nostalgia so prevalent in Edwardian attitudes to England, his attitude is dignified by his lack of cynicism and his innocent desire to sell tradition to an evidently ready market. Wells' wry depiction here connects Teddy's bogus remedy with this coining of tradition – both are harmless in their way but each also offers an illusory form of hope.

Wells offers his clearest critique of the age's emptiness and insubstantiality in the account of the building of Crest Hill. This project, designed by Teddy as a monument to the power of his wealth, is instead, according to his nephew, a physical index of 'vulgar magnificence and crudity and utter absurdity! It was as idiotic as the pyramids' (Wells 1909/1994: 314). The construction of Crest Hill is abandoned following the collapse of Teddy's business empire, and this imbues the house with further symbolic resonance, inspiring George to pronounce it 'the compactest image, and sample of all that passes for Progress, of all the advertisement-inflated spending, the aimless building up and pulling down, the enterprise and promise of my age' (315). The bankrupt nature of present-day fakery, and the impossibility (and inadvisability) of reinstating, in any meaningful way, the old England of which Lady Grove was a relic, leaves the narrator a space in which to speculate about the fate of the nation in a post-country-house era. In breaking away from those models of middle-class social reorganisation that characterised the conclusions of other novels in this section, Wells looks elsewhere for possible answers, pointing instead towards science as the probable determining factor in England's fate. The all-encompassing vision of England's future with which he concludes *Tono-Bungay* suggests at a stroke the insufficiency and irrelevance of the more fine-grained and arguably self-interested social projections of his fellow Edwardian writers. The final pages of *Tono-Bungay*, in which George Ponderevo pilots the destroyer that he has built, tears down the Thames 'into the great spaces of the future'. This confident embracing of the future appears a provocative challenge to the nostalgic refusal of modernity so prevalent elsewhere in Edwardian writing. The irrelevance to the twentieth century of Worsted Skeynes, Howards End, Bladesover, Lady Grove, (and even that vain gesture towards the future, Crest Hill) appears complete from this water-borne perspective, one sonically charged by the craft's turbines which 'fall to talking in unfamiliar tongues' (352). Wells' holistic interpretation of the Condition of England anticipates in its breath of vision the centrality of the machine in the coming century. The Great War, while confirming that centrality in comprehensive and devastating terms, also brought to a conclusive end the dreams of England that were kept alive in the country-house novel and fostered more generally by Edwardian writers.

Afterword

My aim throughout this book has been to try to interpret Edwardian literature on its own terms, seeking to recapture the original significance of the novels, poems and plays discussed here by contextualising their writing and reception. The organising concept of the 'Emporium' has offered an enabling framework for this project, allowing separate departments of literary culture to be viewed both individually and also as part of a larger and connected enterprise. What these 'departments' confirm discretely and collectively are the problems inherent in taking too seriously Virginia Woolf's tongue-in-cheek claim for December 1910 as a starting point for artistic development in Britain in the twentieth century. The lasting influence of these inflexible interpretations of Woolf's thesis has hampered our understanding of what lies on the other side of this putative watershed. Philipp Blom's study of European history, *The Vertigo Years: Change and Culture in the West, 1900–1914* (2008), presents a compelling challenge to those who have interpreted Woolf's 1910 starting point in rigid ways. Blom's case for antedating the temporal centre of artistic gravity from 1910 to the beginning of the twentieth century is established in the following terms:

> In a large part, the uncertain future facing us early in the twenty-first century arose from the inventions, thoughts and transformations of those unusually rich fifteen years between 1900 and 1914, a period of extraordinary creativity in arts and sciences, of enormous change in society and in the very image people had of themselves. Everything that was to become important during the twentieth century – from quantum physics to women's emancipation, from abstract art to space travel, from communism and fascism to the consumer society, from industrialised slaughter to the power of the media – had already made deep impressions in the years before 1914, so that the rest of the century was little more than an exercise, wonderful and hideous by turn, in living out and exploring these new possibilities. (Blom 2008: 3)

Although Blom's conceptualisation of the period after 1914 as a mere 'exercise' of the 'new possibilities' established in the pre-war period is somewhat hyperbolic, his general thesis is convincing. This resetting of the temporal compass encourages the sort of open-mindedness in which fresh literary history such as my own can be received. Only when freed from the long-established belief in the marginal nature of Edwardian writing can we become fully cognisant of the range and textures of work emerging at this time. Equipped with this sharper understanding, we are better able to comprehend the interconnectedness of the Edwardians with their surrounding literary periods. By filling in these gaps in our knowledge we can begin to construct a more complete and nuanced narrative of our cultural heritage.

With a deeper understanding of this period's literature comes fresh scrutiny regarding its designation as 'Edwardian'. The potentially problematic and misleading nature of this label was something that the narrator of Rose Macaulay's novel *Told by an Idiot* considered as early as 1923:

> Well, the Edwardians, like the Elizabethans, the Jacobeans, the Carolines, the Georgians, the Victorians, and the neo-Georgians, were a mixed lot. This attempt to class them, to stigmatise them with adjectives, is unscientific, sentimental, and wildly incorrect. But, because it is rather more interesting than to admit frankly that they were merely a set of individuals, it will always be done. (185–6)

In spite of its relative meaninglessness as a form of classification, the term 'Edwardian' remains widely used today: one only has to recall the marketing of the popular British television series *Downton Abbey* to recognise its enduring application. This being the case, it appears expedient for critics like myself to embrace 'Edwardian' as a shorthand method for identifying and drawing attention to the period's literary culture. At the very least, it offers a way of beginning conversations with those who might remain sceptical about the artistic legacy of the twentieth century's first decade. The subtitle of this book, *The Great Edwardian Emporium*, works to some extent then as an act of salesmanship on my part. In keeping with those writers identified by Woolf as materialists, my aim here has been to draw attention to something tangible and worthy of inspection. Only after the goods in this textual emporium are closely examined by open-minded consumers can considerations of their quality and value begin to be addressed.

Works Cited

Abercrombie, Lascelles (ed.) (1933), *Edwardian England A.D. 1901–1910*, London: Ernest Benn.

Adcock, A. St John (1900a) *In the Wake of the War*, London: Hutchinson.

Adcock, A. St John (1900b), *The Luck of Private Foster*, London: Hodder & Stoughton.

Allen, F. M. (1900), *London's Peril*, London: Downey.

Andom, R. (1901), *Troddles and Us and Others*, London: Jarrold.

Andom, R. (1909), *On Tour with Troddles*, London: Jarrold.

Anonymous [Laurence Housman] (1900a), *An Englishwoman's Love-Letters*, London: John Murray.

Anonymous (1900b), *From the Front: Stories from the Seat of War*, London: Sands.

Anonymous (1900c), 'Literature', *Athenaeum*, 3814 (1 December), 716.

Anonymous (1900d), 'Monthly Reports of the Wholesale Bookselling Trade', *Bookman*, 18(105) (June), 72.

Anonymous (1900e), *The New Battle of Dorking*, London: Grant Richards.

Anonymous (1900f), 'Novels' *Saturday Review*, 90(2354) (8 December), 728.

Anonymous (1900g), 'Recent Novels', *The Times*, 36116 (14 April), 9.

Anonymous (1900h), 'Smart Society', *Pall Mall Gazette*, 11(149) (22 December), 3.

Anonymous (1901a), 'Messrs. Duckworth & Co. have just published', *Athenaeum*, 3841 (8 June), 712.

Anonymous (1901b), 'News Notes', *Bookman*, 19(112) (January), 109–10.

Anonymous (1901c), *The Sack of London in the Great French War of 1901*, London: F.V. White.

Anonymous (1902a), 'Fiction', *Times Literary Supplement*, 40 (17 October), 308.

Anonymous (1902b), 'Juvenile Literature', *Athenaeum*, 3912 (18 October), 519.

Anonymous (1902c), 'The Literary Week', *Academy*, 62(1552) (1 February), 104.

Anonymous (1903a), 'Literature', *Athenaeum*, 3932 (7 March), 298–300.

Anonymous (1903b), 'Novel Notes', *Bookman*, 25(146) (November), 104.

Anonymous (1903c), 'The World of Books', *London Quarterly Review*, 9(1) (January), 182–3.

Anonymous [E. V. Lucas] (1904a) 'Books for Boys', *Times Literary Supplement*, 148 (11 November), 348.

Anonymous (1904b), 'Fiction', *Speaker*, 24 December, 319–20.

Anonymous (1904c), 'The Poems of Mr. Alfred Noyes', *Speaker*, 10 December, 270.

Anonymous (1904d), 'Wholesale Reports of the Bookselling Trade', *Bookman*, 27(157) (October), 6.

Anonymous (1905a), 'The Drama', *Academy*, 69(1743) (30 September), 1010.

Anonymous (1905b), 'New Books of the Month', *Bookman*, 28(167) (August), 176–8.

Anonymous (1906a), 'News Notes', *Bookman*, 30(179) (August), 160.

Anonymous (1906b), 'Shorter Notices of Books', *Times Literary Supplement*, 257 (14 December), 418.

Anonymous (1906c), 'The Soul of the Urban', *Saturday Review*, 101(2614) (9 June), 728–9.

Anonymous (1907a), 'Fiction', *Academy*, 73(1840) (31 August), 849.

Anonymous (1907b), 'Insular Fiction', *Edinburgh Review*, 205(419) (January), 192–211.

Anonymous ('A Man of Letters') (1907c), 'The Fleshly School of Fiction: A Protest against the Degradation of the Modern Novel', *Bookman*, 33(193) (October), 25–7.

Anonymous (1907d), 'News Notes', *Bookman*, 31(185) (February), 199–203.

Anonymous (1907e), 'Supplement', *Saturday Review*, 104(2719) (7 December), iv.

Anonymous (1908a), 'Broad and "Long"', *Academy*, 74(1879) (30 May), 832.

Anonymous (1908b), 'Broad and "Long"', *Academy*, 75(1897) (5 September), 227–8.

Anonymous (1908c), 'Fiction', *Academy*, 75(1906) (14 November), 473–4.

Anonymous (1908d), 'New Books', *Bookman*, 35(205) (October), 51–2.

Anonymous (1908e), 'The Three-Colour Process', *Edinburgh Review*, 208(425) (July), 209–29.

Anonymous [Walter de la Mare] (1910), 'Fiction', *Times Literary Supplement*, 453 (15 September), 328.

Anstey, F. (1900), *The Brass Bottle*, London: Smith Elder.

Anstey, F. (1903), *Only Toys*, London: Grant Richards.

Anstey, F. (1906), *Salted Almonds*, London: Smith Elder.

Austin, Alfred (1900), 'Mafeking', *The Times*, 36,147 (21 May), 6.

Austin, Alfred (1902), *Haunts of Ancient Peace*, London: Macmillan.

Austin, Alfred (1905), 'Wardens of the Wave', *The Times*, 37,842 (19 October), 13.

Austin, Alfred (1907), *The Garden That I Love, Second Series*, London: Macmillan.

Avery, Gillian and Briggs, Julia (eds) (1989), *Children and Their Books*, Oxford: Clarendon Press.

Baden-Powell, Robert (1908), *Scouting for Boys*, London: Horace Cox.

Balfour, Andrew (1902), *Cashiered and Other War Tales*, London: J. Nisbet.

Balzac, Honoré de (1833/2009), *Eugénie Grandet*, Oxford: Oxford World's Classics.

Bannerman, Helen (1899), *The Story of Little Black Sambo*, London: Grant Richards.

Barclay, Florence L. (1909), *The Rosary*, London: G. P. Putnam's.

Barker, Harley Granville (1910/1977), *The Madras House*, London: Eyre Methuen.

Barker, Harley Granville (1987), *Plays by Granville Barker, The Marrying of Ann Leete, The Voysey Inheritance, and Waste*, ed. Dennis Kennedy, Cambridge: Cambridge University Press.

Barrie, J. M. (1902), *The Little White Bird*, London: Hodder & Stoughton.

Barrie, J. M. (1906), *Peter Pan in Kensington Gardens*, London: Hodder & Stoughton.

Barrie, J. M. (1999), *Peter Pan and Other Plays*, Oxford: Oxford World's Classics.

Barry, Kevin (ed.) (2000), *James Joyce: Occasional, Critical, and Political Writing*, Oxford: Oxford World's Classics.

Barry, William (1910), 'The Cleansing of Fiction', *Bookman*, 37(220), January, 178–80.

Batchelor, John (1982), *The Edwardian Novelists*, London: Duckworth.

Baum, L. Frank (1900), *The Wonderful Wizard of Oz*, Chicago, New York: George M. Hill.

Belloc, Hilaire (1907), *Cautionary Tales for Children*, London: Eveleigh Nash.

Belloc, Hilaire (1910), *Verses*, London: Duckworth.

Belloc, Hilaire (1981), *Complete Verse*, London: Duckworth.

Bennett, Arnold (1898), *Journalism for Women: A Practical Guide*, London: John Lane: The Bodley Head.

Bennett, Arnold [E.A.] (1898), *A Man from the North*, London: John Lane: The Bodley Head.

Bennett, Arnold [EAB] (1901a), 'The Fallow Fields of Fiction', *Academy*, 1519 (15 June), 517–18; 1521 (22 June), 557–8; 1524 (20 July), 57–8.

Bennett, Arnold [E.A.] (1901b), *Fame and Fiction*, London: Grant Richards.

Bennett, Arnold (1902/1967), *Anna of the Five Towns*, Harmondsworth: Penguin Books.

Bennett, Arnold (1902), *The Grand Babylon Hotel*, London: Chatto & Windus.

Bennett, Arnold (1903/n.d.), *How to Become an Author*, London: The Literary Correspondence College.

Bennett, Arnold (1903), *Leonora*, London: Chatto & Windus.

Bennett, Arnold (1904), *A Great Man*, London: Chatto & Windus.

Bennett, Arnold (1905), *Tales of the Five Towns*, London: Chatto & Windus.

Bennett, Arnold (1906), *Whom God Hath Joined*, London: A. Nutt.

Bennett, Arnold (1907), *The Grim Smile of the Five Towns*, London: Chapman and Hall.

Bennett, Arnold (1908), *Buried Alive*, London: Chapman and Hall.

Bennett, Arnold (1908/1990), *The Old Wives' Tale*, Harmondsworth: Penguin Books.

Bennett, Arnold [Jacob Tonson] (1910a), 'Books and Persons (An Occasional Causerie)', *New Age*, 8(2) (10 November), 40–1.

Bennett, Arnold (1910b/1984), *The Card*, London: Everyman.

Bennett, Arnold (1910c), *Clayhanger*, London: Methuen.

Bennett, Arnold (1911), *Hilda Lessways*, London: Methuen.

Bennett, Arnold (1916), *These Twain*, London: Methuen.

Bennett, Arnold (1932a), *The Journals of Arnold Bennett, 1896–1910*, London: Cassell.

Bennett, Arnold (1932b), *The Journals of Arnold Bennett, 1911–1921*, London: Cassell.

Bennett, Arnold and Phillpotts, Eden (1906), *The Sinews of War*, London: T. Werner Laurie.

Bensusan, Inez (1909/1911), *The Apple: An Episode of To-day*, London: Actresses' Franchise League.

Bergonzi, Bernard (1973/1974), *The Turn of a Century*, New York: Barnes & Noble.

Binyon, Laurence (1908), *London Visions*, London: Elkin Mathews.

Blackwood, Algernon (1906), *The Empty House*, London: Eveleigh Nash.

Blom, Philipp (2008), *The Vertigo Years, Change and Culture in the West, 1900–1914*, London: Phoenix.

Booth, Michael R. and Kaplan, Joel H. (eds) (1996), *The Edwardian Theatre*, Cambridge: Cambridge University Press.

Boothby, Guy (1901), *A Cabinet Secret*, London: F. V. White.

Brazil, Angela (1906), *The Fortunes of Philippa*, London: Blackie.

Briggs, Julia (1987), *A Woman of Passion: The Life of E. Nesbit*, New York: New Amsterdam Books.

Buchan, John (1910/1947), *Prester John*, Edinburgh: Thomas Nelson.

Bullock, Shan F. (1907), *Robert Thorne: The Story of a London Clerk*, London: T. Werner Laurie.

Burnett, Frances Hodgson (1905), *A Little Princess*, London: Frederick Warne.

Burnett, Frances Hodgson (1910/1911), *The Secret Garden*, London: William Heinemann.

Cairnes, William Elliot (1901), *The Coming Waterloo*, London: Archibald Constable.

Carroll, Lewis (1865/1907), *Alice's Adventures in Wonderland*, London: William Heinemann.

Chesney, George (1871), *The Battle of Dorking: Reminiscences of a Volunteer*, Edinburgh: William Blackwood.

Chesterton, G. K. (1905), *Heretics*, London: John Lane: The Bodley Head.

Chesterton, G. K. (1908), *All Things Considered*, London: John Lane: The Bodley Head.

Chesterton, G. K. (1910), 'Our Notebook', *Illustrated London News*, 136(3689) (1 January), 4.

Chesterton, G. K. (1927), *The Collected Poems of G. K. Chesterton*, London: Burns, Oates & Washbourne.

Childers, Erskine (1903), *The Riddle of the Sands*, London: Smith Elder.

Clarke, Allen (1904), *Starved into Surrender*, London: C. W. Daniel.

Clarke, I. F. (1970), *Voices Prophesying War, 1763–1984*, London: Panther Arts.

Clarke, Ian (1989), *Edwardian Drama*, London: Faber and Faber.

Classen, Constance (ed.) (2005), *The Book of Touch*, Oxford: Berg.

Cockburn, Claud (1972), *Bestseller: The Books that Everyone Read, 1900–1939*, London: Sidgwick & Jackson.

Cole, Sophie (1910), *A Wardour Street Idyll*, London: Mills and Boon.

Conrad, Joseph (1899), *Heart of Darkness, Blackwood's Edinburgh Magazine*, 165 (February) 193–220; (March) 479–502; (April) 634–57.

Conrad, Joseph (1899–1900/1981), *Lord Jim*, Harmondsworth: Penguin Books.

Conrad, Joseph (1904), *Nostromo*, London: Harper and Brothers.

Conrad, Joseph (1907/2004), *The Secret Agent*, Oxford: Oxford World's Classics.

Corelli, Marie (1902), *A Christmas Greeting*, New York: Dodd, Mead.

Corelli, Marie et al. (1905), *Letters on the Simple Life*, London: S. W. Partridge.

Cossins, George (1900), *A Boer of To-Day: A Story of the Transvaal*, London: George Allen.

Cross, Victoria (1901/2006), *Anna Lombard*, London: Continuum.

Cross, Victoria (1908), *Five Nights*, London: John Long.

Crosse, Victoria (1895), *The Woman Who Didn't*, London: John Lane: The Bodley Head.

Crowell, Norton B. (1955), *Alfred Austin: Victorian*, London: Weidenfeld & Nicolson.

Curtis, A. C. (1902), *A New Trafalgar: A Tale of the Torpedo Fleet*, London: Smith Elder.

Danby, Frank (1904), *Baccarat*, London: William Heinemann.

Davies, W. H. (1908), *Nature Poems and Others*, London: A. C. Fifield.

Dawson, A. J. (1907), *The Message*, London: Grant Richards.

de la Mare, Walter (1906), *Poems*, London: John Murray.

Ditchfield, P. H. (1908/1994), *The Charm of the English Village*, London: Senate.

Douglas Brown, George [Douglas, George] (1901), *The House with the Green Shutters*, London: John MacQueen.

Dowie, Ménie Muriel (1901), *Love and His Mask*, London: William Heinemann.

Doyle, Arthur Conan (1905), *The Return of Sherlock Holmes*, London: George Newnes.

Drabble, Margaret (1975), *Arnold Bennett: A Biography*, London: Futura Publications.

Eldridge Miller, Jane (1994), *Rebel Women: Feminism, Modernism and the Edwardian Novel*, London: Virago Press.

Ellis, Havelock (1900), *Studies in the Psychology of Sex*, Vol. 1, *Sexual Inversion*, London, Watford and Leipzig: The University Press.

Ellmann, Richard (1960), *Edwardians and Late Victorians*, New York: Columbia University Press.

Farrar, Frederic W. (1858), *Eric, or Little by Little*, Edinburgh: Adam & Charles Black.

Fernihough, Anne (2013), *Freewomen and Supermen: Edwardian Radicals and Literary Modernism*, Oxford: Oxford University Press.

Fitzpatrick, J. Percy (1907), *Jock of the Bushveld*, London: Longmans, Green.

Flower, Desmond (1934), *A Century of Best Sellers, 1830–1930*, London: National Book Council.

Forster, E. M. (1910/1989), *Howards End*, London: Penguin.

Freud, Sigmund (1910), *Three Contributions to the Sexual Theory*, trans. A. A. Brill, New York: The Journal of Nervous and Mental Disease Publishing Company.

Fuller, J. F. C. (1937), *The Last of the Gentleman's Wars*, London: Faber and Faber.

Galsworthy, John (1906), *The Man of Property*, London: William Heinemann.

Galsworthy, John (1907/1919), *The Country House*, London: William Heinemann.

Galsworthy, John (1909), *Plays: Volume 1: The Silver Box, Joy, Strife*, London: Duckworth.

Gaunt, Mary (1910), *The Uncounted Cost*, London: T. Werner Laurie.

Gavin, Adrienne E. and Humphries, Andrew F. (eds) (2008), *Childhood in Edwardian Fiction: Worlds Enough and Time*, Basingstoke: Palgrave.

Gillies, Mary Ann (2007), *The Professional Literary Agent in Britain, 1880–1920*, Toronto: University of Toronto Press.

Gissing, George (1905), *Will Warburton: A Romance of Real Life*, London: Archibald Constable.

Glyn, Elinor (1900/1901), *The Visits of Elizabeth*, London: Duckworth.

Glyn, Elinor (1905), *The Vicissitudes of Evangeline*, London: Duckworth.

Glyn, Elinor (1906), *Beyond the Rocks*, London: Duckworth.

Glyn, Elinor (1907/1996), *Three Weeks*, London: Virago.

Glyn, Elinor (1909), *Elizabeth Visits America*, London: Duckworth.

Glyn, Elinor (1909), *One Night*, London: Duckworth.

Glyn, Elinor (1910/1911), *High Noon*, London: Duckworth.

Glyn, Elinor (1910), *His Hour*, London: Duckworth.

Grahame, Kenneth (1908/1999), *The Wind in the Willows*, Oxford: Oxford World's Classics.

Greene, Graham (1970), *Collected Essays*, London: Penguin.

Grimble, Simon (2004), *Landscape, Writing and 'The Condition of England' – 1878–1917, Ruskin to Modernism*, Lampeter: Edwin Mellen Press.

Grimm, The Brothers (1909), *The Fairy Tales of the Brothers Grimm*, London: Constable.

Gross, John (1969), *The Rise and Fall of the Man of Letters*, London: Macmillan.

Gubar, Marah (2010), *Artful Dodgers: Reconceiving the Golden Age of Children's Literature*, Oxford: Oxford University Press.

Haggard, H. Rider (1905), *A Gardener's Year*, London: Longmans, Green.

Hamilton, Cicely (1908/2003), *Diana of Dobson's*, Peterborough, ON: Broadview Editions.

Hamilton, Cosmo (1908), *Keepers of the House*: London: John Long.

Hardy, Thomas (1903), *Poems of the Past and the Present*, London: Macmillan.

Hardy, Thomas (1904), *The Dynasts: A Drama of the Napoleonic Wars, in Three Parts, Nineteen Acts, & One Hundred and Thirty Scenes, Part First*, London: Macmillan.

Hartley, L. P. (1944/1971), *The Shrimp and the Anemone*, London: Faber and Faber.

Hayens, Herbert (1902), *Scouting for Buller*, Edinburgh: Thomas Nelson.

Henty, G. A. (1901), *With Buller in Natal*, London: Blackie.

Henty, G. A. (1902), *With Roberts to Pretoria*, London: Blackie.

Hepburn, James (ed.) (1966), *Letters of Arnold Bennett, Volume I, Letters to J. B. Pinker*, Oxford: Oxford University Press.

Hepburn, James (ed.) (1968), *Letters of Arnold Bennett, Volume II, 1889–1915*, Oxford: Oxford University Press.

Hewlett, Maurice (1908), *Halfway House*, London: Chapman and Hall.

Hewlett, Maurice (1909), *Open Country*, London: Macmillan.

Hewlett, Maurice (1910), *Rest Harrow*, London: Macmillan.

Hichens, Robert (1904/1920), *The Garden of Allah*, London: Methuen.

Hichens, Robert (1904), *The Woman with the Fan*, London: Methuen.

Hill, Headon (1903), *Seaward for the Foe*, London: Ward Lock.

'Home Counties' (1905), *Country Cottages: How to Build, Buy and Fit Them Up*, London: William Heinemann.

Hornung, E. W. (1992), *The Collected Raffles*, London: Everyman's Library.

Housman, Laurence (1907), *Stories from the Arabian Nights*, London: Hodder & Stoughton.

Howard, Ebenezer (1902), *Garden Cities of To-morrow*, London: Swan Sonnenschein.

Howard, Keble (1906), *The Smiths of Surbiton*, London: Chapman and Hall.

Howarth, Anna (1902), *Nora Lester*, London: Smith Elder.

Howells, William Dean (1910), 'Mr. Pett Ridge's Clever Books', *North American Review*, 191 (1 January), 64–74.

Hueffer, Ford Madox (1906), *The Heart of the Country*, London: Alston Rivers.

Hueffer, Ford Madox (1907), *The Spirit of the People: An Analysis of the English Mind*, London: Alston Rivers.

Hueffer, Ford Madox (1911), *Ancient Lights and Certain New Reflections, Being the Memories of a Young Man*, London: Chapman and Hall.

Hughes, Thomas (1857), *Tom Brown's School Days*, Cambridge: Macmillan.

Hull, E. M. (1919), *The Sheik*, London: E. Nash & Grayson.

Hume, Fergus (1900), *A Traitor in London*, London: John Long.

Hunter, Jefferson (1982), *Edwardian Fiction*, Cambridge, MA: Harvard University Press.

Hynes, Samuel (1968/1991), *The Edwardian Turn of Mind*, London: Pimlico.

Hynes, Samuel (1972), *Edwardian Occasions*, London: Routledge & Kegan Paul.

Irving, Washington (1905), *Rip Van Winkle*, London: William Heinemann.

Jackson, Kate (2001), *George Newnes and the New Journalism in Britain, 1880–1910*, Aldershot: Ashgate.

James, Henry (1914), 'The Younger Generation', *Times Literary Supplement*, 635 (19 March), 133–4.

Jekyll, Gertrude (1900), *Home and Garden*, London: Longmans, Green.

Jekyll, Gertrude (1902), *Roses for English Gardens*, London: Country Life and George Newnes.

Jekyll, Gertrude (1904), *Some English Gardens*, London: Longmans, Green.

Jerome, Jerome K. (1900), *Three Men on the Bummel*, Bristol: J. W. Arrowsmith.

Jerome, Jerome K. (1901), *The Observations of Henry*, Bristol: J. W. Arrowsmith.

Jerome, Jerome K. (1905), *Idle Ideas in 1905*, London: Hurst & Blackett.

Jerome, Jerome K. (1907), *The Passing of the Third Floor Back and Other Stories*, London: Hurst & Blackett.

Johns, Rev. C. A. et al. (1905), *I Go A-Walking Through the Lanes and Meadows*, Edinburgh: T. N. Foulis.

Johns, Rev. C. A. et al. (1907), *I Go A-Walking Through the Woods and O'er the Moor*, Edinburgh: T. N. Foulis.

Jones, Rufus Matthew (1905), *Quakerism and the Simple Life*, London: Headley Bros.

Kaplan, Carola M. and Simpson, Anne B. (1996), *Seeing Double: Revisioning Edwardian and Modernist Literature*, Basingstoke: Macmillan.

Keating, Peter (1989/1991), *The Haunted Study*, London: Fontana Press.

Kemp, Sandra, Mitchell, Charlotte and Trotter, David (eds) (1997), *Edwardian Fiction: An Oxford Companion*, Oxford: Oxford University Press.

Kenyon, Frederic G. (ed.) (1897), *The Letters of Elizabeth Barrett Browning*, London: Macmillan.

Kipling, Rudyard (1894), *The Jungle Book*, London: Macmillan.

Kipling, Rudyard (1895), *The Second Jungle Book*, London: Macmillan.

Kipling, Rudyard (1899), *Stalky & Co.*, London: Macmillan.

Kipling, Rudyard (1901/1998), *Kim*, Oxford: Oxford World's Classics.

Kipling, Rudyard (1902), *Just So Stories*, London: Macmillan.

Kipling, Rudyard (1903), *The Five Nations*, London: Methuen.

Kipling, Rudyard (1904), *Traffics and Discoveries*, London: Macmillan.

Kipling, Rudyard (1906/1987), *Puck of Pook's Hill*, Harmondsworth: Penguin.

Kipling, Rudyard (1910), *Rewards and Fairies*, London: Macmillan.

Kipling, Rudyard (1990), *The Complete Verse*, London: Kyle Cathie.

Kipling, Rudyard (1999), *War Stories and Poems*, Oxford: Oxford World's Classics.

Krebs, Paula M. (2004), *Gender, Race, and the Writing of Empire*, Cambridge: Cambridge University Press.

Lang, Andrew (1889), *The Blue Fairy Book*, London: Longmans, Green.

Lawrence, D. H. (1915), *The Rainbow*, London: Methuen.

Le Queux, William (1906), *The Invasion of 1910*, London: Eveleigh Nash.

Lear, Linda (2008), *Beatrix Potter, The Extraordinary Life of a Victorian Genius*, London: Penguin.

Leverson, Ada (1908), *Love's Shadow*, London: Grant Richards.

Locke, W. J. (1905), *The Morals of Marcus Ordeyne*, London: The Bodley Head.

London, Jack (1903), *The Call of the Wild*, New York: Macmillan.

London, Jack (1906), *White Fang*, London: Macmillan.

Lowe, Charles (1910), 'About German Spies', *The Contemporary Review*, 97 (January), 42–56.

Lucas, E. V. (1899), *The Open Road*, London: Grant Richards.

Lucas, E. V. (1904), *Highways and Byways in Sussex*, London: Macmillan.

Lurie, Alison (1991), *Not in Front of the Grown-Ups: Subversive Children's Literature*, London: Sphere Books.

Macaulay, Rose (1923/1986), *Told by an Idiot*, London: Virago.

MacCarthy, Desmond (1907), *The Court Theatre 1904–1907: A Commentary and Criticism*, London: A. H. Bullen.

MacCarthy, Fiona (1981), *The Simple Life: C. R. Ashbee in the Cotswolds*, London: Lund Humphries.

McCrum, Robert (2004), *Wodehouse: A Life*, London: Viking.

McDonald, Jan (1986), *The 'New Drama' 1900–1914*, Basingstoke: Macmillan.

Machen, Arthur (1906), *The House of Souls*, London: Grant Richards.

Machen, Arthur (1907), *The Hill of Dreams*, London: Grant Richards.

Mackenzie, Norman and Mackenzie, Jeanne (1973), *The Time Traveller: The Life of H. G. Wells*, London: Weidenfeld & Nicolson.

Mackey, Margaret (1998), *The Case of Peter Rabbit: Changing Conditions of Literature for Children*, New York: Garland.

MacQueen-Pope, W. (1947), *Carriages at Eleven*, London: Hutchinson.

Maeterlinck, Maurice (1902), 'Motor-Car Impressions', *Harper's*, 104(621) (February), 397–9.

Malet, Lucas (1901), *The History of Sir Richard Calmady*, London: Methuen.

Malet, Lucas (1906), *The Far Horizon*, London: Hutchinson.

Marriott, Charles (1903), *The House on the Sands*, London: John Lane: The Bodley Head.

Marrot, Harold V. (1935), *The Life and Letters of John Galsworthy*, London: William Heinemann.

Marshall, H. E. (1905), *Our Island Story*, London: T. C. & E. C. Jack.

Masefield, John (1910), *The Tragedy of Nan and Other Plays*, London: Grant Richards (includes *The Campden Wonder*).

Masterman, C. F. G. (1909/1910), *The Condition of England*, London: Methuen.

Maugham, W. Somerset (1902/1967), *Mrs Craddock*, Harmondsworth: Penguin.

Melville, Lewis (1904), 'Literary Geography', *Bookman*, 27(159) (December), 127–8.

Millard, Kenneth (1991), *Edwardian Poetry*, Oxford: Clarendon Press.

Mirbeau, Octave (1907), *La 628-E 8*, Paris: Fasquelle.

Mitford, Bertram (1900), *Aletta: A Tale of the Boer Invasion*, London: George Bell.

Montgomery, L. M. (1908), *Anne of Green Gables*, Boston: L. C. Page.

Montgomery, L. M. (1909), *Anne of Avonlea*, Boston: L. C. Page.

Morgan, Kenneth O. (2002), 'The Boer War and the Media (1899–1902)', *Twentieth Century British History*, 13(1): 1–16.

Morrah, Herbert (ed.) (1900), *The Literary Year-Book and Bookman's Directory 1900*, London: George Allen.

Morrah, Herbert (ed.) (1901), *The Literary Year-Book and Bookman's Directory 1901*, London: George Allen.

Nesbit, E. (1899/1958), *The Story of the Treasure Seekers*, Harmondsworth: Penguin.

Nesbit, E. (1901), *Nine Unlikely Tales for Children*, London: T. Fisher Unwin.

Nesbit, E. (1901/1934), *The Wouldbegoods*, London: Ernest Benn.

Nesbit, E. (1902/1979), *Five Children and It*, Harmondsworth: Puffin.

Nesbit, E. (1904/1976), *The Phoenix and the Carpet*, Harmondsworth: Puffin.

Nesbit, E. (1906/1975), *The Railway Children*, Harmondsworth: Puffin.

Nesbit, E. (1906/1996), *The Story of the Amulet*, London: Puffin.

Nesbit, E. (1907), *The Enchanted Castle*, London: T. Fisher Unwin.

Nesbit, E. (1908), *The House of Arden*, London: T. Fisher Unwin.

Nesbit, E. (1909), *Harding's Luck*, London: Hodder & Stoughton.

Nesbit, E. (1910), *The Magic City*, London: Macmillan.

Nesbit, E. (1911/1933), *The Wonderful Garden*, London: Ernest Benn.

Newbolt, Henry (n.d.), *Collected Poems, 1897–1907*, Edinburgh: Thomas Nelson.

Newbolt, Henry (1905), 'Trafalgar Day', *The Times*, 21 October, 11.

Newte, Horace W. C. (1908), *The Square Mile*, London: Alston Rivers.

NHW (1911) Review of Arnold Bennett, *The Card*, *T.P.'s Weekly*, 17 March 1911, 327.

Nietzsche, Friedrich (1903), *The Dawn of Day*, London: T. Fisher Unwin.

Nietzsche, Friedrich (1907), *Beyond Good and Evil Prelude to a Philosophy of the Future*, Edinburgh: T.N. Foulis.

Nisbet, Hume (1900), *The Empire Makers*, London: F. V. White.

Norway, Arthur H. (1897), *Highways and Byways in Devon and Cornwall*, London: Macmillan.

Nowell-Smith, Simon (ed.) (1964), *Edwardian England, 1901–1914*, London: Oxford University Press.

Noyes, Alfred (1904), *Poems*, Edinburgh: William Blackwood.

Noyes, Alfred (1925), *Collected Poems, Volume 1*, Edinburgh: William Blackwood.

Offin, T. W. (1900), *How the Germans Took London*, Chelmsford: E. Durrant.

Orwell, George (1976), *Inside the Whale and Other Essays*, Harmondsworth: Penguin.

Orwell, George (1998), *I Belong to the Left, 1945*, London: Secker & Warburg.

Pain, Barry (1900), *Eliza*, London: S. H. Bousfield.

Pain, Barry (1903), *Eliza's Husband*, London: Chatto & Windus.

Pakenham, Thomas (1982), *The Boer War*, London: Futura.

Palmer, Herbert (1938), *Post-Victorian Poetry*, London: J. M. Dent.

Parrinder, Patrick (ed.) (1972), *H. G. Wells, The Critical Heritage*, London: Routledge & Kegan Paul.

Pater, Calvin (1905), *How to Live the Simple Life*, London: T. Werner Laurie.

Perkins, David (1976), *A History of Modern Poetry, From the 1890s to the High Modernist Mode*, Cambridge, MA: The Belknap Press of Harvard University Press.

Phillpotts, Eden (1906), *My Garden*, London: Country Life.

Pinero, Arthur Wing (1906/1907), *His House in Order*, London: William Heinemann.

Plowden, William (1973), *The Motor Car and Politics in Britain*, Harmondsworth: Penguin.

Potter, Beatrix (1902), *The Tale of Peter Rabbit*, London: Frederick Warne.

Potter, Beatrix (1903), *The Tailor of Gloucester*, London: Frederick Warne.

Potter, Beatrix (1903), *The Tale of Squirrel Nutkin*, London: Frederick Warne.

Potter, Beatrix (1904), *The Tale of Benjamin Bunny*, London: Frederick Warne.

Potter, Beatrix (1904), *The Tale of Two Bad Mice*, London: Frederick Warne.

Potter, Beatrix (1905), *The Tale of the Pie and the Patty-Pan*, London: Frederick Warne.

Potter, Beatrix (1908), *The Tale of Jemima Puddle-Duck*, London: Frederick Warne.

Potter, Beatrix (1908), *The Tale of Samuel Whiskers or, The Roly-Poly Pudding*, London: Frederick Warne.

Potter, Beatrix (1909), *The Tale of the Flopsy Bunnies*, London: Frederick Warne.

Powell, Kerry (ed.) (2004), *The Cambridge Companion to Victorian and Edwardian Theatre*, Cambridge: Cambridge University Press.

Pritchett, V. S. (1942), *In My Good Books*, London: Chatto & Windus.

Pugh, Edwin (1895), *A Street in Suburbia*, London: Heinemann.

Pugh, Edwin (1904), *The Fruit of the Vine*, London: John Long.

Pugh, Edwin (1908), *The Broken Honeymoon*, London: John Milne.

Pugh, Edwin (1910), *The Mocking Bird*, London: John Milne.

Pykett, Lyn (1995), *Engendering Fictions: The English Novel in the Early Twentieth Century*, London: Edward Arnold.

Quiller-Couch, Arthur (1910), *The Sleeping Beauty and Other Fairy Tales from the Old French*, London: Hodder & Stoughton.

Rainey, Lawrence, Poggi, Christine and Wittman, Laura (2009), *Futurism: An Anthology*, New Haven, CT: Yale University Press.

Ransome, Arthur (1906), *Nature Books for Children*, 3 vols, London: Anthony Treherne.

Ratcliffe, Sophie (2013), *P. G. Wodehouse: A Life in Letters*, London: Arrow Books.

Read, Donald (1999), *The Power of the News: The History of Reuters*, Oxford: Oxford University Press.

Reed, Talbot Baines (1881/1887), *The Fifth Form at St. Dominic's*, London: Religious Tract Society.

Ridge, W. Pett (1895), *A Clever Wife*, London: Richard Bentley.

Ridge, W. Pett (1898), *Mord Em'ly*, London: C. Arthur Pearson.

Ridge, W. Pett (1899), *Outside the Radius*, London: Hodder & Stoughton.

Ridge, W. Pett (1901), *London Only*, London: Hodder & Stoughton.

Ridge, W. Pett (1903), *Up Side Streets*, London: Hodder & Stoughton.

Ridge, W. Pett (1904), *Next Door Neighbours*, London: Hodder & Stoughton.

Ridge, W. Pett (1905), *On Company's Service*, London: Hodder & Stoughton.

Ridge, W. Pett (1906), *The Wickhamses*, London: Methuen.

Ridge, W. Pett (1907), *Name of Garland*, London: Methuen.

Ridge, W. Pett (1907), *Nearly Five Million*, London: Hodder & Stoughton.

Ridge, W. Pett (1908), *Sixty-Nine Birnam Road*, London: Hodder & Stoughton.

Ridge, W. Pett (1910), *Light Refreshment*, London: Hodder & Stoughton.

Ridge, W. Pett (1910), *Nine to Six-Thirty*, London: Methuen.

Ridge, W. Pett (1923), *A Story Teller: Forty Years in London*, London: Hodder & Stoughton.

Roberts, Morley (1901), *Taken by Assault or The Fugitives*, London: Sands.

Robins, Elizabeth (1909), *Votes for Women!* London: Mills and Boon.

Rose, Jonathan (1986), *The Edwardian Temperament 1895–1919*, Athens: Ohio University Press.

Rowling, J. K. (2000), 'From Mr Darcy to Harry Potter by way of Lolita', *Sunday Herald*, 21 May, n.p. Available at: http://www.accio-quote.org/arti cles/2000/autobiography.html (accessed 24 April 2016).

Russell, T. Baron (1903), *Borlase & Son*, London: John Lane: The Bodley Head.

Sambourne, Linley (1896), 'Alfred the Little', *Punch*, 110 (11 January), 14.

Scott, Dixon (1911), 'New Books', *Manchester Guardian*, 23 February, 7.

Seton, Christine and Wilbraham, Estra (1901), *Two Babes in the City*, London: E. Arnold.

Seton, E. Thompson (1904), *Monarch, the Big Bear of Tallac*, New York: Charles Scribner's Sons.

Seton, E. Thompson (1909), *The Biography of a Silver-Fox*, London: Archibald Constable.

Shakespear, Olivia (1910), *Uncle Hilary*, London: Methuen.

Sharp, Cecil (1907), *English Folk Songs, Some Conclusions*, London: Simpkin, Novello.

Sharp, Cecil (1907), *The Morris Book*, London: Novello.

Sharp, William (1904), *Literary Geography*, London: Pall Mall Publications.

Shaw, George Bernard (1903/1928), *Man and Superman. A Comedy and a Philosophy*, London: Constable.

Shaw, George Bernard (1905/1960), *Major Barbara*, London: Penguin.

Shaw, George Bernard (1907), *John Bull's Other Island, and Major Barbara: also How He Lied to Her Husband*, London: Constable.

Shaw, George Bernard (1911), *The Doctor's Dilemma; Getting Married; and The Shewing-up of Blanco Posnet*, London: Constable.

Shaw, George Bernard (1949), *Misalliance, The Dark Lady of the Sonnets, & Fanny's First Play*, London: Constable.

Sinclair, May (1907), *The Helpmate*, London: Constable.

Sinclair, May (1908), *The Judgement of Eve*, London: Harper & Brothers.

Smith, David C. (ed.) (1998), *The Correspondence of H. G. Wells, Volume 1, 1880–1903*, London: Pickering & Chatto.

Snaith, J. C. (1907), *William Jordan Junior*, London: John Collis.

Springfield, Lincoln (1924), *Some Piquant People*, London: T. Fisher Unwin.

Stacpoole, H. de Vere (1908), *The Blue Lagoon*, London: T. Fisher Unwin.

Strang, Herbert (1907), *King of the Air; or, to Morocco on an Airship*, Oxford: Oxford University Press.

Strang, Herbert (1909), *Swift and Sure: The Story of a Hydroplane*, London: Hodder & Stoughton.

Strang, Herbert (1910), *The Cruise of the Gyro-Car*, London: Hodder & Stoughton.

Strang, Herbert (1910), *Round the World in Seven Days*, London: Hodder & Stoughton.

Stuart, J. A. (1901), *The Eternal Quest*, London: Hutchinson.

Swanwick, H. M. (1907), *The Small Town Garden*, London: Sherratt and Hughes.

Swift, Jonathan (1909), *Gulliver's Travels*, London: J. M. Dent.

Swinnerton, Frank (1909), *The Merry Heart*, London: Chatto & Windus.

Swinnerton, Frank (1910), *The Young Idea*, London: Chatto & Windus.

Swinnerton, Frank (1935), *The Georgian Literary Scene*, London: William Heinemann.

Swinnerton, Frank (1937), *Swinnerton: An Autobiography*, London: Hutchinson.

Temple Thurston, E. (1908), *Sally Bishop*, London: George Bell.

Thomas, Edward (1902), *Horae Solitariae*, London: Duckworth.

Thomas, Edward (1903), *Oxford*, London: A&C Black.

Thomas, Edward (1905), *Beautiful Wales*, London: A&C Black.

Thomas, Edward (1906/1982), *The Heart of England*, Oxford: Oxford University Press.

Thomas, Edward (1906), 'New Books', *Bookman*, 30(177) (June), 111–12.

Thomas, Edward (1907), *The Pocket Book of Poems and Songs for the Open Air*, London: Grant Richards.

Thomas, Edward (1909), *Richard Jefferies, His Life and Work*, London: Hutchinson.

Thomas, Edward (1909/1984), *The South Country*, London: Everyman's Library.

Thomas, Edward (1911), *Maurice Maeterlinck*, London: Methuen.

Tracy, Louis (1901), *The Invaders*, London: C. Arthur Pearson.

Trevena, John (1910), *Bracken*, London: Alston Rivers.

Trilling, Lionel (1965), *E. M. Forster*, New York: New Directions.

Trodd, Anthea (1991), *A Reader's Guide to Edwardian Literature*, Hemel Hempstead: Harvester Wheatsheaf.

Trotter, David (1993/1998), *The English Novel in History 1895–1920*, London: Routledge.

Tweedsmuir, Susan (1966), *The Edwardian Lady*, London: Gerald Duckworth.

Upton, Florence K. (1901), *The Golliwogg's 'Auto-Go-Cart'*, London: Longmans, Green.

Upton, Florence K. (1902), *The Golliwogg's Air-Ship*, London: Longmans, Green.

van Wyk Smith, M. (1978), *Drummer Hodge: The Poetry of the Anglo-Boer War, 1899–1902*, Oxford: Clarendon Press.

Wales, Hubert (1907), *The Yoke*, London: John Long.

Wall, Barbara (1991), *The Narrator's Voice: The Dilemma of Children's Fiction*, Basingstoke: Macmillan.

Waller, Philip (2006/2008), *Writers, Readers, & Reputations: Literary Life in Britain 1870–1918*, Oxford: Oxford University Press.

Watson, William (1902), *Ode on the Day of the Coronation of King Edward the Seventh*, London: John Lane: The Bodley Head.

Watson, William (1903), *For England: Poems Written during Estrangement*, London: John Lane: The Bodley Head.

Weales, Gerald (ed.) (1962), *Edwardian Plays*, New York: Hill and Wang.

Wells, F. M. (1901), *The Suburban Garden*, London: Sampson Low, Marston.

Wells, H. G. (1895a), *The Stolen Bacillus and Other Incidents*, London: Methuen.

Wells, H. G. (1895b), *The Time Machine*, London: William Heinemann.

Wells, H. G. (1896), *The Island of Doctor Moreau*, London: William Heinemann.

Wells, H. G. (1897), *The Invisible Man*, London: C. Arthur Pearson.

Wells, H. G. (1898), *The War of the Worlds*, London: William Heinemann.

Wells, H. G. (1901/1902), *Anticipations*, London: Chapman & Hall.

Wells, H. G. (1905/1998), *Kipps*, London: Everyman.

Wells, H. G. (1905/1994), *Love and Mr. Lewisham*, London: Everyman.

Wells, H. G. (1909/1994), *Tono-Bungay*, London: Everyman.

Wells, H. G. (1909/2005), *Ann Veronica*, London: Penguin.

Wells, H. G. (1910/1999), *The History of Mr. Polly*, London: Everyman.

Wells, H. G. (1914a), *An Englishman Looks at the World*, London: Cassell.

Wells, H. G. (1914b), *The Wife of Sir Isaac Harman*, New York: Macmillan.

Wells, H. G. (1934/1984), *Experiment in Autobiography*, 2 vols, London: Faber and Faber.

West, Rebecca (1928), *The Strange Necessity: Essays and Reviews*, London: Jonathan Cape.

Wexler, Joyce Piell (1997), *Who Paid for Modernism? Art, Money, and the Fiction of Conrad, Joyce and Lawrence*, Fayetteville: The University of Arkansas Press.

Whitten, Wilfred [John O'London] (1904), 'Intellectual Honesty', *T.P.'s Weekly*, IV(86) (1 July), 17.

Wiener, Martin J. (1982), *English Culture and the Decline of the Industrial Spirit, 1850–1980*, Cambridge: Cambridge University Press.

Wiggin, Kate Douglas (1903), *Rebecca of Sunnybrook Farm*, Boston and New York: Houghton Mifflin.

Williams, Archibald (1902), *The Romance of Modern Invention*, London: C. Arthur Pearson.

Williams, Archibald (1904), *The Romance of Modern Engineering*, London: C. Arthur Pearson.

Williams, Archibald (1904), *The Romance of Modern Locomotion*, London: C. Arthur Pearson.

Williams, Archibald (1905), *The Romance of Modern Exploration*, London: Seeley.

Williams, Archibald (1906), *The Romance of Modern Mechanism*, London: Seeley.

Williams, Archibald (1907), *The Romance of Modern Mining*, London: Seeley.

Williams, Mrs Leslie (1901), *A Garden in the Suburbs*, London: John Lane: The Bodley Head.

Williamson, C. N. and A. M. (1902/n.d.), *The Lightning Conductor: The Strange Adventures of a Motor-Car*, Edinburgh: Thomas Nelson.

Williamson, C. N. and A. M. (1905), *My Friend the Chauffeur*, London: Methuen.

Williamson, C. N. and A. M. (1906), *The Car of Destiny*, London: Methuen.

Williamson, C. N. and A. M. (1907), *The Botor Chaperon*, London: Methuen.

Williamson, C. N. and A. M. (1909), *The Motor Maid*, London: Hodder & Stoughton.

Wilson, A. E. (1951), *Edwardian Theatre*, London: Arthur Baker.

Wilson, Harris (ed.) (1960), *Arnold Bennett & H. G. Wells: A Record of a Personal and Literary Friendship*, London: Rupert Hart-Davis.

Winckler, Paul A. (1980), *Reader in the History of Books and Printing*, Englewood, CO: Indian Head.

Winter, John Strange (1902), *A Blaze of Glory*, London: F. V. White.

Wodehouse, P. G. (1901), 'School Stories', *Public School Magazine*, August, 125.

Wodehouse, P. G. (1903), *A Prefect's Uncle*, London: A&C Black.

Wodehouse, P. G. (1903), *Tales of St. Austin's*, London: A&C Black.

Wodehouse, P. G. (1905), *The Head of Kay's*, London: A&C Black.

Wodehouse, P. G. (1907), *The White Feather*, London: A&C Black.

Wodehouse, P. G. (1909/1932), *Mike*, London: A&C Black.

Wodehouse, P. G. (1910/1950), *Psmith in the City*, London: A&C Black.

Wodehouse, P. G. (1950), *Psmith in the City*, London: A&C Black.

Wodehouse, P. G. (1953), *Performing Flea*, London: Herbert Jenkins.

Wodehouse, P. G. (1986), *The Golden Bat and Other School Stories*, Harmondsworth: Penguin.

Wodehouse, P. G. (1987), *The Pothunters and Other School Stories*, Harmondsworth: Penguin.

Wood, Walter (1906), *The Enemy in Our Midst*, London: John Long.

Woodhead, Lindy (2008), *Shopping, Seduction, & Mr Selfridge*, London: Profile Books.

Woolf, Virginia [originally anonymous] (1919), 'Modern Novels', *Times Literary Supplement*, 899 (10 April), 189–90.

Woolf, Virginia (1980), *The Diary of Virginia Woolf, Volume 3, 1925–1930*, ed. Anne Oliver Bell, London: The Hogarth Press.

Woolf, Virginia (1988), *The Essays of Virginia Woolf, Volume 3, 1919–1924*, ed. Andrew McNeillie, London: The Hogarth Press.

Young, A. B. Filson (1904), *The Complete Motorist*, London: Methuen.

Index